Presidential Decisionmaking
in Foreign Policy

Other Titles of Interest

A Danger of Democracy: The Presidential Nominating Process, Terry Sanford

† *The Illusion of Presidential Government,* edited by Hugh Heclo and Lester M. Salamon

† *Presidents, Secretaries of State, and Crises in U.S. Foreign Relations: A Model and Predictive Analysis,* Lawrence S. Falkowski

† *National Interests and Presidential Leadership: The Setting of Priorities,* Donald E. Nuechterlein

Crisis Resolution: Presidential Decision Making in the Mayaguez *and Korean Confrontations,* Richard G. Head, Frisco W. Short, and Robert McFarlane

† *U.S. Policy in International Institutions: Defining Reasonable Options in an Unreasonable World,* Revised Student Edition, edited by Seymour Maxwell Finger and Joseph R. Harbert

† *Psychological Models in International Politics,* edited by Lawrence S. Falkowski

Political Psychology and Biopolitics: Assessing and Predicting Elite Behavior in Foreign Policy Crises, Gerald W. Hopple

† *Biopolitics: Search for a More Human Political Science,* Thomas C. Wiegele

† *Theories of Comparative Politics: The Search for a Paradigm,* Ronald H. Chilcote

† *Politics, Values, and Public Policy: The Problem of Methodology,* Frank Fischer

† *Biology and the Social Sciences: An Emerging Revolution,* edited by Thomas C. Wiegele

Lend-Lease, Loans, and the Coming of the Cold War: A Study of the Implementation of Foreign Policy, Leon C. Martel

† Available in hardcover and paperback.

Westview Special Studies in International Relations

Presidential Decisionmaking in Foreign Policy: The Effective Use of Information and Advice
Alexander L. George

This study first examines various ways in which the judgments of foreign-policy decisionmakers are distorted by the misuse or nonuse of information and policy analysis, particularly as individual executives or small policymaking groups try to cope with the stresses of making difficult decisions. Professor George then discusses methods of organizing and managing the policymaking process in order to reduce the likelihood of such distortions. Calling attention to the impact that different presidential styles and personality characteristics have on the nature and functioning of policymaking and advisory systems, he concludes with a look at how collegial (as opposed to formalistic) relationships within a policymaking group can improve the quality of both policy analysis and policy decisions.

Alexander L. George is Graham H. Stuart Professor of International Relations at Stanford University. Among his many articles and books is *Deterrence in American Foreign Policy,* which won the Bancroft Prize in 1975.

Presidential Decisionmaking in Foreign Policy: The Effective Use of Information and Advice

Alexander L. George

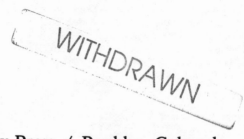

Westview Press / Boulder, Colorado

Westview Special Studies in International Relations

Published in 1980 in the United States of America by
  Westview Press, Inc.
  5500 Central Avenue
  Boulder, Colorado 80301
  Frederick A. Praeger, Publisher

Library of Congress Cataloging in Publication Data:
George, Alexander L.
  Presidential decisionmaking in foreign policy.
  (Westview special studies in international relations)
  1. Presidents—United States—Decisionmaking. 2. United States—Foreign relations—Decisionmaking. I. Title. II. Series: Westview special studies on international relations and U.S. foreign policy.
JK570.G46   353.008'92   79-16824
ISBN 0-89158-380-7
ISBN 0-89158-510-9 pbk.

Printed and bound in the United States of America

10   9   8   7   6   5

For my wife, Juliette,
with enduring love and gratitude

Contents

List of Tables and Figures................................*xi*

Preface ....*xiii*

Introduction: The President's Search
for Quality Decisions — A Framework 1

**Part One
Sources of Impediments to
Information Processing** 15

1. Introduction to Part One 17

2. Psychological Aspects of Decisionmaking:
   Adapting to Constraints on Rational Decisionmaking.........25

3. The Importance of Beliefs and Images 55

4. The President and His Advisers: Structure,
   Internal Processes, and Management of Small Groups 81

5. Organizational Behavior and Bureaucratic Politics
   as Sources of Impediments to Information Processing 109

6. Some Possible (and Possibly Dangerous) Malfunctions
   of the Advisory Process 121

**Part Two
Ways of Reducing Impediments
to Information Processing** 137

7. Introduction to Part Two...............................139

8. Presidential Management Styles and Models 145

9. The Devil's Advocate: Uses and Limitations 169

10. The "Formal Options" System 175

11. Multiple Advocacy 191

12. The Collegial Policymaking Group 209

13. The Concept of National Interests: Uses and Limitations, *Alexander L. George and Robert O. Keohane* 217

14. Policy-Relevant Theory 239

    Index 263

Tables and Figures

Tables

1. Three Management Models 165

2. Roles, Role Conflict, and Role Overload 198

3. Types of National Interests (for the United States) 223

Figures

1. Trade-Off Dilemmas in Presidential Decisionmaking 2

2. The Competitive Model (FDR) 150

3. The Formalistic Model (Truman) 152

4. The Formalistic Model (Eisenhower) 154

5. The Formalistic Model (Nixon) 156

6. The Collegial Model (JFK) 158

7. The Flow of Policymaking in the Noniterative System 180

8. The Flow of Policymaking in the Iterative System 182

Preface

This is a study of presidential decisionmaking in foreign policy, a subject that has absorbed me since I was a graduate student in the Political Science Department at the University of Chicago in the days before Pearl Harbor. In a seminar on the psychology of politics taught by Nathan Leites I became interested in the role that a leader's personality can play in his political behavior. My research paper for the seminar was a study of Woodrow Wilson from this standpoint. Some years later, with the invaluable help of my wife, Juliette L. George, whose contribution to the enterprise went well beyond that of coauthor, the seminar paper became a biography, *Woodrow Wilson and Colonel House: A Personality Study* (New York: John Day Co., 1956).

By this time I had become deeply involved in foreign policy and national security research, first as a research analyst in U.S. military government in Germany and then as a member of the Social Science Department of the Rand Corporation. A continuing challenge of the many years spent at Rand was the task of bringing scholarly analysis to bear effectively upon high-level policymaking. At Rand policy research was not defined exclusively in terms of narrow applied research. Emphasis was given to the need for basic research that would improve the knowledge base and contribute to the development of theory and methodology.

Before leaving Rand in 1968 to join the Political Science Department at Stanford University, I had started a project aimed at bridging the gap between theory and practice. One of its objectives was the development of policy-relevant theory in well-defined issue-areas of foreign policy. My premise was that policymakers need theory and in fact do use it in making decisions, though often they operate with primitive theories of questionable validity that are, moreover, not well articulated. Another objective was to understand better the rules of thumb and shortcuts that political leaders resort to in their efforts to make rational decisions when laboring under the well-known "cognitive limits" on rationality. These interests, which originated while I was at Rand, led eventually to a number of books and articles on related subjects: coercive diplomacy, deterrence, crisis management, the "operational codes" of political leaders, multiple advocacy, and policy-relevant forecasting.

In 1970 I attended the Conference on Coping and Adaptation held at Stanford University under the sponsorship of the Department of Psychiatry with the support of the National Institute of Mental Health. The conference stimulated me to view political decisionmaking from a different perspective, and I wrote a paper, "Adaptation to Stress in Political Decision Making: The Individual, Small Group, and Organizational Contexts," for the volume based upon the conference proceedings. This early paper, in fact, provides an important part of the framework for the present book.

In 1974 Peter Szanton, then research director of the Commission on the Organization of the Government for the Conduct of Foreign Policy, a joint presidential-congressional committee, asked me to undertake a study for the commission on a topic that it had entitled "Minimizing Irrationality" and defined as follows:

> Recent work in several disciplines provides new insight into the tendencies of personal and bureaucratic factors (and in the case of crises, physiological and additional psychic factors) to distort the judgment of decision makers. Drawing on recent work in the political, behavioral and psychological sciences, this study would address two questions: (1) to what extent are current organizational, procedural and staff arrangements unnecessarily vulnerable to such pressures; (2) what alternative arrangements might either shield decision makers from such pressures or open their deliberations to others less likely to be affected by them? Answers would be sought as to arrangements both for response to crises, and for more routine decision making.

Additional definition and refinement of the study was achieved as a result of a planning conference held at Stanford University in mid-June 1974. This conference was attended by the research director of the commission, Peter Szanton, and seven consultants. They were Professor Graham Allison, Harvard University; Professor Paul Hammond, then head of the Social Science Department, the Rand Corporation; Professor Charles Hermann, associate director, the Mershon Center, Ohio State University; Professor Ole Holsti, Political Science Department, Duke University; Professor Richard T. Johnson, Graduate School of Business, Stanford University; Professor Thomas Schelling, Harvard University;

and Dr. Richard Smoke, then a post-doctoral fellow with the Institute of Personality Assessment, University of California at Berkeley. Others who were invited but could not attend were Professor John Steinbruner, then at Harvard University, and Professor Robert Jervis, Political Science Department, UCLA.

The consensus that emerged from the planning conference was that the intended purposes of the study would be best addressed by focusing on possible impediments to optimal (or effective) information processing within the foreign-policymaking system in the executive branch, and that attention should be focused upon the ways in which these impediments might affect the quality of major decisions made at the highest levels of policymaking. While this definition of the study did not reject the possibility that gross irrationalities of the type that concern professional psychiatrists may occur in individuals who participate in policymaking systems, it directed attention instead to the variety of other types of impediments that can distort information processing and the evaluation of alternative options.

The study for the commission, to which a number of other scholars contributed, was entitled "Towards A More Soundly Based Foreign Policy: Making Better Use of Information." It was issued in 1975 as Appendix D in Volume 2 of the Appendixes that were published for the commission by the U.S. Government Printing Office. Having been encouraged by a number of acquaintances to prepare a publication based on this report that would be more readily available for wider use, I revised and updated it in the past year.

The present book differs from the original report in several respects. It includes a new introduction, "The President's Search for Quality Decisions—A Framework," in which I discuss in more detail the difficult problem of trying to understand the role of various personality variables in an executive's decisionmaking and leadership behavior. Chapter 7, "Presidential Management Styles and Models," is also entirely new. Several chapters have been considerably expanded. Chapter 5 provides a more detailed discussion of the effects of bureaucratic politics on the quality of information and advice that reach the president. The nature and role of policy-applicable theory (Chapter 13) are now discussed in detail and are illustrated with reference to crisis management, coercive diplomacy, deterrence, and détente.

Chapter 3, "The Importance of Beliefs and Images," has been revised to include new material on the relevance of recent developments in cognitive psychology and attribution theory for the study of political decisionmaking. Less-extensive revisions and additions have been made in other chapters.

I keenly regret that limitations of space have made it necessary to drop from the present version of the study two important specialized chapters that appeared in the original report. These are David K. Hall's chapter on "The 'Custodian-Manager' of the Policymaking Process," which is based on a forthcoming Ph.D. dissertation in political science at Stanford University, and the stimulating proposal "Maintaining the Quality of Decision-Making in Foreign Policy Crises," prepared by Margaret G. Hermann and Charles F. Hermann.

It is perhaps useful to add a word or two about the nature of this study, which attempts an ambitious synthesis of a great deal of material that bears in one way or another on the tasks of understanding and improving the quality of presidential-level decisionmaking in the sphere of foreign policy and national security. A tremendous body of significant research and writing on decisionmaking and on the related task of developing more effective policymaking procedures has accumulated in the last several decades. This literature is voluminous and often highly specialized. Those who have contributed to it include not only persons with practical experience in foreign policymaking, but also many specialists in the behavioral sciences — psychologists, political scientists, sociologists, economists, organizational theorists, and decision theorists. They have utilized many different kinds of data and have employed a variety of research approaches in studying the behavior of individual decisionmakers, small groups engaged in problem solving or policymaking, and complex organizations.

Much of this specialized literature has been examined in preparing this study, but the use made of it has necessarily been selective. Judgment has been exercised regarding the relative significance of different studies for present purposes. No doubt this judgment is imperfect and will be questioned. Moreover, despite a conscientious effort to locate all sources containing significant information, undoubtedly important materials have been missed.

The reader will want to keep in mind that while this study has benefited greatly from the contributions of academic specialists, it is not written primarily for the community of research scholars. References to relevant literature and footnotes are not lacking in this report, but they have been kept to a minimum.

It was my good fortune to have had the assistance of many others in planning and preparing the original report for the commission. In addition to the contributions to that report by David K. Hall and Margaret and Charles Hermann, Professor Robert Keohane, my colleague at Stanford University, coauthored with me Chapter 13, "The Concept of National Interest." A briefer version of what is now Chapter 14 was prepared by Dr. Richard Smoke. In addition, Joseph Atkinson, then of

Yale University, and Professor Anne McMahon, then of the Sociology Department at Stanford, assisted in the preparation of Chapter 4.

Altogether, over twenty persons read one or more chapters of the original report and prepared comments. They are Joseph Atkinson, Lincoln P. Bloomfield, Davis Bobrow, Thomas V. Bonoma, Chester L. Cooper, Eric Davis, Lloyd S. Etheredge, Stephen Genco, David Hamburg, Grant Hilliker, Ole R. Holsti, Irving L. Janis, Robert Jervis, Curtis Kamman, Richard Lazarus, Joshua Lederberg, Joseph S. Nye, Jr., E. Raymond Platig, Austin Ranney, Robert L. Rothstein, John Steinbruner, and Aaron Wildavsky.

I wish to express my appreciation to the following persons for their willingness to be interviewed when I was collecting additional data for the commission report and for sharing with me their insights into problems of policymaking or for calling relevant materials to my attention: Drs. Herbert J. Spiro, Carl Nydell, E. Raymond Platig, Pio Uliassi, and Sven Groennings – all of the State Department; Professor Arnold A. Rogow, Graduate School and University Center, City University of New York; Drs. Leonard Wainstein and John Ponturo, Institute of Defense Analysis; Drs. Andrew Marshall and Alfred Goldberg, Department of Defense; Dr. Irving M. Destler, the Brookings Institution; Dr. Bertram S. Brown, director, National Institute of Mental Health; Dr. Francis Barnes, M.D., and Dr. Bryant Wedge, M.D., both of Washington, D.C.; Dr. William Davidson, M.D., Institute for Psychiatry and Foreign Affairs, Washington, D.C.; Dr. Chester L. Cooper, Woodrow Wilson International Center, Smithsonian Institution; Professors Henry S. Rowen and Alain C. Enthoven, Graduate School of Business, Stanford University; Drs. Vincent P. Zarconne and Jared R. Tinklenberg, Psychiatry Department, Stanford University.

It is a pleasure to acknowledge my longstanding indebtedness to Dr. David A. Hamburg, M.D., formerly head of the Department of Psychiatry and Behavioral Sciences, Stanford University, and currently president of the Institute of Medicine, National Academy of Sciences, for introducing me to the study of problems of stress and coping, and for the help he has given me in conceptualizing certain aspects of the present study and in assisting me with some of the interviews.

For unfailingly cheerful and efficient secretarial and administrative help I am indebted, as so often in the past, to Mrs. Lois Renner and Mrs. Barbara Sullivan.

It should be noted, finally, that some important matters that can affect policymaking are *not* taken up in this report. We do not deal here with problems associated with the physical and mental health of policymakers, the effects of sleep disorders on cognitive processes, the effects of aging on the performance of political leaders, the effects of drugs and medications taken for various purposes, the effects of "jet lag," etc. Preliminary data were gathered on some of these matters, but it became quickly evident that to provide useful and responsible analysis of these questions would require highly specialized competence and much more time and resources than were available for the present study. Given the importance of these matters, it is hoped that they will become the focus of a separate study at some point in the future.

Alexander L. George

Introduction:
The President's Search for
Quality Decisions — A Framework

This book focuses on the task of improving the quality of information, analysis, and advice available to a president and his leading advisers for making important foreign-policy decisions. Before proceeding, however, it is well to recognize that the search for high-quality decisions in foreign policy, as in domestic policy, is often complicated by the need to be attentive to other considerations as well.

Trade-Offs Between Quality, Acceptability, and Decisionmaking Resources

Like it or not, every president must struggle with the difficult task of attempting to harmonize his search for high-quality decisions with two other requirements for being an effective leader and decisionmaker.[1] Thus, a president must be sensitive to the need to achieve sufficient consensus in support of his policies and decisions within his own administration, in Congress, and with the public. The amount of support required will vary for different presidential policies and actions as will a president's judgment of the minimal level of consensus that he needs on different occasions.[2] One hopes that on many occasions there will be no serious conflict between the quality of a decision and its acceptability and hence no necessity for the president to make a difficult trade-off decision whether to sacrifice some of the quality of a preferred policy for greater acceptability or, conversely, to accept the risk of low acceptability and inadequate support in order to pursue a policy or action that he and his advisers regard as more advantageous from the standpoint of the national interest. But the need for minimal levels of support and consensus on behalf of foreign policy is an ever-present constraint on the president's ability to seek and to choose high-quality policies.[3]

Similarly, a president's search for quality in his foreign-policy decisions must be sensitive to the constraints of time and to the proper use of available policymaking resources. In many instances the search for a higher-quality decision cannot or should not be prolonged insofar as the failure to make a timely decision may itself reduce the likelihood of achieving a successful outcome. Nor should the search for a higher-quality decision on one policy question be allowed to consume a disproportionate share of the manpower, and the analytical and intelligence resources that must be available to attend to other urgent policy questions.

Given these important constraints on the president's ability to dedicate himself exclusively to the search for high-quality decisions, a number of dilemmas are encountered. Just as there are often trade-offs between the search for quality decisions and the need for consensus and support, so, too, difficult trade-offs will be encountered between the search for greater quality and the prudent management of time and other policymaking resources. And, finally, it must be recognized that presidential decisionmaking often encounters still another trade-off dilemma: that between a desire to achieve greater acceptability for the chosen policy and the expenditure of precious time and other policymaking resources that would be incurred in the effort to develop greater support for that policy.

We have identified three competing desiderata that impinge in varying degrees on presidential decisionmaking. They often create genuine dilem-

Figure 1. Trade-Off Dilemmas in Presidential Decisionmaking

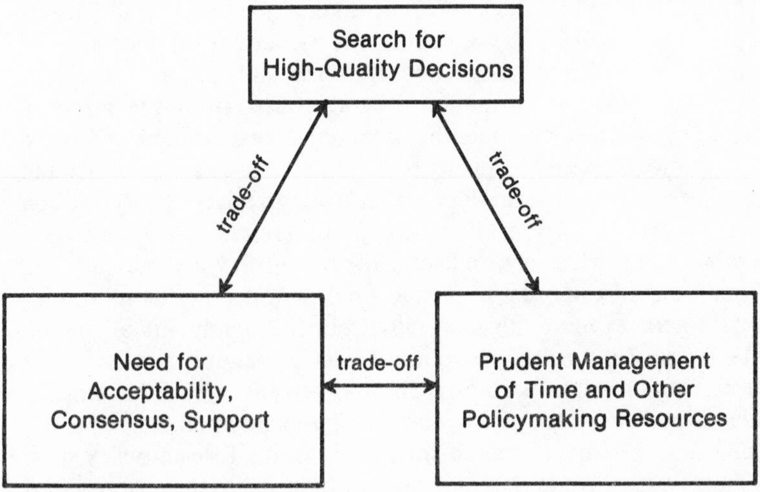

mas, forcing the executive to exercise difficult, often quite painful trade-off judgments. An "effective" decisionmaker must be sensitive to all three desiderata; he is obliged to weigh their relative importance in any given situation; and he is called upon to exercise good judgment in making trade-offs among them. The resulting complexity of presidential decisionmaking is depicted in Figure 1.

The Criterion of a "Quality" Decision

We have spoken thus far of the search for "high-quality" decisions without defining that desideratum. In the sphere of foreign policy this criterion is usually identified with the concept of "national interest"—i.e., a high-quality decision is one in which the president correctly weighs the national interest in a particular situation and chooses a policy or an option that is most likely to achieve national interest at acceptable cost and risk. Presumably, therefore, it is the criterion and proper understanding of national interest that should guide policymakers in their search for high-quality decisions. We will discuss later the serious limitations of the concept of national interest from this standpoint.[4]

Human nature and politics being what they are, the abstract concept of "national interest" has many competitors when it comes to the president's own subjective conception of a high-quality decision. The policy issues with which an executive must deal often arouse in him a variety of motives and interests that are in fact extraneous to the values associated with even a very broad conception of the national interest. Foreign-policy issues and the circumstances in which they arise may activate the policymaker's personal motives and values and bring to the fore his political interests or those of his administration or political party. This is not surprising, since the way in which the president deals with a particular policy problem may have important consequences for his sense of personal well-being or his political fortunes. Thus, whether he is fully cognizant of it or not, a president may stretch the desideratum of "high quality" to include consideration of whether the decision he makes will have one or more of the following consequences:

- satisfy or frustrate his personal values;
- provide an outlet for expressing deep-seated motives and impulses;
- obtain approval or disapproval from persons who are significant figures in his life;
- enhance or damage his self-esteem;
- advance or set back his career prospects;
- strengthen or weaken his political and bureaucratic resources.

At times, these personal and political stakes in a foreign-policy issue may lead the president in the same direction as his objective conception of where the national interest lies. But it must be recognized that they also are capable of diluting, if not distorting, his search for a high-quality decision based on the criterion of national interest. At the same time, however, various safeguards against such possibilities do exist. In the first place, the president must justify his foreign-policy decisions with reference to the criterion of the national interest in a manner that is credible to his associates, to Congress, and to public opinion. His awareness of this necessity can serve as an important brake on the tendency to allow personal needs or political interests to dilute his search for quality decisions. Then, too, much of presidential decisionmaking is institutionalized in ways that reduce or contain such tendencies. The operation of organizational, procedural, and staff arrangements in support of presidential decisionmaking serves to structure and discipline a president's choices; thereby, they reduce—though certainly they do not eliminate—the possibility that personal motives and interests will intrude into and distort his judgment.[5]

The Role of Personality in Decisionmaking

This study does not reject the possibility that gross irrationalities of the type that concern psychiatrists may occur in presidents and other leading participants in policymaking.[6] However, this possibility is not singled out for detailed examination. Instead, the present study directs attention to other impediments that can lower the quality of information, analysis, and advice available for making important foreign-policy decisions and that can distort the president's judgment in making such choices. Before proceeding with the major focus of our inquiry, however, some additional observations may be offered regarding the role of personality factors in high-level policymaking.

Many individuals—even those who enjoy remarkably successful careers in politics, business, academia, or some other occupation—operate with complex motivational patterns that often include deficits or vulnerabilities in their self-esteem for which they attempt to obtain compensation in the pursuit of their careers and in the day-to-day performance of tasks associated with their occupations. Moreover, all individuals employ psychological devices to cope with the anxiety, fear, or guilt that they experience from time to time in certain situations.

In fact, it often is not at all difficult to find evidence that an individual's character-rooted needs—whether it be an unusual need for affection, respect, aggression, rectitude, power, security, etc.—or his ego defenses are being expressed in the performance of tasks associated with his position. From this it is tempting to infer that the way in which that person performed was determined in part, if not wholly, by the personal needs or motives in question. While this may be a correct explanation on occasion, it is also important to recognize that the *expression* of personality needs is a necessary *but insufficient* condition for establishing the critical causal importance of those personality factors for the behavior in question. The fact that a political leader strives for or achieves gratification of personal needs in his performance of a political role does not automatically bestow decisive causal importance to the personality variable.

Performance in executive positions such as the presidency is sensitive to a variety of constraints. A given behavior may be no more than a response to the logic of the situation—i.e., a requirement of the situation rather than a requirement of personality. Or it may be a response to the expectations of others as to how an incumbent president should behave in a particular situation or in situations of a given type. Executive behavior, in other words, is sensitive to *situational* and *role* variables as well as to character-rooted needs or to psychodynamic patterns for adapting to stressful experiences.

In addition, it must be recognized that an individual's personality system itself includes more than character-rooted needs and ego defenses (such as projection, denial, repression) that are employed to cope with anxiety, fear, and guilt. Thus, an executive's political behavior will be shaped also by a variety of *cognitive beliefs* (ideology, world view, beliefs about correct political strategy and tactics, etc.) that he has acquired during the course of his education, personal development, and socialization into political affairs. In other words, much of an individual's behavior as a political decisionmaker will reflect what he has learned along the way either through direct or vicarious experience and will be shaped also by the values and behavioral patterns that he has acquired by modeling himself on prestigious persons.

Still another important component of the total personality of a political decisionmaker is the set of *skills* that he has acquired, which, he has come to believe, provide him with relevant tools and resources for effectively meeting the role demands of a political leader and an executive. These skills, and the successful use of them on previous occasions, provide the individual with *a sense of personal efficacy* for addressing at least some of the role tasks associated with executive leadership.

These examples indicate that the task of assessing the impact of an executive's personality on his performance is complex and thereby caution against the common tendency to explain too much of an individual's performance in terms of personality flaws. Personality itself, as indicated, is not a simple concept, but rather an intricate system comprised of the individual's character-rooted needs and motives, his sense of self (or "identity") and the various self-esteem vulnerabilities and needs that accompany it, the skills and adaptative patterns that the individual has acquired for relating to other individuals and for coping with or mastering a variety of tasks and situations, and the cognitive beliefs and knowledge in terms of which he organizes his experiences, plans his activities, and diagnoses and responds to new situations. Awareness of the complexity of personality — whether its complexity is expressed in these terms or by using other concepts — should serve to discourage the tendency to explain behavior by going for "the jugular of the unconscious" and other forms of psychological reductionism that bypass attention to the situational, institutional, and role contexts in which the executive functions.

Having said this, however, it is still the case that much of value can be learned by studying presidents from the standpoint of the fit or lack of fit between various components of personality and the different role and situational requirements of the enormously complex job of being president.[7] Fascinating evidence indicates that a number of individuals who served as president were aware to some extent, in some cases even to a considerable extent, of a lack of fit between some of their personality characteristics and some of the demands of the presidential role. Just as brilliant performance of some presidential tasks can be traced to a "fit" between personality components and role requirements, so, too, can inadequate performance of some presidential tasks be traced to "malfits" between personality and role. The example of William Howard Taft, a poignant one from a human standpoint, will suffice to illustrate the point.[8]

The fact that Taft's personal qualities did not fit well the requirements of the presidential role was evident to him as well as to others even before he became president. He wrote to his wife in 1906, while he was a member of Theodore Roosevelt's cabinet, saying that "politics, when I am in it, makes me sick" (p. 76). Nonetheless, Taft's ambitious wife helped Roosevelt drag Taft into running as the Republican presidential candidate in 1908. Taft's eighty-year-old mother, on the other hand, knew her son well enough to write to him in 1907, trying to discourage him from agreeing to become Roosevelt's hand-appointed successor: she pointedly observed that "Roosevelt is a good fighter and enjoys it, but the malice of politics would make you miserable" (p. 76). This proved to be an accurate prediction!

Taft also had a temperamental antipathy to self-dramatization, and this caused him simply to ignore reporters during his first weeks in the White House. Taft's abhorrence of drama or emotion discouraged him from trying to learn the techniques of public relations. He had no ability and little interest in shaping the news as an instrument of power and leadership. One biographer notes that at times Taft was reluctant to read the newspapers for fear that he would have to comment!

Taft also ruled out many other standard techniques of influence. He was loathe to use patronage or to appeal to the public over the heads of Congress. "His creed was—don't play politics, fight for what is right, and seek to be a source of unity rather than of discord" (p. 89).

For a variety of reasons Taft did not think that he could be a particularly effective president. He lacked a sense of efficacy—i.e., the skills and resources—relevant to many of the role requirements of the presidency. Not surprisingly, he succumbed to the temptation to cope with this lack of fit between personality and role by frequently lapsing into passivity and complacency. His friend Archie Butt wrote that Taft "believes that many things left to themselves will bring about the same result as if he took a hand in their settlement" (p. 92).

Psychologists note that individuals caught in an unpleasant situation from which they cannot remove themselves physically often resort to removing themselves psychologically. There are many evidences of Taft's effort to "escape the field" in order to minimize the unpleasant aspects of the job of being president. As one biographer puts it: "He ate too much, wanted to sleep too long, preferred playing bridge to work, and was always reluctant to leave the golf course. . . . He loved to travel because it got him out of Washington and away from problems but complained that he was expected to make speeches on his tours" (p. 95).

If there was a lack of fit between certain components of Taft's personality and the requirements of the presidency, interestingly enough the opposite was the case when he became chief justice, a position for which he was much better suited temperamentally and for which there was a much better fit between personality and role requirements. Thus, as chief justice, Taft did not experience the self-doubts that had plagued him in the presidency. As chief justice, far from attempting to "escape the field," he worked harder and longer and was much happier than he had been as president. Taft was a much stronger and more effective chief justice because his motives, incentives, and skills were more fitted for a judicial rather than a political position.

The interaction between personality, situation, and role can take many forms, and it is by no means the case that the impact of personality on performance of the executive role is always deleterious. In fact, the opposite may be the case. Thus, personal motives and needs aroused in a particular situation may serve to alert the individual to perceive more acutely the political opportunities (or threats) presented by that situation. The possibility that such a situation affords for gratifying a personality need may also help to energize the individual to meet difficult situational tasks and role requirements. As a result, personality factors may facilitate and improve the individual's performance of role requirements.

There is, of course, a danger that the arousal of powerful personality needs may distort the individual's reality testing and his judgment of whether and how the situation threatens important policy objectives or offers opportunities for furthering those goals. Highly relevant in this regard is the strength and operation of the individual's ego controls—that is, his ability to regulate the expression of personal needs, anxieties, and defenses in order to prevent them from distorting his effort to appraise situations realistically and deal with them appropriately. It is important to recognize that the effectiveness of ego controls is not to be gauged by their success in denying any expression at all to personal needs in one's political functioning. This would be impossible in any case. Rather, what is more likely is that in the process of maturation most successful adult personalities have developed ego controls that are generally strong enough to curb the expression of personal needs unless the behavior that would gratify those needs is also consistent with the requirements of the situation and the demands of the role task. In other words, an individual's personality needs may be subjected to effective reality-testing and disciplined by that person's awareness of role and situational requirements before they are allowed expression in his behavior. Personality needs can be said to have a dysfunctional, adverse effect on the performance of official duties only when there is reason to believe that ego controls have failed and that the needs and motives have led him to a distorted or inadequate perception of role and situational requirements, or to a choice of inferior ways of meeting those requirements.[9]

In addition to this preventive control function, the so-called "ego" component of personality has a positive function as well. During the course of an individual's maturation and development, he typically formulates a variety of constructive strategies for harnessing in more positive directions the expression of deep-seated personal needs and motives.[10]

Some years ago, when political scientists were exposed to early developments in ego psychology, they were struck by the fact that arousal of a leader's anxieties and ego defenses could severely impair his ability to deal rationally with a situation. As a result, political scientists—and some psychiatrists and psychologists as well—tended to regard any display of ego defenses (such as denial, projection, or rationalization) by a political leader in a stressful situation as a telltale sign that his ability to cope rationally and effectively with that situation had been impaired. Decisions made under these circumstances were regarded with suspicion, and any inadequacy perceived in the substance of the decision was explained as being the unfortunate by-product of the leader's resort to ego defenses to cope with his anxieties. Explanatory hypotheses of this kind often oversimplified and distorted the role of unconscious emotional factors in decisionmaking.[11]

Recent developments in ego psychology and in studies of the nature of coping processes offer political scientists a much more refined and discriminating understanding of these matters. Many of the classical ego-defense mechanisms can be used constructively by an individual in the total process of coping. Defensive operations such as withdrawal, denial, or projection do not necessarily preclude intelligent and reasonable adaptation to a difficult situation. Rather, these defensive maneuvers may give the individual time to regroup ego resources and provide him with the short-run, tactical ego support that sustains him momentarily until he can return to employing more constructive ego capacities such as information seeking, role rehearsal, or planning in order to deal with the problem.[12]

Psychological aspects of policymaking are important, but the present study will attempt to accommodate them within a social-psychological framework rather than by means of a narrow psychiatric approach. It must be immediately noted, however, that there does not exist a single social-psychological approach that deals comprehensively and in an integrated manner with all of the possible impediments to information processing in a complex policymaking system. Accordingly, by necessity the present study has had to formulate an eclectic framework of its own within which to discuss and evaluate the many different kinds of findings and theories that are relevant to one or another aspect of the overall problem addressed.[13]

The first part of our framework identifies the five procedural tasks that must be well performed within a policymaking system if the top executive is to receive information, analysis, and advice of reasonably good quality. The second component of the framework provides a refined and differentiated model of the policymaking system that will enable the reader to see more clearly the sources of impediments to the performance of these five critical tasks.

Five Critical Procedural Tasks in Effective Decisionmaking

Certain procedures generally are considered to be desirable in decision-making. While adherence to these procedures does not guarantee high-quality decisions in any given instance, nor does the failure to do so necessarily result in a poor decision, most specialists in decisionmaking believe that adherence to these procedures is likely to increase the probability of obtaining decisions of higher quality.

While specialists employ somewhat different terminologies in describing the desirable characteristics of decisionmaking procedure, there is substantial agreement that a policymaking process should accomplish the following tasks:

1. Ensure that sufficient information about the situation at hand is obtained and that it is analyzed adequately so that it provides policymakers with an incisive and valid diagnosis of the problem.

2. Facilitate consideration of all the major values and interests affected by the policy issue at hand. Thus, the initial objectives established to guide development and appraisal of options should be examined to determine whether they express adequately the values and interests imbedded in the problem and, if necessary, objectives and goals should be reformulated.

3. Assure a search for a relatively wide range of options and a reasonably thorough evaluation of the expected consequences of each. The possible costs and risks of an option as well as its expected or hoped for benefits should be carefully assessed; uncertainties affecting these calculations should be identified, analyzed, and taken into account before determining the preferred course of action.

4. Provide for careful consideration of the problems that may arise in implementing the options under consideration; such evaluations should be taken into account in weighing the attractiveness of the options.

5. Maintain receptivity to indications that current policies are not working out well, and cultivate an ability to learn from experience.

With these procedural desiderata of a good policymaking system in mind, we turn now to differentiating and refining the internal components of a policymaking system so as to identify better the sources of impediments to the performance of these procedural tasks.

The Three Interrelated Subsystems of the Policymaking System: Individual, Small Group, and Organization

Efforts to find ways of improving the performance of a policymaking system will be facilitated by employing a more complex and differentiated model of that system that takes into account individual, group, and organizational behavior within the executive branch. Efforts at rational calculation of policy take place in three interrelated contexts or subsystems within the policymaking system: *the individual context* (e.g., the chief executive, secretary of state); *the small group context* of the face-to-face relationships into which the executive enters with a relatively small number of advisers; and the *organizational context* of hierarchically organized and coordinated processes involving the various departments and agencies concerned with foreign-policy matters in the executive branch.[14]

The investigator must take into account the fact that these three subsystems are interrelated. Thus, the individual-executive, the small decisionmaking group, and the organization units often interact with each other in producing foreign-policy outputs. Each of these three subsystems is capable of generating a special set of adaptive and maladaptive ways of coping with the cognitive and procedural tasks of decisionmaking. Part of the research task is to identify distinctive dynamic processes of this kind associated with each of these subsystems. It also will be necessary to consider how the distinctive dynamic processes associated with each subsystem can adversely or favorably affect information processing within the other two subsystems.

The task outlined here is a formidable one. Despite advances in relevant portions of theories of individual psychology, small group dynamics, and organizational behavior, the linkage and synthesis of these three theories is still primitive. A much more satisfactory integration of relevant elements of individual psychology and of group dynamics than is presently available will be needed eventually for identifying the variety of interaction patterns between the individual-executive and small group that can affect efforts to cope with the different kinds of stress that impinge on foreign-policy behavior. Much the same has to be said regarding the need for a better integration of theories of small group dynamics and organizational behavior and theories of executive leadership and organizational behavior.

Within the broad conceptual framework that has been outlined, the study proceeds in two parts. In Part 1 the sources of impediments to information processing are identified and illustrated in (1) the dynamics of individual decisionmaking behavior, focusing in particular on the top executive; (2) the way in which the top executive structures the small policymaking or advisory group with which he interacts, manages its internal processes, and regulates its communications with outsiders; and (3) the patterns of behavior that emerge in the rest of the executive branch and how these patterns affect the flow of information and advice upwards to the top executive and his small advisory group and the implementation of top-level policies and decisions.

From these sources spring impediments to performance within the policymaking system of the five critically important procedural tasks. But knowledge of the sources of impediments is not sufficient by itself for practical purposes; what is needed, in addition, is a list of the symptoms of inadequate information processing to which these impediments give rise.

Since the sources of impediments cannot be eliminated easily, the practical task is to institute preventive measures to reduce or minimize the impact that they are allowed to have upon policymaking. For this purpose, knowledge of the symptoms of inadequate information processing and appraisal identified in Part One can be helpful. It can sensitize those who participate in policymaking and those who are responsible for maintaining effective procedures for policymaking to quickly spot indications that information processing has become defective and to take corrective action. Part Two of the study takes up various ways in which the policymaking system can be structured and managed in order to avoid impediments to information processing or at least to minimize their harmful effects on the workings of the policymaking process.

Notes

1. This section draws upon two books by Norman R. F. Maier, *Problem-Solving Discussions and Conferences* (New York: McGraw-Hill, 1963) and *Problem Solving and Creativity in Individuals and Groups* (Belmont, Calif.: Brooks/Cole, 1970); Victor H. Vroom and Philip W. Yetton, *Leadership and Decision Making* (Pittsburgh, Pa.: University of Pittsburgh Press, 1973); Ole R. Holsti and Alexander L. George, "The Effects of Stress on the Performance of Foreign Policy-makers," in Cornelius P. Cotter, ed., *Political Science Annual*, vol. 6 (Indianapolis: Bobbs-Merrill, 1975), pp. 273-74. It should be kept in mind that a president's search for quality decisions in foreign policy proceeds in the context of an extremely complex set of duties and responsibilities. An incisive discussion of the president's overall "job description" is provided by Thomas E. Cronin, *The State of the Presidency* (Boston: Little, Brown & Co., 1975), Chapter 9.

2. Different types of decisions would appear to call for different ranking of these criteria. For example, a nuclear test ban treaty requires broad support in Congress and the Pentagon to be effective, its consequences unfold rather slowly, and it is easily reversible should other adherents be found in violation of its provisions; it therefore appears to place a high premium on acceptance, and less on quality, time, or expenditure of resources. In contrast, decisions such as those made during the Cuban missile crisis seem to require primary emphasis on quality and time, whereas concern for acceptance and expenditure of resources are probably less critical considerations, at least in the short run. The important point is that only in the most trivial decisions can policymakers maximize quality and acceptance, while minimizing the expenditure of time and resources.

3. For a fuller discussion of the need for a widely shared consensus on the fundamentals of foreign policy if the president is to be able to conduct a coherent, consistent policy over a period of time, *see* Alexander L. George, "Domestic Constraints on Regime Change in U.S. Foreign Policy: The Need for Policy Legitimacy" (in press).

4. *See* Chapter 13.

5. This thesis is ably argued by Sidney Verba, "Assumptions of Rationality and Non-Rationality in Models of the International System," *World Politics* 14 (1961):93-117.

6. This section draws from a more detailed discussion in Alexander L. George, "Assessing Presidential Character," *World Politics* 26 (1974):234-82. *See also* A. L. George, "Power as a Compensatory Value for Political Leaders," *Journal of Social Issues* 24 (July 1968); and Lloyd S. Etheredge, *A World of Men: The Private Sources of American Foreign Policy* (Cambridge, Mass.: MIT Press, 1978).

7. A useful framework for conceptualizing the relationship between personality and role in terms of "fit" or "malfit" is presented in Edwin J. Thomas, "Role Theory, Personality, and the Individual," in E. R. Borgata and W. Lambert, eds., *Handbook of Personality Theory and Research* (Chicago: Rand McNally, 1968). *See also* Michael Maccoby, *The New Corporate Leaders: The Gamesman* (New York: Simon and Schuster, 1976).

8. The brief sketch of William Howard Taft presented here is drawn from the longer profile of him in Erwin C. Hargrove, *Presidential Leadership: Personality and Political Style* (New York: Macmillan, 1966), pp. 77-96. Personality variables are treated sensitively and, with the recent experience of presidential abuse of power in the Vietnam war and the Watergate affair in mind, also with reference to the problem of securing greater accountability in presidential performance in Hargrove's more recent book, *The Power of the Modern Presidency* (New York: Knopf, 1974). In this book, one of the most important revisionist reassessments of the strong, "heroic" model of the presidency, Hargrove reexamines and modifies his earlier assumption that effective performance in the presidency requires an individual with a "power-oriented" personality. On this point *see also* Richard Neustadt's post-Watergate reflections in his *Presidential Power: The Politics of Leadership with Reflections on Johnson and Nixon* (New York: Wiley, 1976). I have discussed some of these issues in an

unpublished paper, "The 'Power Problem' of the Presidency" (February 1976).

9. Complicating factors also should be noted: (1) the role and situational requirements that impinge on a political actor may contain conflicting or ambiguous elements that make it more difficult for him to exercise effective control and constructive regulation of his personality needs; (2) the politician's role may itself include aberrant requirements that activate personality motives and needs that ordinarily are kept under control. In other words, as Willard Gaylin, M.D., has emphasized, the nature of politics and what it takes to be successful in politics — as in business — may attract sociopathic and paranoid personality types: "The capacity to be ruthless, driving and immoral, if also combined with intelligence and imagination, can be a winning combination in politics as well as commerce. . . . Sociopathic and paranoid personality traits that are most dangerous in people of power are precisely those characteristics most suitable for the attainment of power in a competitive culture such as ours" ("What's Normal?," *New York Times Magazine,* 1 April 1973).

10. As Brewster Smith, Jerome Bruner, and Robert White noted many years ago, the early psychoanalytic account of ego defense mechanisms "failed to mention the tremendous importance of constructive strategies [employed by 'normal' individuals] as a means of avoiding the vicissitudes that make crippling defenses necessary. . . . [They] often prevent things from occurring that might disrupt them or, more positively, they . . . plan events in such a way [so as to] operate effectively. . . ." (*Opinions and Personality* [New York: Wiley, 1956], p. 283; *see also* p. 22).

11. For a systematic discussion of the circumstances under which ego-defensive needs are likely to manifest themselves in an actor's political behavior, *see* Fred I. Greenstein, *Personality and Politics: Problems of Evidence, Inference, and Conceptualization* (Chicago: Markham, 1969), pp. 57-61.

12. For a fuller discussion, *see* George, "Adaptation to Stress in Political Decision-making: The Individual, Small-Group, and Organizational Contexts," in G. V. Coelho, D. A. Hamburg, and J. Adams, eds., *Coping and Adaptation* (New York: Basic Books, 1974). *See also* Holsti and George, "The Effects of Stress."

13. The framework employed in the present study draws upon that developed in the author's earlier publications: *see* George, "Adaptation to Stress." For a recent review of social psychological approaches to decisionmaking, *see* Samuel A. Kirkpatrick, "Psychological Views of Decision Making," in Cornelius P. Cotter, ed., *Political Science Annual,* vol. 6 (Indianapolis: Bobbs-Merrill, 1975).

14. It should be noted that we will not attempt to deal with still other subsystems that interact with the three noted here — i.e., Congress, public opinion, and allied and neutral governments. Similarly, while much of the analysis that follows presumably relates to decisionmaking in other national contexts as well, parts of it may have more limited applicability for other nations (e.g., in small countries that have small or virtually nonexistent foreign-policy bureaucracies).

Part One
Sources of Impediments to Information Processing

1
Introduction to Part One

The study considers, first, the *sources* of possible impediments to information processing. The most useful way of identifying these sources is to begin by taking note of the fact that a policymaking system is comprised of *individuals* who often come together in *small groups* within the framework of an *organization* that is characterized by hierarchy, division of labor, and specialization. It is not surprising, therefore, that sources of impediments to information processing are to be found in (1) the dynamics of individual behavior; (2) the ways in which small policymaking groups are structured, their internal processes managed, and their communications with outsiders regulated; and (3) the patterns of behavior that emerge in complex organizations.

Part One of the study draws together in a systematic way available knowledge regarding the variety of often maladaptive ways in which individuals, small groups, and organizations deal with decisionmaking tasks. Many of these impediments stem from the very cognitive processes by means of which the human mind attempts to deal with complex policy problems that are characterized by value-complexity and uncertainty.

This is the focus of Chapter 2, "Psychological Aspects of Decisionmaking," which discusses different ways in which individuals attempt to make decisions when policy issues are clouded by value complexity or when there is insufficient information and knowledge by means of which to calculate the expected consequences of different options. Thus, when a policy issue engages multiple competing values, the decisionmaker may find it difficult to devise a course of action that promises to safeguard all of these values and interests; he may be forced, instead, to determine his value priorities and choose among them. Value trade-off dilemmas of this kind are difficult to resolve by analytical techniques; they may create considerable frustration and psychological stress for the conscientious decisionmaker. To cope with or ward off the ensuing emotional malaise, he may resort to defensive modes of dealing with the value complexity imbedded in the policy issue.

We distinguish and discuss three different ways in which a policymaker may attempt to deal analytically or psychologically with value-complexity. First, he may attempt to *resolve* the value conflict, at least to his own satisfaction, by devising a course of action that seems to satisfy all of the competing values, either genuinely or in a spurious and illusory way. A second way is to *accept* the value conflict as unavoidable and to face up to the necessity to make a difficult trade-off choice. This, too, can be psychologically comforting for, after all, by doing so the decisionmaker is fulfilling one of the difficult responsibilities of leadership. But whether the decisionmaker correctly perceives the value-conflict as unavoidable and whether he deals adequately with the trade-off is another matter. Finally, the decisionmaker may find the value conflict imbedded in the policy issue so difficult to resolve and so distressing to contemplate that he may seek to *avoid* recognizing its existence or to play down its importance. This strictly defensive mode of coping may succeed in reducing or banishing the psychological malaise he would otherwise feel, but it may do so only at the cost of markedly impairing information processing and appraisal of options.

The decisionmaker is faced with another kind of difficulty when there is insufficient information about the situation and inadequate knowledge by means of which to assess the expected consequences of available options. Forced to act in the face of these uncertainties, when so much may be at stake, the decisionmaker may experience considerable malaise.

Studies of decisionmaking under conditions of uncertainty indicate that there are a variety of psychological devices that can be employed by the individual to reduce or avoid the malaise of having to decide what to do in the face of incomplete information and inadequate knowledge. One of these devices, "defensive avoidance," provides an escape from worrying by not exposing oneself to cues that evoke awareness of a decisional dilemma. Defensive avoidance can take the form of procrastination—i.e., when a person seizes upon the fact that there is no immediate necessity for a decision to put the problem out of his mind, foregoing the opportunity for additional information search, appraisal, and realistic contingency planning.

Another type of defensive avoidance, "bolstering," may be resorted to when a decision cannot be put off because external pressures or a strict deadline demands action. In these circumstances, the individual may make the task of choosing easier for himself by reevaluating the options before him, increasing the attractiveness of one option (which he will then select) and doing the opposite for competing options (which he will reject). "Bolstering," or "spreading the alternatives" as it is sometimes called, can result in distortion of information-processing and option appraisal. This is particularly likely when the decisionmaker, acting to cut short the malaise of a decisional dilemma, rushes his final choice, thereby foregoing the possibility of using the remaining time to obtain still additional information and advice. Supportive bolstering by sycophantic (or equally stressed) subordinates to the top decisionmaker can aggravate this danger.

In addition to these modes of defensive avoidance, which provide psychological assistance to enable a policymaker to come to a decision, there are a variety of cognitive aids to decision and simple decision rules that enable an individual to cope with the intellectual problem of what to do in the face of an issue that is clouded by uncertainty. The following six such aids to decision are discussed and illustrated in Chapter 2: (1) the use of a "satisficing" rather than an "optimizing" decision rule; (2) the strategy of incrementalism; (3) "consensus politics"—i.e., deciding on the basis of what enough people want and will support rather than via an attempt to master the complexity of the policy issue; (4) use of historical analogies; (5) reliance upon ideology and general principles as guides to action; (6) application of beliefs about correct strategy and tactics.

While each of these aids to decision can facilitate the policymaker's choice, they can also have indirect and important consequences for the quality of information processing. There is a danger that an executive will resort *prematurely* to one of his favorite aids to decision or *rely too heavily* on it in reaching a decision. The result may well be to cut himself off from the possibility of benefiting from a broader or in-depth analysis of the problem that advisers or the organizational information-processing system can provide.

Chapter 3, "The Importance of Beliefs and Images," views information processing from the perspective of cognitive psychology. The very processes of perception, cognition, calculation, and choice are subject to inherent limits. The mind cannot perform without structuring reality, thereby often oversimplifying or distorting it. Nor, as cognitive psychologists have emphasized, can the mind function without seeking to make beliefs consistent with each other and incoming information consistent with existing beliefs. This deeply rooted striving for consistency (though it admits of exceptions) necessarily limits the flexibility and ingenuity with which an individual can recognize and deal with novel and complex features of foreign policy problems. Thus, information processing for policymaking can be seriously impaired by the strong tendency displayed by individuals (and organizations, as well) to see only what they expect or want to see (the role of expectations or "mind-sets") and the tendency to assimilate incoming information to one's existing images, hypotheses, and theories.

Distorted information processing of this kind can contribute to an un-justified and dangerous lowering of one's guard—as, for example, when warning indicators of a military attack are rejected as inconsistent with preexisting beliefs. Or, equally, it can lead to an unjustified and costly raising of one's guard—as, for example, when an opponent's failure to cooperate is misread as evidence in support of a preexisting belief regarding his hostility. A number of historical examples of these processes are presented in Chapter 3, and particular attention is given there to the critical importance in foreign policy of understanding the opponent's perspective. One's image of the adversary includes an understanding of his ideology, his "operational code," and his mode of calculating utility and assessing risks. An incorrect image of the opponent can distort the appraisal of even good factual information on what he may do. Chapter 3 cites examples of this from the history of the Cold War.

To recognize the fact that all individuals must develop beliefs and con-structs that simplify and structure the external world and that consistency-striving in processing information is pervasive in human behavior does not, however, require us to take a deterministic or fatalistic view with regard to the effects on policymaking. That some manifestations of a policymaker's consistency-striving are excessive and possibly harmful in decisionmaking is something that he, or certainly other participants in policymaking, are capable of recognizing and possibly correcting. The practical question is how to design and manage the policymaking process in order to avoid forms of consistency-striving that are likely to severely narrow, distort, or curtail information process-ing and appraisal. Chapter 3 identifies a number of recognizable in-dicators that consistency-striving may have become excessive and that, therefore, greater vigilance in information processing may be required.

In Chapter 4, "The President and His Advisers: Structure, Internal Processes, and Management of Small Groups," attention turns from the dynamics of individual behavior to small group processes. It is well known that foreign-policy decisions are typically made in the setting of a small group in which the executive interacts with a relatively small number of close advisers. This chapter identifies additional sources of possible impediments to information processing and option appraisal that may be rooted in the structure, internal processes, and management of small policymaking groups.

Small groups tend to have simpler internal role structures—that is, less differentiation of tasks, less division of labor and specialization within the group, and less formalized modes of procedure. Accordingly, there is less need of coordinating the activities of participants in small decision-making groups, and more of the time and energy of members can be focused directly on the problem-solving task. But the fact that relatively few individuals comprise the decisionmaking group may also mean that fewer policy options will be considered insofar as a smaller range of values, beliefs, and attitudes are then represented in the group and a reduced amount of knowledge and analytical skills is present within the group. To enhance the performance of small decisionmaking groups, therefore, it is often critical not only that a flow of relevant, timely information and advice be provided the group from outside sources but, equally important, that members of the group remain open and receptive to it.

Top-level officials and advisers comprising a small decisionmaking group tend to have broader perspectives and a less parochial view than individuals identified with departmental and agency interests. This may serve to improve the quality of decisions taken. But the smallness and hierarchical position of such groups may lead to new constraints and impediments. For when decision evolves to the top of an organization, there is some risk that harassed senior officials will lose contact with sources of information and experts at lower levels. Specialists on organizational behavior have noted a marked tendency for the critical uncertainties identified in policy analyses provided by experts at lower levels of the organization to be left out, deemphasized, or presented in an oversimplified manner when summaries of these analyses are transmitted upwards to top-level officials. To safeguard against these possibilities, the executive may be well advised to assign the role of "expert's advocate" to someone in the small decisionmaking group who is indeed well qualified to appreciate the complexities of the experts' reports and whose function it is to make sure that the group does not oversimplify the analytical summaries obtained from elsewhere in the organization.

The smallness of a decision group can be harmful also if it leads to increased pressure for conformity. Small groups are likely to be more cohesive because they provide fewer opportunities for subgrouping and the intragroup conflicts associated with it. A particular danger in small decision groups is that irrelevant status characteristics or power-prestige differences among members may importantly influence their relationships, interactions, and performance of the tasks of policy analysis and appraisal of options.

Students of small group behavior used to emphasize the benefits of "cohesion," i.e., the members' positive valuation of the group and their motivation to continue to belong to it. While a certain degree of cohesiveness, solidarity, mutual esteem, and liking may be necessary for group performance, it is increasingly recognized that highly cohesive groups are not necessarily high-performance groups. This is particularly so when, as in foreign-policymaking, the group is under pressure to deal with situations in which the stakes are high. In these circumstances members of the group may begin to act as if maintaining group cohesion and well-being were the overriding goal to the detriment of task-oriented activities.

Recent emphasis on the hazards of high group cohesion has led to the delineation of two different patterns of group conformity: firstly, the long familiar pattern of group pressure on individual members which leads them to hesitate to express doubts and misgivings regarding the dominant view being expressed out of fear of recrimination, anxiety about presenting a disloyal self-image, or fear of eviction from the group; and secondly, a less obvious pattern, labelled "Groupthink" by Professor Irving Janis, in which conformity springs from strong group cohesion brought about or accentuated by a threatening, stressful environment. These two patterns of conformity pressures within the group can significantly lower group performance by introducing impediments to information processing and option appraisal. Historical examples of both types of conformity pressures, taken from recent American foreign policy, are cited in Chapter 4.

While conformity pressures are most likely to occur in small groups, smallness per se is not necessarily disruptive of effective information processing. What is critical is that the norms operating within the group emphasize the necessity for considering a reasonably wide range of options, for making realistic estimates of potential dangers and opportunities, and for avoiding the hazards of conformity pressures and practices which may lead to a premature stifling of diverse viewpoints. In Chapter 4 and elsewhere in the report, various suggestions are made for enhancing the quality of information processing and option appraisal within small decisionmaking groups.

Chapter 5, "Organizational Behavior and Bureaucratic Politics," examines the larger subsystem within which the search for effective foreign policy takes place. Far from fulfilling the hopes of an earlier generation that modern principles of organization would strengthen the quest for more rational policies, the structural features of hierarchy, specialization, and centralization that characterize all complex organizations have produced chronic pathologies of information processing and appraisal. The various impediments that stem from patterns of organizational behavior and "bureaucratic politics" are briefly listed in Chapter 5.

It is useful to be aware of the nature of impediments to information processing that can spring from individual behavior, from the structure and management of small policymaking groups, and from the stubborn dynamics of complex organizations. But knowledge of the *sources* of impediments is not sufficient by itself for practical purposes; what is needed, in addition, is a list of the *symptoms* of inadequate information processing to which these impediments give rise. Since the sources of impediments cannot be easily eliminated, the practical task is to institute preventive measures to reduce or minimize the impact which they are allowed to have upon policymaking. For this purpose knowledge of the symptoms of inadequate information processing and appraisal can be helpful. It can sensitize those who participate in policymaking and those who are responsible for maintaining effective procedures for policymaking to quickly spot indications that information processing has become defective and to take corrective action.

To this end Chapter 6, "Some Possible (and Possibly Dangerous) Malfunctions of the Advisory Process," lists and illustrates nine types of "malfunctions" to which policymaking systems are prone. These malfunctions are not of a hypothetical kind; the chapter cites evidence which suggests that they occurred in recent historical cases of U.S. foreign-policymaking. These process malfunctions are of a general kind; they can occur under any model for organizing the foreign-policymaking system—whether a highly centralized, White House–oriented system, a State-centered system, or a looser decentralized system. Whichever of these alternative organizational models is adopted, provision should be made within it to monitor the policymaking process in the interest of timely identification and correction of these malfunctions. Each process malfunction tends to have an adverse effect on one or another of the five important procedural tasks associated with effective decisionmaking that were listed earlier. The nine types of malfunctions identified thus far include the following situations:

1. When the decisionmaker and his advisers agree too readily on the nature of the problem facing them and on a response to it.
2. When advisers and policy advocates take different positions and debate them before the executive, but their disagreements do not cover the full range of relevant hypotheses and alternative options.
3. When there is no advocate for an unpopular policy option.
4. When advisers to the executive thrash out their disagreements over policy without the executive's knowledge and confront him with a unanimous recommendation.
5. When advisers agree privately among themselves that the ex-

ecutive ought to face up to a difficult decision, but no one is willing to alert him to the need to do so.

6. When the executive, faced with an important problem to decide, is dependent upon a single channel of information.

7. When the key assumptions and premises of a plan which the executive is asked to adopt have been evaluated only by advocates of that option.

8. When the executive asks advisers for their opinions on a preferred course of action but does not request a qualified group to examine more carefully the negative judgment offered by one or more advisers.

9. When the executive is impressed by the consensus among his advisers on behalf of a particular option but fails to ascertain how firm the consensus is, how it was achieved, and whether it is justified.

While the historical illustrations chosen to illustrate these malfunctions in Chapter 6 are drawn from presidential-level decisionmaking in the sphere of foreign policy, similar malfunctions no doubt occur at lower levels in the organization as well. Nor are these malfunctions confined to the area of foreign policy or to policymaking in government. Rather, the theory of malfunctions and the recommendation that efforts be made to monitor policymaking to identify the emergence of such malfunctions and to take appropriate preventive action are presented here as having general applicability to a variety of policymaking systems.

2
Psychological Aspects of Decisionmaking: Adapting to Constraints on Rational Decisionmaking

Much of foreign policymaking consists of efforts to calculate the utility of alternative courses of action.[1] Rational calculation of this kind requires (1) *information* about the situation; (2) *substantive knowledge* of cause-and-effect relationships that is relevant for assessing the expected consequences of alternative courses of action; and (3) a way of applying the *values* and interests engaged by the problem at hand in order to judge which course of action is "best" and/or least costly and which, therefore, should be chosen.

These three requirements are imperfectly met by the way in which most foreign-policy issues present themselves. As a result, the policymaker must proceed under the handicap of severe constraints on the possibility of meeting these requirements of rational decisionmaking. These constraints are often referred to as the problems of "value-complexity" and "uncertainty."

Considerable psychological stress—in the form of anxiety, fear, shame, or guilt—can be evoked in a decisionmaker who struggles to cope with these two types of constraints on his ability to work out a good solution to the policy problem that confronts him. It is a central thesis of this chapter that a policymaker often experiences decisional conflicts in attempting to deal with the value complexity and uncertainty imbedded in a problem and that the resulting psychological stress, depending on how the decisionmaker copes with it, can impair adaptive responses to policy issues.[2]

The policymaker can deal with the psychological stress of decisionmaking in either of two ways: (1) by utilizing *analytical* modes of coping with value-complexity and uncertainty or (2) by resorting to *defensive* modes of coping with the malaise they engender. This chapter discusses these different modes of coping with value-complexity and uncertainty and calls attention to their implications for the quality of information processing and appraisal. The following chapter will discuss the role which certain types of beliefs and images held by decisionmakers play in information processing. We shall defer for subsequent chapters a discussion of the ways in which small-group dynamics and organizational processes can affect the individual decisionmaker's quest for effective policies. The reader should keep in mind that the individual decisionmaker's efforts to process and appraise information can be affected in many ways by processes associated with the small advisory groups in which he participates and by the organizational behavior around him.

Value-Complexity and Uncertainty: Some Definitions

A brief statement of what is meant by "value-complexity" and by "uncertainty" is useful at the outset. *"Value-complexity" refers to the presence of multiple, competing values and interests that are imbedded in a single issue.* When this is the case, it is difficult, if not impossible, for the decisionmaker to formulate a single yardstick that encompasses and aggregates all of the competing values and interests. Lacking a single criterion of utility, the decisionmaker may experience great difficulty judging which course of action is "best" on an overall basis. He is confronted instead by a value-tradeoff problem which can be extremely difficult and painful to deal with. In order to do so he may attempt to order his value priorities and decide which of the competing values and interests to pursue in the given situation at the expense of the other values and interests that are also at stake. Value tradeoff decisions of this kind are often extremely stressful for the decisionmaker. Neither the analytical nor the defensive modes of coping with value-complexity adopted by the decisionmaker may be conducive to sound policy even though they may be successful in relieving or reducing the malaise he experiences.

As we shall note in Chapter 13, the decisionmaker's effort to apply the criterion of "national interest" in deciding what course of action is "best" does not enable him to escape the problem of value-complexity or to cope with it easily and satisfactorily. For, not only has the concept of national interest been stretched to encompass a variety of values and interests, even the more rigorously delimited notion of "vital" or irreducible" national interests includes several fundamental values that compete and conflict with each other in many situations which foreign-policymakers must deal with.

Finally, we take note of the fact that the effect of value-complexity on decisionmaking can be considerably accentuated by what has been referred to as "value extension,"[3] i.e., the all too familiar tendency of policy issues to arouse a variety of motives and interests that are extraneous to values associated with even a very broad conception of the "national interest." Thus, foreign-policy issues and the circumstances in which they arise may arouse the policymaker's personal motives and values, his political interests, or those of the administration or political party to which he belongs. This is not surprising since the way in which a policymaker deals with a particular foreign-policy problem can indeed have important consequences for his personal well-being and political fortunes: thus, it can:

- satisfy or frustrate personal values held by the policymaker;
- provide an outlet for expressing his deep-seated motives and impulses;
- obtain approval or disapproval from those who are significant figures in his life;
- enhance or damage his self-esteem;
- advance or set back his career prospects;
- strengthen or weaken his bureaucratic resources.

At times the policymaker's personal stakes in a foreign-policy issue may lead him in the same direction as his objective conception of where the national interest lies. But often, whether he is aware of his personal motives and interests or attempts to repress such awareness, they add to the problem of value-complexity and exacerbate his value conflicts. As a result, the dilemma of choice the decisionmaker experiences can become accentuated, and the value trade-off problem he faces in trying to decide what to do may become even more difficult. Finally, the decisionmaker may be willing or unwilling, able or unable, to prevent his personal motives and interests from affecting his perception of the policy problem and his judgment in dealing with it.

"Uncertainty," as the term is used here, refers to the lack of adequate information about the situation at hand and/or the inadequacy of available general knowledge needed for assessing the expected outcomes of different courses of action. Uncertainty complicates the task of making good assessments of the problem facing the decisionmaker and the additional task of deciding how to deal with it. In the face of uncertainty the decisionmaker has difficulty in making reliable cost-benefit appraisals of the alternative courses of action under consideration. He is faced with the necessity of choosing from among the options without a firm basis for confidence in his judgment. Uncertainty of this kind adds to the stress of decisionmaking. This is an important consideration to keep in mind when focusing upon emotional and psychological factors that can affect decisionmaking. Some of the ways available to individuals and organizations for coping with stress induced by uncertainty can seriously degrade the quality and effectiveness of the decisions that emerge.

Together, the presence of value-complexity and uncertainty impose severe limits on the possibility of raising policymaking to the level of rationality associated with models of "pure" rationality in decision theory.[4] Very often, both value-complexity and uncertainty are present in a problem which the policymaker is trying to decide. For purposes of analysis and presentation, however, we shall deal with them separately in this chapter.

Dealing with Value-Complexity

There are, as decision theorists have emphasized, analytical ways of dealing with value-complexity in choice situations in order to strive for as "efficient" and acceptable a solution to such problems as possible. We shall not review this technical literature here, nor attempt to judge how germane it is for different types of foreign-policy problems. Such analytical techniques may be relevant in principle but, for various reasons, difficult to apply in practice in the settings in which foreign-policy decisions are made.

Precisely because it is so difficult to employ objective analysis to deal with value-complexity, the top executive is expected by others in the policymaking group to reconcile competing values and interests by going through an "internal debate." The hope is that a subjective ordering and aggregation of the competing values by the executive will enable him to offer a satisfactory solution to what would otherwise be left to be settled entirely via conflict and bargaining among the actors within the policymaking system. To the extent that the top executive accepts and discharges this unique task of leadership, he may be able to make a decisive contribution to lessening the social-political tensions and costs associated with making policy in a highly pluralistic political system. As Dean Pruitt has noted, the executive is in a better position to deal with value conflict than a small group or an organization because his own intrapersonal tensions are "more easily resolved, since [he] can better subordinate one value to another."[5]

Of course, the executive may be unwilling to accept this task; or, if he does, he may not encompass all the social values that are vying for satisfaction in the political arena or may not give some of their values the weight in his own calculus that others think they deserve. Even when the executive is reasonably successful in "resolving" the value conflict through an "internal debate," it may require considerable skill at communication on his part to be credited by those concerned with having made the best decision in the overall national interest. (One can appreciate in this context the utility to the executive of the concept of "national interest" for justifying his decisions to the public. For further discussion see Chapter 13.)

Internal debate and subjective aggregation of competing values and interests do not always work. The top executive may search for but be unable to find a course of action that promises to safeguard all of the multiple stakes aroused for him by that issue. Faced with this dilemma, he may attempt to deal with it strategically as, for example, by assigning higher priority to achieving some of the values and interests at stake and by utilizing available information and analytical skills as best he can for this purpose. But even a strategic approach for dealing with difficult value trade-offs may not be wholly successful and may result in the decisionmaker experiencing considerable frustration, anxiety, self-doubts, etc. To cope with the ensuing emotional stress, he may react defensively in ways that may further prejudice the possibilities for a more satisfactory response to the policy problem. In sum, the decisionmaker may deal with value-complexity analytically and strategically; or he may resort to defensive psychological modes of coping with the emotional stress of being faced by difficult value trade-off problems. It is also possible that his response will include elements of both analytical-strategic and defensive modes of coping.

It is useful to distinguish three different ways in which a policymaker may attempt to deal with the malaise associated with value-complexity. First, he may *resolve* the value conflict, at least in his own mind, by devising a course of action that constitutes either a genuinely creative analytical solution to the problem or a spurious and illusory resolution of it that may also be psychologically comforting even though analytically defective. A second way is to *accept* the value conflict as unavoidable and to face up to the need to make the difficult trade-off choice as part of one's role requirements as a decisionmaker. This, too, can be psychologically comforting; but whether the decisionmaker is correct in perceiving the value conflict as unavoidable and whether he deals adequately with the trade-off is another matter. Finally, the decisionmaker may seek to *avoid* a value conflict by denying its existence or playing down its importance. This strictly defensive mode of coping may succeed in reducing or banishing psychological stress, but is may do so only at the cost of markedly impairing information processing and appraisal. Let us examine these three models of dealing with value-complexity more closely.

Value-Conflict Resolution

This way of dealing with value-complexity takes the form of attempting to satisfy, to some extent at least, all of the competing values and interests of which one is aware. This is usually a formidable task, if not an impossible one. But, if the policymaker is successful in doing so, the rewards are considerable; not only does he achieve a high-quality decision, he derives inner psychological satisfaction from doing so and may also expect political benefits from satisfying many different constituencies. Particularly in a democracy or in a pluralistic policymaking system the executive is under strong temptation and indeed often under strong political pressure to try to reconcile conflicting values imbedded in an issue he must decide. In these circumstances, the inventive executive may indeed come up with a creative, novel option that genuinely resolves the apparent value conflict, demonstrating thereby that the values in question were really congruent. More often, the best that can be done is the lesser, but still significant achievement of reconciling the value conflict through some kind of compromise. The weaker solution of value compromise may result in a policy that sacrifices the quality of the decision for greater acceptability.[6]

The resolution of value conflict may be attained in one of two ways: (1) by inventing a single policy that yields some satisfaction for each of the multiple interests and values at stake; or (2) by staging or scheduling satisfaction for these values/interests via a series of separate actions or polices over a longer period of time. In the latter case, the policymaker realizes that the value trade-off problem cannot be avoided entirely. His initial action is designed to promote only some of the competing values/interests; he may try to promote the remaining values/interests damaged or neglected by his initial policy by additional actions shortly thereafter. This type of "scheduling" may prove to be beneficial or damaging to foreign policy objectives, depending on circumstances and the perspicacity of the policymaker. Inept "scheduling," of course, may produce a policy that is incoherent and inconsistent.

We have to recognize that, however effective in relieving the policymaker's psychological stress, efforts to resolve value conflicts may in fact be unrealistic, spurious, and illusory. Some value conflicts simply cannot be resolved. Efforts to do so may actually impede the search for effective policies, resulting in highly questionable compromises of all or most of the values imbedded in the issue. A decision-maker who impulsively or rigidly strives to resolve or reconcile value conflicts shirks thereby his responsibility to determine value priorities and to make reasoned trade-off choices. Thus, while value-conflict resolution is the best strategy when it is possible and skillfully done, it is often not feasible, and other strategies for dealing with the problem posed by conflicting values are then preferable.

Value-Conflict Acceptance

In this way of dealing with a complex mix of values the decisionmaker faces up to the fact that a difficult choice among them must be made. It is important, however, that he should not determine value priorities *prematurely;* rather, he should maintain unimpaired receptivity to information that illuminates the full range of values imbedded in the issue. Only then should he proceed to make a reasoned, conscientious determination of value priorities in order to resolve the trade-off problem that confronts him.

To do so requires the policymaker to accept the fact that he has to put aside or give lesser weight to some salient values and interests in order to advance those judged to be of greater importance or, at least, those with the greatest chance of being realized in the situation at hand. Ideally, he does so without engaging in a fruitless effort to achieve a genuine, full resolution of the value conflict or resorting to defensive psychological mechanisms of denying or minimizing the conflict.

Some decisionmakers are evidently better able than others to deal with value conflicts in this manner. It is, of course, one of the major role tasks of a leader that he accept the responsibility to make difficult trade-off choices of this kind. Harry Truman appears to have been unusually successful in avoiding the stresses of decisionmaking by identifying with this leadership requirement. Identification with the role may bring with it an understanding and acceptance of the fact that one cannot be an executive without facing up to the fact that there will be occasions on which one simply cannot make a good decision without sacrifice of some of one's own interests or those of others. We may recall that it was Truman who made the difficult decision (which cost him a great deal politically but evidently not much by way of psychological distress) to withdraw U.S. backing from Chiang Kai-shek in 1949 and who later resisted strong domestic pressure (again at high political cost to himself and his party but without much evidence of emotional stress) to expand the Korean War against the Chinese mainland.

By identifying with the role of executive and viewing oneself as being a role player, the individual may find it possible to make difficult decisions with greater detachment and also with greater sensitivity to priorities among competing interests and values. At the same time, being a good role player may enable the individual to experience less stress and less personal damage when he is obliged to make a decision that sacrifices

some interests. For then he may see these losses as an unavoidable consequence of fulfilling his role requirements, which oblige him to make the
best possible decision that focuses on the most important of the various
stakes at issue. Finally, by fulfilling difficult role requirements of this
kind, as Truman did, the individual may in fact derive personal satisfaction—if not also the respect and praise of others—that bolsters and pro-
tects his self-esteem.

But, as with the first mode of dealing with the analytical difficulty and
psychological stress of value-complexity which has already been discussed, this second mode, too, may be performed ineptly so far as its impact on foreign policy is concerned. Critical in this respect is whether the
decisionmaker is correct in perceiving a value conflict as being
unavoidable. As a matter of fact, he may arrive at this conclusion
prematurely without adequate information or analysis of the policy problem. Being a good role player, insofar as concerns fulfilling the requirement to make difficult decisions when necessary, does not guarantee
good judgment; nor did it prevent Truman, who tended to be overly
eager to appear "decisive," from acting impulsively on occasion.

In sum, the two ways for dealing with value-complexity that we have
discussed thus far may be successful in relieving or avoiding
psychological malaise, but their consequences for the quality of a leader's
decisions is another matter and can be either beneficial or harmful. This
danger is much more pronounced when the decisionmaker seeks to *avoid*
a value conflict by denying its existence or minimizing its true importance. It is to this defensive mode of coping with value-complexity that
we now turn.

Value-Conflict Avoidance

To avoid or minimize the psychological malaise created for him by
perception of important value conflicts an individual may resort to the
tactics of ignoring or playing down some of the competing values and interests that are imbedded in the decisional problem. Defensive
maneuvers of this kind have received considerable attention in
psychological studies of decisional stress. A variety of psychological
devices are available to any individual for reducing his perception of a
value conflict that would otherwise create severe stress. These
mechanisms are described in various psychological theories of balance,
consistency, dissonance, and conflict. The two which seem of greatest
importance here are "cognitive restructuring" and "devaluation."

In the first of these, cognitive restructuring, the individual finds a way
of turning aside incoming information that calls attention to or heightens
a value conflict. Thus, he may ignore, discount, deny, forget, or uninten-

tionally misinterpret information about some of the competing values. In "devaluation," on the other hand, the individual downgrades one of the values or interests that he or others close to him hold. Doing so minimizes the value conflict he would otherwise experience and makes it more manageable, psychologically and analytically. Devaluation may lead the individual to reduce or abandon his identification with significant others who are going to be damaged as a result of his ignoring their interests or values. The decisionmaker may cut out of his consultations those holding the devalued values, or refuse to credit the information they put before him, or even denigrate them before others.

Avoiding value conflicts in these two ways is more likely to impede information processing than other mechanisms that may also be utilized for the same purpose.[7] Thus, cognitive restructuring and devaluation are likely to distort the decisionmaker's perception of the full range of values imbedded in the issue and hamper appraisal of options that best deal with the multiplicity of values and interests at stake.

Cognitive restructuring exemplifies a more general tendency displayed by individuals and organizations to see what they expect to see and to assimilate incoming information to preexisting images, beliefs, hypotheses, and theories. We deal in some detail with this tendency, often referred to by cognitive psychologists as "consistency-striving," in the next chapter. Here we shall illustrate how consistency-striving may contribute to the decisionmaker's avoidance of value trade-off problems.[8]

Truman's decision to use the Seventh Fleet to "neutralize" Formosa early in the Korean War provides a possible example of how policymakers can avoid recognizing a value trade-off problem. Truman and his advisers could think immediately of several good reasons for interposing the Seventh Fleet between Formosa and the Chinese mainland; but the historical record gives no indication whatsoever that they recognized, let alone discussed, that other U.S. interests would be jeopardized by this move. The "neutralization" of Formosa involved the United States once more in the Chinese civil war. While offered as a temporary move, the use of the Seventh Fleet for this purpose set into motion a reversal of Truman's policy of disengaging the United States from the fate of the Nationalist regime which had fallen back from the mainland to Formosa.[9]

Choices are indeed easier when there is no need to consider value trade-offs. Avoidance of value complexity is particularly likely, as Jervis notes, when a decisionmaker initially considers only one or two of the values involved in the problem at hand and comes to favor a particular policy for dealing with it because it seems appropriate for safeguarding or enhancing those particular values. Later, when he becomes aware that other important values and interests are also imbedded in the problem, he may proceed to bolster his premature adherence to a favored policy option by finding questionable or ill-considered arguments for believing that the same action will also somehow safeguard, or at least not seriously damage, the other values and interests. As a result, the process of information "search" and "appraisal" is inhibited and cut short before the decisionmaker has examined the range of values at stake more fully and weighed the evidence of a conflict among them more carefully.

Psychological avoidance of hard choices may be detected also in instances when foreign-policymakers fail to recognize that the set of goals they are pursuing are in fact likely to be inconsistent with one another. Thus, for example, as World War II drew to an end American policymakers were disposed to agree that the Soviet Union's security requirements made it necessary for her to have friendly regimes on its borders in Eastern Europe; but, at the same time, American leaders also strongly embraced the idea of free elections in Eastern Europe. President Roosevelt appears to have avoided a clear recognition of the likely incompatibility of these two goals—and hence a dilemma for U.S. policy—by embracing the optimistic but highly questionable expectation, which he stated at the Yalta Conference, that free elections in Eastern Europe would result in governments "thoroughly friendly to the Soviet [Union] for years to come." Roosevelt's unwillingness to contemplate that Eastern European governments formed via free elections might be hostile to the Soviet Union made it possible for U.S. foreign policy to embrace what were in fact mutually incompatible objectives, thus laying the groundwork for further exacerbation of Soviet-American relations later on.[10]

As this case illustrates, the failure of policymakers to perceive an admittedly difficult value trade-off spawns unrealistic policies that can prove damaging to the realization of either of the conflicting objectives. It is well to recognize that excessive consistency-striving is often abetted, as in the case just cited, by the *political* constraints under which policymakers operate. To face up to the necessity for choice can sometimes entail severe political costs, whichever way the value trade-off is resolved. Perception of value conflicts can be blurred, moreover, when— as is often the case when policymakers attempt to assess the "national interest"—the values in question are vague or ill-defined. Perception of value trade-offs can be muted also when the impact of the policy chosen upon the values in question will not be felt immediately and when the longer-term consequences of the policy cannot be reliably predicted.

Dealing with Uncertainty

When the information and knowledge needed for making an important decision are inadequate, this, too, can create emotional stress for the executive.[11] Thus, in a pioneering essay on political decisionmaking many years ago, three political scientists called attention to the need to look for the "devices" employed by decisionmakers to minimize "the psychological tensions which accompany decisionmaking under circumstances of uncertainty and lack of complete information." Continuing, they asked: "How do decisionmakers learn to live with the possibility of 'unacceptable error'? And what effects do the devices used to cope with uncertainty have on their deliberations?"[12] We shall list and discuss briefly a number of well-known ways in which individuals deal with uncertainty in making decisions. Some of these devices serve to minimize psychological tension for the decisionmaker without necessarily helping him to deal effectively with the situation.

Calculated Procrastination

It is understandable that in the face of stress induced by uncertainty executives often find it difficult to act. Indeed, some leaders go so far as to conclude that the best strategy of leadership is to do as little as possible, hoping that the problems that seem to require their attention will go away or find some other solution.

Of the many executives in political life or in other sectors of society who have adopted this philosophy as a strategy for dealing with decisional uncertainty, it will suffice to take note of Calvin Coolidge's well-known principle of "calculated inactivity." As one political scientist has put it, Coolidge's strategy in the presidency "was to 'sit down and keep still' in the face of problems rather than to confront them, to 'remain silent until an issue is reduced to its lowest terms, until it boils down to something like a moral issue.' 'If you see ten troubles coming down the road, you can be sure that nine will run down into the ditch before they reach you and you have to battle with only one.' "[13]

The philosophy of "calculated procrastination" may be surprisingly effective under some circumstances, but it carries with it the risk that the executive will be confronted by acute crises more often than would otherwise have been the case had he taken action on a timely basis to deal with emerging problems.

Defensive Procrastination

While some executives adopt the general *strategy* of "calculated procrastination" to deal with uncertainty in a variety of situations, many more executives will resort to the *tactic* of procrastination only on occa-sion.[14] It is useful in this connection to distinguish between "rational (or calculated) procrastination" and "defensive procrastination." When the relative merits of alternative courses of action for dealing with a par-ticular problem are clouded by uncertainty, it may be quite rational to postpone making a decision if (a) there is no time pressure to do so, or (b) there is reason to hope that more information and a better appraisal of the problem and of the options may be available later on; or (c) there is reason to believe that the situation itself may improve.

"Defensive procrastination" occurs, on the other hand, when a person seizes upon the fact that there is no immediate necessity for a decision to escape from the decisional conflict that the uncertainty has created by putting the problem out of his mind and turning his attention to other matters. (Delegating the problem to an assistant or to a committee, in ef-fect for "burial," can facilitate defensive procrastination.) A person who engages in "defensive procrastination" displays lack of interest in the issue thereafter, with the consequence that he foregoes further informa-tion search, appraisal, and contingency planning. In contrast, the person who engages in "rational procrastination" sees to it that active search, ap-praisal, and contingency planning continue.

In brief, whereas the defensive procrastinator "leaves the field" in order to escape the unpleasantness of uncertainty, the rational pro-crastinator *uses* the time the lack of a deadline offers, taking steps to reduce the uncertainty that plagues the decision he will have to make.

Examples of both kinds of procrastination can be found in the conduct of foreign policy. In the management of conflict relations with other states, decisionmaking is often geared to externally imposed time pressure, by deadlines implicit in rapidly developing situations or deliberately created by other actors in the international arena. Viewed from this standpoint, international crises may have a necessary and useful catalytic function in forcing foreign-policymakers to come to grips with and to decide difficult issues on which they would rather pro-crastinate. A similar function may be performed, of course, by a variety of other events — for example, congressional budget hearings, summit meetings, press conferences, etc.

At the same time, however, several examples can be cited of the deci-sionmaker's resort to defensive procrastination when the time pressure and urgency that had initially galvanized him into addressing a difficult issue was removed with the passing of the crisis. Thus, when the Tai-wan Strait crisis reached a peak of war tension in March 1955, Eisen-hower sent a high-level delegation to Formosa to persuade Chiang Kai-shek to thin out his forces on the Offshore Islands. When the crisis suddenly calmed down, Eisenhower's interest in the problem quickly evaporated. This despite the fact that there was every reason to expect that the crisis would probably erupt again in the future, with the prospect that Chiang's heavy deployment of troops on the Offshore Islands would once again complicate U.S. policy. In fact, after the crisis was over Chiang proceeded to *increase* the size of his forces on the Offshore Islands without objection from Washington. As a result, when tension in the Taiwan Strait erupted again in 1958 the administration had even less freedom of action than in 1955. Again Eisenhower sent a high-level emissary to Chiang, but with the waning of the crisis the salience of the issue declined and, once again, the administration turned its attention to other matters.[15]

Dealing with Uncertainty Under Time Pressure

We have noted that in the face of uncertainty imbedded in complex issues executives often find it difficult to act. How *does* a leader overcome such inhibitions? There are, after all, many situations in which the policymaker has to decide what to do even when the relative merits of alternative options are by no means clear and when he perceives serious risks in any course of action. Self-imposed deadlines and time pressures facilitate choice in such situations, but they do not by themselves make it easier for the decisionmaker to cope with the malaise of having to make an important decision in a matter that is laden with uncertainty.[16] What, we may ask, does forced choice under these circumstances do to the quality of search and appraisal?

Social psychologists who have studied decisionmaking under circumstances of this kind have noted two different ways in which information processing and appraisal can be impaired. One type of impairment results from "hypervigilance"; the other from "defensive avoidance." The first refers to a paniclike state of mind that is accompanied by a marked loss of cognitive efficiency. The second refers to psychological devices used to escape from current worrying about a decision by not exposing oneself to cues that evoke awareness of a decisional conflict or dilemma that is fraught with potential losses. While hypervigilance is relatively rare, defensive avoidance is a highly pervasive tendency that is encountered in many different types of decisions whether in business, family affairs, or in politics.[17]

We have already discussed one type of defensive avoidance, namely, "defensive procrastination." Another manifestation of defensive avoidance is what is sometimes called "bolstering," a phenomenon that occupies a prominent role in the theory of cognitive dissonance and in related social psychological theories.[18]

"Bolstering"

"Bolstering" refers to the psychological tendency under certain conditions of decisional stress to increase the attractiveness of a preferred (or chosen) option and doing the opposite for options which one is inclined to reject (or has rejected). Thus, the expected gains from the preferred alternative are magnified and its expected costs/risks are minimized. Similarly, the expected gains from rejected alternatives are downgraded, their expected costs/risks are magnified.

It is important to note that bolstering makes the decisionmaker's task of choosing what to do easier; it reduces the malaise of making a decision that is clouded by uncertainty.[19] It does so by *"spreading the alternatives,"* i.e., making one option seem more attractive than the alternative options. Thus, bolstering is accompanied by *distorted information-processing and appraisal.*

Bolstering can occur before a decision is made as well as, perhaps more often, afterwards.[20] Predecisional bolstering occurs when the decisionmaker believes that a firm deadline for decision is approaching and when he believes that he will not obtain additional relevant information of much consequence. He will then move towards closure by selecting what he regards as the least objectionable alternative and then consolidate his choice by reinterpreting the uncertainties to make it appear more attractive than it has seemed to be earlier.

It should be noted that the decisionmaker's belief that there is little time left to make the decision and his belief that no additional useful information can be expected may both be in error. In order to cut short the stress and malaise of a decisional dilemma he may rush his decision, thereby foregoing the possibility of using the remaining time to obtain still additional information and advice. In other words, anxiety and stress may push the decisionmaker towards premature closure, cutting off search and appraisal in the interest of resolving his decisional dilemma via bolstering. Supportive bolstering by sycophantic (or equally troubled) subordinates can aggravate this danger.[21]

It has to be recognized, of course, that bolstering can be of positive value to the decisionmaker if it is preceded by search and appraisal that is as thorough as circumstances permit. Then a last-minute bolstering—one that does not cut short search and appraisal—can help the decisionmaker to avoid suffering gnawing self-doubts that can further drain his time and energy. Of course, if carried too far in this respect, last-minute bolstering may render the decisionmaker less capable of monitoring the consequences of his decision and less inclined to reconsider his policy on the basis of evidence that it is not working.

A variety of rationalizations and other psychological devices may be utilized by the decisionmaker who resorts to bolstering in order to achieve the comforting feeling that the action he is taking is likely to lead to a successful outcome. An *incomplete* list includes the following:

1. He may convert the genuine uncertainty that exists as to the likelihood of different outcomes into spuriously calculated risks to which he assigns probabilities.
2. He may distort the estimate of the probability of future events, exaggerating the likelihood that his action will lead to a favorable outcome and minimizing the likelihood of an unfavorable outcome.
3. He may exaggerate in his own mind possibilities open to him for reversing his decision, should it turn out badly, or for limiting or correcting whatever undesirable effects it may have.
4. He may reevaluate some of the negative consequences his decision may entail by attributing certain longer-range benefits to them.
5. He may engage in wishful thinking as to the likelihood that the risks of his policy will materialize, if at all, only in the long-run whereas its benefits will emerge more quickly.
6. He may attempt to convince himself that if his policy fails, its failure will at least not be highly and widely visible or that he will not in any case be held personally responsible for its failure.
7. He may believe that even if his policy fails in the end, it will have done enough good to have been worthwhile.[22]

The shallowness of rationalizations of this kind is always clearer in the aftermath of a policy fiasco. Thus Kennedy and his advisers, heavily bolstering the decision to allow the Bay of Pigs invasion, managed to convince themselves that the United States' role in the invasion would not become known. During the Korean War, Truman and Acheson bolstered their decision to allow MacArthur to occupy North Korea by assuming that, should the Russians or Chinese intervene, they would be able to reverse the decision or at least limit the undesirable consequences. And in 1965 President Johnson and many of his advisers bolstered their decision to use air power against North Vietnam with the optimistic expectation that a prolonged bombing campaign would not be necessary and that the war would end "soon."

The Use of Aids to Decision and Simple Decision Rules

In addition to "bolstering," which provides *psychological* assistance for enabling the policymaker to come to a decision, there are a variety of *cognitive aids* that enable him to cope with the intellectual problem of deciding what to do in the face of uncertainty.[23]

Most individuals have learned to diagnose new situations even when the available information is ambiguous or incomplete. And most individuals have also acquired ways of choosing among alternative courses of action even when limitations of knowledge and information exclude the possibility of assessing the expected outcomes by applying a comprehensive, rigorous, analytic model. Let us review quickly some of the major decision rules and strategies employed to cope with decisional uncertainty.

The use of a "satisficing" rather than an "optimizing" decision rule. Because the search for a course of action that will yield the highest possible payoff is often impractical, most people settle for a course of action that is "good enough," one that offers a sufficient rather than a maximum payoff.[24] Not only does the use of "satisficing" as a decision rule fit the severe limitations of man's capacity to process information—and, only to a lesser extent, that of organizations as well—it is also an appropriate way of adjusting to the fact that to apply an "optimizing" decision rule requires enormous quantities of information and analytical resources such as are often simply not available or could be obtained only at great cost.

A distinction needs to be made between the most limited application of the "satisficing" criterion, in which the decisionmaker selects the first option coming to his attention that offers some degree of improvement over the present state of affairs, and "satisficing" after a more persistent search for an option that does better than others that have been considered.

The strategy of "incrementalism." Incrementalism converts the "satisficing" decision rule for dealing with uncertainty for any single decision problem into a strategy covering a whole sequence of decisions aimed at improving the present state of affairs gradually by means of small steps.[25] The incremental approach recommends itself to leaders when they find it difficult to obtain agreement on longer-range objectives and when the knowledge and information needed to devise more comprehensive plans to achieve them is in any case lacking. Under these circumstances, a decisionmaker employing the incremental strategy will consider a narrow range of policy alternatives that differ only slightly from existing policies and aim at securing marginal rather than dramatic improvements. The strategy relies on feedback as part of a "remedial," "serial," "exploratory" attack on the problem at issue—hence, the description of incrementalist strategy as "the art of muddling through."

While the incrementalist approach may recommend itself to the policymaker as a way of hedging against uncertainty and as a conservative strategy that avoids the risks of seeking more far-reaching changes, it nonetheless entails risks of its own that are not always recognized. The marginal improvements sought may be proven illusory or grossly insufficient. Incrementalism may degenerate into a costly series of trial-and-error actions that fail to secure a cumulative improvement in the situation. Reliance upon incrementalism may encourage policies that attack symptoms and offer marginal relief rather than deal with root causes. There is, in brief, no guarantee that the decisionmaker will somehow muddle through successfully. And, by focusing on securing marginal improvements in the near future, the policymaker may fail to see opportunities for larger gains by means of strategies geared to longer-range objectives. Further, particularly in foreign policy but also in domestic policy, incrementalism can be dangerously myopic insofar as the actions taken to achieve short-term gains, as in U.S. policy in Vietnam, may turn out to be steps on a slippery slope to highly unfavorable outcomes.

Clearly, then, some way must be found to distinguish sloppy, myopic incrementalism from a more sophisticated variant of this strategy. To this end, several caveats seem appropriate:

1. Incrementalism is *not* a substitute for *policy analysis* that encompasses longer-range considerations and generates a *planning context* within which, then, incremental decisions are made.

2. The incremental approach requires *criteria* by means of which the decisionmaker can judge the results of past decisions in order to make needed corrections in policy.

3. The strategy of incrementalism assumes — and requires! — that the decisionmaker will retain freedom and flexibility to make important corrections of policy after the consequences of his earlier move have emerged. (This assumption often proves to be unjustified in practice — as in the case of Truman's provisional decision to unify Korea by force in the late summer of 1950 — for corrections of policy often have a heavy political and/or economic cost attached to them.[26] Once established, policies often acquire a momentum that is difficult to control or reverse.)

The strategy of sequential decisionmaking. This strategy attempts to bring incremental decisionmaking into a framework of sophisticated policy planning, thereby giving policymakers an opportunity to avoid or minimize the worst consequences of sloppy, myopic incrementalism.[27] It does so in two ways: (1) by breaking up a big policy decision into a series of smaller-step decisions over time and (2) by attempting to deal with different uncertainties at optimal points in the sequence of interrelated decisions.

In developing an appropriate decision strategy for dealing with a complex policy problem, it is important for the policymaker to determine what has to be decided now and what can be left for decision later. Making the component decisions seriatim in this way often enables the policymaker to develop options that did not exist at the outset and to obtain better inputs from his analysts and experts for some aspects of the evolving policy later on.

This strategy attempts to turn to account the fact that the informational and analytical requirements differ for different parts of an evolving policy. By breaking up a big decision into smaller component decisions, the strategy uses the available time to improve the quality of some of the analytical inputs needed for later component decisions. For the policymaker to deal intelligently with uncertainties imbedded in the problem, it is useful, as systems analysts have emphasized, to distinguish among the various types of uncertainty. In addition to statistical uncertainty, there are technological and economic uncertainties as well as uncertainties with regard to human behavior and future environments. Stratagems for dealing with one type of uncertainty are not appropriate for coping with other types of uncertainty.[28]

One should not ignore the possible risks and costs of attempting to create a variety of options and to retain as much policy flexibility as possible. The policymaker who employs this decision strategy may find that the options he has created for planning purposes often create or attract support from influential actors in the policymaking system and the public, thereby achieving a momentum that may force the policymaker's hand.[29] But while the practice of "flexible options" may have been oversold or misapplied on occasion in the past, the strategy of sequential decisionmaking with which it is associated nonetheless constitutes a more sophisticated variant of the strategy of incrementalism in that it attempts to find a way of coping with and avoiding the worst consequences of "muddling through."

"Consensus Politics." The policymaker may decide what to do on the basis of what enough people want and will support rather than attempt to master the cognitive complexity of the problem by means of analysis. In the search for an effective decision there is often a potential trade-off between the substantive "quality" of a decision and its "acceptability" to those whose support the decisionmaker feels he would like to have or, indeed, must have. When the search for a "quality" option is handicapped by the difficulty of calculating expected outcomes, the policymaker may fall back on the decision rule of "consensus." In effect, then, the decisionmaker bypasses the thorny trade-off dilemma between "quality" and "acceptability" by making the criterion of "acceptability" a substitute for that of "quality."

Use of historical analogies. Many thoughtful observers have remarked about the universal human tendency to force the present into constructs of the past. Thus, "history does not repeat itself in the real world but it does repeat itself in the 'reality world' of the mind."[30]

It is indeed striking to note the extent to which political leaders have attempted to follow the injunction to learn the "lessons" of history. As the diplomatic historian Ernest May noted some years ago, "Eagerness to profit from the lessons of history is the one characteristic common in the statecraft of such diverse types as Stanley Baldwin, Adolf Hitler, Harry Truman, Charles de Gaulle, and John F. Kennedy." Each of these statesmen "was determined to hear the voice of history, to avoid repeating the presumed mistakes of the past."[31]

Our purpose here is not to call attention once more to the lessons of an earlier historical case or of misapplying the correct lessons of that case to a new situation which differs from it in important respects. Rather, attention is drawn to the fact that policymakers often cope with the difficulty of comprehending and dealing with new situations by resorting to historical analogies. Thus, an earlier historical case that had made a particularly strong impression on the policymaker becomes an aid to diagnosing the present situation and for deciding what is the best or necessary way with which to respond to it. Very often it is relatively recent history—events that the statesman personally experienced earlier in his life or which he experienced vicariously through contact with significant figures in his intellectual development—that provides the models or analogies to which the decisionmaker turns most readily. Very often, too, it is the "remembered history" of his generation on which he draws. Thus, as World War II began to draw to a close and Franklin Roosevelt addressed himself to the peace that would follow, he was influenced particularly by a desire to avoid the mistakes Woodrow Wilson had made at the end of World War I. As for Harry Truman, when the Korean War unexpectedly broke out in late June of 1950, he quickly oriented himself by viewing it in terms of its presumed parallel with the events of the 1930s, when the democracies had failed to act in the face of totalitarian aggression against Manchuria, Ethiopia, and Austria, thus encouraging the totalitarian powers to go further until World War II broke out.[32]

The role that historical analogy played in the deliberations leading to President Johnson's intervention in the Dominican crisis of April 1965 is emphasized in all accounts of the crisis. Fear of another Castro in the Caribbean strongly shaped the perceptions and judgments of American policymakers on this occasion. Johnson probably acted as he did, not because he thought that the probability of a Communist victory in the Dominican Republic was high, but rather because he attached high value to avoiding such an outcome. In other words, he was unwilling to accept even a relatively low risk of a Communist takeover. At the same time, however, the president's known concern over the possibility of another Castro heightened the sensitivity of those reporting on events in the Dominican Republic to any possible evidence of Communist influence and led to distorted information search and appraisal. Commenting on this, Abraham Lowenthal notes how pervasive the tendency is for policymakers to rely on historical analogies, "lessons of history," and simplifying concepts: "Policy-makers seize on evils they have experienced and wish to avoid in order to organize their information about events they do not have the time to analyze from scratch . . . unfamiliar problems are discussed in terms of the familiar."[33]

Other scholars as well have called attention to the risks associated with the policymaker's reliance on historical analogies. Often the causal linkage which the policymaker assumes to have been present in the past case is questionable in and of itself; or else he overgeneralizes the causal relationship that was indeed present in a historical case and misapplies it to a new situation that differs in important respects. One way of avoiding these habits is to absorb the lessons of many different historical cases into a richer, differentiated theory that is comprised of *contingent* generalizations, i.e., the conditions under which a particular causal relationship of policy relevance does and does not hold. For example, the simple generalization: "if appeasement, then World War III," should be converted into conditional generalizations: "Under what conditions is appeasement likely to lead to a larger war? And, under what conditions is appeasement likely to achieve useful foreign-policy objectives without leading to a major war?" (For further discussion of the need for policy-relevant theory of this kind, *see* Chapter 14.)

Ideology and General Principles as Guides to Action. Other sources of relatively simple decision rules for coping with decisional complexity and the uncertainties that hamper calculation of outcomes are to be found in the ideological beliefs and moral principles of the policymaker. They provide a generalized, deductive belief system which, applied to a particular situation, can help the decisionmaker to cut through its complexity to illuminate whether, when, and how he should respond to it.

Thus, for example, Cordell Hull, secretary of state under Franklin D. Roosevelt, had memorized as a youth a set of maxims from Jefferson and Gladstone. "As I faced the stupendous problems to be dealt with abroad," Hull wrote of his first month in office, "it gave me some relief and greater confidence to feel that I was strongly grounded on the fundamental propositions that should govern relations among nations. I proceeded to assemble and classify these principles, all of which the President, too, believed in strongly, and to make practical application of them at appropriate times."[34]

Hull's principles no doubt served to simplify and structure the problem of action he faced repeatedly as secretary of state. Whether they also enabled him to exercise consistently good judgment in foreign policy is another matter. Arthur Schlesinger, Jr., for one, wrote critically of the use to which Hull put his "principles": "often . . . they served as a means of avoiding problems until he could find an aspect reducible to his set of principles, or of disguising, even from himself, some of his less creditable impulses. . . . Hull's moral world was bounded, in other words, not by the facts or by original moral convictions, but by the copy-book maxims into which he absorbed both the facts and his emotions."[35]

Beliefs about correct strategy and tactics. The problem of action in the face of uncertainty is eased for the decisionmaker by fundamental beliefs he holds about (a) the nature of international politics and conflict; (b) the extent to which historical developments can be shaped by intelligent or misguided action; and (c) axioms regarding correct strategy and tactics for dealing with friendly and unfriendly actors in domestic and world political arenas. Most political actors have developed relatively stable views on many of these matters. These beliefs are part of the "cognitive map" which enables them to process information and engage in appraisals of alternative courses of action.

The term "operational code" has been employed in referring to beliefs of this kind held by a particular statesman or policy elite. But the term is somewhat a misnomer insofar as it implies or permits the inference that a leader's "operational code" consists of a set of recipes or rules for action that he applies mechanically in his decisionmaking. Rather, beliefs of this kind serve as a prism or filter that influences the actor's perception and diagnosis of political situations and that provides norms and standards to guide and channel his choices of action in specific situations. The function of an operational code belief system in decisionmaking, then, is to provide the actor with "diagnostic propensities" and "choice propensities." Neither his diagnosis of situations nor his choice of action for dealing with them is rigidly prescribed and determined by these beliefs. Rather, their function is to *simplify* and *channel* the task of processing information, inventing and appraising options, and choosing the action that seems best in the circumstances. Stated in another way, these beliefs serve to adapt the actor's effort to engage in optimal informational processing and in rational calculation to the complexity and uncertainty that are characteristic of so much political decisionmaking.

The old Bolsheviks, for example, developed a set of beliefs which led them to employ a special kind of optimizing strategy in relations with opponents, both domestic and external.[36] It was unnecessary and undesirable in their view to approach the task of selecting the objectives of political action by trying first to calculate precisely the probability of achieving each of the alternative objectives that might be pursued in a given situation. Further, the old Bolsheviks believed that one should not limit the choice of objective to one that appears quite likely or certain of realization. Rather, one should be willing to pursue more ambitious objectives that were possible of achievement, even though the probability of a successful outcome was uncertain and difficult to calculate. By following these maxims one would safeguard against falling into an overly conservative approach to political action, typified by the tendency to pare down the goals of action to those that seemed highly feasible and likely to be achieved.

Resort to an optimizing strategy of this kind did not imply neglect of risk and cost calculations. The old Bolshevik "code" assigned important limits to the preferred optimizing strategy. Thus, for example, the risks of pursuing ambitious objectives could be controlled by *limiting the means* employed on their behalf. (In contrast, in one influential American approach to international politics, a *limitation of objectives* was considered particularly important for keeping limited conflicts with adversaries such as the Soviet Union from expanding dangerously.)

There were, as a result, important differences between Soviet and U.S. approaches to the calculation and acceptance of risks during the period of the Cold War. Soviet leaders acted on the premise, derived from the old Bolshevik "code," that in the struggle to make important gains one can often accept *seemingly* high risks — such as the danger of war — so long as the undesired outcome is several steps removed in a possible temporal sequence and so long as, in addition, one can control the sequence of events that might lead to that undesired outcome. These beliefs about correct strategy and tactics led Soviet leaders on a number of occasions (e.g., the Berlin crises) to engage in what they regarded as low-risk, controlled-risk actions to advance their interests as part of an "optimizing" strategy. To Western leaders and audiences, however, these same actions appeared to indicate that Soviet leaders were engaging in high-risk actions and were indeed prepared to risk war. The risk of war, however, was in fact several steps removed; and Soviet leaders, applying their own approach to risk-calculation and risk-acceptance, could well believe that they retained the possibility of moderating their actions, terminating the crisis or redirecting it into safer channels, should it become necessary to do so.

It is clear that during the Cold War the two sides often operated with fundamentally different notions of what constituted a rational approach to risk-calculation and risk-acceptance under conditions of uncertainty.

Interpreting Soviet behavior from the standpoint of their own approach to risk-calculation led Western leaders and publics on more than one occasion to distorted judgments regarding Soviet intentions and the willingness of Soviet leaders to incur high risks.

• • •

Each of the seven cognitive aids to decisionmaking that have now been discussed can enable the policymaker to cope in some way with the intellectual problem he faces when the decision he must make is clouded with uncertainty. The substantive quality of the decision is, of course, another matter. Leaving aside a direct answer to this question, let us consider instead the implications of the policymaker's use of these cognitive aids and simple decision rules for his ability to benefit from the contribution that close advisers and the organizational information-processing system can make to his search for an effective decision.

The first thing to be noted is the danger that the executive will resort *prematurely* to one of his favored cognitive aids or simple decision rules — for example, a historical analogy or a maxim of correct strategy, a "satisficing" or a "consensus" decision rule — or *rely too heavily* on it in making his decision. The result may well be to cut himself off from the possibility of benefiting from a broader or in-depth analysis of the problem that advisers or the organizational information-processing system can provide. Cognitive aids and decision rules may be indispensable, but they carry the risk of serving as filters that screen, channel, or block the executive's receptivity to information and advice from others. The cognitive aid or decision rule an executive leans on in order to reach a decision can easily serve to define in a narrow way his informational needs in that situation. He will tend to pay less attention or give less weight to available information and advice that is not directly relevant and usable with respect to the cognitive aid or decision rule he utilizes in order to cut through the intellectual complexity and "confusion" surrounding the problem at hand. This has important implications for the design and management of advisory relationships and organizational information-processing systems.

International Crises as a Source of Stress

Diplomatic confrontations and military crises can be extremely stressful for policymakers and, depending on how policymakers cope with the emotions aroused, can impair information processing and performance of the cognitive tasks associated with policymaking.[37]

Let us consider first the characteristics of crises and confrontations that can generate high levels of stress:

First, stress is generated by the fact that an international crisis typically entails *a strong threat to major values and interests* that top officials are responsible for safeguarding.

A second source of stress is present when, as is so often the case, the crisis comes as a *surprise* to policymakers—that is, with little warning. Even crises that have been anticipated to some extent can have quite a shock effect insofar as they present novel features that were not foreseen.

A third source of stress stems from the fact that crises often require *quick decisions.* Short response time is typical of many international crises, and it imposes an additional psychological burden on decision-makers.

Finally, a fourth source of stress is the cumulative *emotional and physical fatigue* that an international crisis often imposes on top policymakers and their staffs. In a crisis, minutes seem like hours, hours like days, days like weeks. The demands on one's energies and emotions are intense; at the same time, opportunities for rest and recuperation are limited. Robert Kennedy's memoir of the Cuban missile crisis makes it clear that tensions during some days reached an almost unbearable intensity: "that kind of [crisis-induced] pressure does strange things to a human being, even to brilliant, self-confident, mature, experienced men. For some it brings out characteristics and strengths that perhaps even they never knew they had, and for others the pressure is too overwhelming."[38] Theodore Sorensen, also a participant in the policymaking group during the missile crisis, reports that he saw firsthand, "during the long days and nights of the Cuban crisis, how brutally physical and mental fatigue can numb the good sense as well as the senses of normally articulate men."[39]

What, then, can be said about the effects of crisis-induced stress on performance of policymaking tasks? Only a brief summary of laboratory and field studies will be presented here. It is true that *mild* levels of stress often facilitate and may actually improve performance, especially if the responses required by the situational task are relatively uncomplicated. But as stress increases to higher levels, performance worsens. This general relationship between stress and performance—often referred to as an "inverted U" curve—is well supported by research findings for a variety of tasks and conditions. At some point, every individual reaches a "threshold" or crossover point at which increased stress no longer improves performance but leads to a more or less rapid decline in performance. However, the point at which the "threshold" is reached varies for different individuals so that, fortunately, one would expect some members of a decisionmaking group to be functioning effectively even though the performance of others has sharply deteriorated. Moreover, the threshold for any given individual varies depending on the nature of the task and the setting in which he or she is experiencing the stress.

While stress affects the performance of a variety of tasks, we are interested here in its effects on the types of complex cognitive tasks associated with foreign-policy decisionmaking. The following is a brief summary of major types of effects that have been noted.

1. *Impaired attention and perception:* (a) important aspects of the crisis situation may escape scrutiny; (b) conflicting values may be overlooked; (c) the range of perceived alternatives is likely to narrow but not necessarily to the best alternatives; and (d) "search" for relevant information and options tends to be dominated by past experience, with a tendency to fall back on familiar solutions that have worked in the past whether or not they are appropriate to the present situation.

2. *Increased cognitive rigidity:* (a) impaired ability to improvise and reduced creativity; (b) reduced receptivity to information that challenges existing beliefs; (c) increased stereotypic thinking; and (d) reduced tolerance for ambiguity, which results in a tendency to cut off information search and evaluation and make decisions prematurely.

3. *Shortened and narrowed perspective:* (a) less attention to longer-range consequences of options; (b) less attention to side effects of options.

4. *Shifting the burden to the opponent:* the belief that one's own options are quite limited and that only the other side has it within its power to prevent an impending disaster.

Many other events and situations that arise in the conduct of foreign policy share some of the same characteristics of threat, surprise, and short response time associated with international crises and, hence, can have similar effects on performance. This is the case, for example, when decisionmakers must meet deadlines on important matters. It is also the case at times when decisionmakers experience role conflicts and role overload. The effects of situationally aroused stress upon performance, therefore, are not confined to international crises. The fundamental constraints of value-complexity and uncertainty that are imbedded in so many foreign-policy problems are themselves capable of generating psychological stress in policymakers that can impair their judgment.

Notes

1. In preparing this chapter, I have drawn on my earlier discussion of some of these problems in A. L. George, "Adaptation to Stress in Political Decision Making," in George V. Coelho, David A. Hamburg, and John E. Adams, eds., *Coping and Adaptation* (New York: Basic Books, 1974).

2. A similar postulate underlies the "conflict theory" developed by Janis and Mann. The desire to avoid the stress of decisional conflicts, they emphasize, is a more general motivation than the consistency-striving postulated in early cognitive dissonance theory. Janis and Mann note, further, that neo-dissonance theory has moved in the direction of this more general motivational concept (I. L. Janis and L. Mann, *Decision Making: A Psychological Analysis of Conflict, Choice, and Commitment* [New York: Free Press, 1977], pp. 17, 420).

3. The concept of "value extension" is taken from the valuable discussion of constraints on rational decisionmaking in John D. Steinbruner, *The Cybernetic Theory of Decision* (Princeton, N.J.: Princeton University Press, 1974), p. 145.

4. For useful discussions of these cognitive limits on rational choice and some of their implications in the arena of political decisionmaking, *see,* for example, James G. March and Herbert A. Simon, *Organizations* (New York: Wiley, 1958); and Charles E. Lindblom, "The Science of 'Muddling Through,'" *Public Administration Quarterly* 29 (spring 1959):79-88. An incisive discussion of these issues is provided in Chapter 2, "The Analytic Paradigm," in Steinbruner, *Cybernetic Theory.*

5. Dean Pruitt, *Problem Solving in the Department of State,* Monograph Series in World Affairs, no. 2 (Denver: University of Denver, 1965), p. 62; *see also* John McDonald, "How the Man at the Top Avoids Crises," *Fortune* 81 (1970):121-22, 152-55.

6. On the trade-off between "quality" and "acceptability" of a decision *see Introduction* to this book.

7. For example, after having made a decision that ignores or gives insufficient weight to some values, the policymaker may attempt to convince those damaged by his action that it was the right or necessary thing to do, or to demonstrate that he is a worthwhile person who is still identified with their interests and welfare, or to resort to acts of expiation or asceticism in order to relieve the self-disapproval or guilt that he experiences as a result of having acted contrary to their interests and values (*see* Janis and Mann, *Decision Making,* pp. 144-47).

8. Robert Jervis deals with the phenomenon of "irrational consistency" and its role in denial of value trade-off problems in considerable detail in his study, *Perception and Misperception in International Politics* (Princeton, N.J.: Princeton University Press, 1976), chapter four.

9. For a detailed discussion, *see* Joseph de Rivera, *The Psychological Dimension of Foreign Policy* (Columbus, Ohio: Charles E. Merrill Publishing Co., 1968), pp. 85-94; *see also* A. L. George and R. Smoke, *Deterrence in American Foreign Policy: Theory and Practice* (New York: Columbia University Press, 1974), chapter 6.

10. This example is taken from Jervis, *Perception and Misperception,* p. 140.

Of course, we cannot be certain of the psychological explanation advanced here for Roosevelt's policy. It is possible that Roosevelt was well aware that the Eastern European governments might prove to be hostile to the USSR but accepted that possibility as a calculated risk.

11. A particularly vivid example of the stress produced for an executive by his inability to cope with decisional complexity is provided by President Warren G. Harding. On one occasion, Harding unburdened himself to a friend: "John, I can't make a damn thing out of this tax problem. I listen to one side and they seem right, and then God! I talk to the other side and they seem just as right, and there I am where I started. I know somewhere there is a book that would give me the truth, but hell, I couldn't read the book. I know somewhere there is an economist who knows the truth, but I don't know where to find him and haven't the sense to know him and trust him when I did find him. God, what a job!" (Quoted by Richard Fenno, *The President's Cabinet* [Cambridge, Mass: Harvard University Press, 1959], pp. 40-41).

12. R. C. Snyder, H. W. Bruck, and B. Sapin, *Foreign Policy Decision-making* (New York: Free Press, 1962), p. 167.

13. Fenno, *President's Cabinet,* pp. 40-41.

14. The discussion of "defensive procrastination" here and the discussion of "hypervigilance," "defensive avoidance," and "bolstering" draw in part on the work of Irving L. Janis. *See* particularly Janis and Mann, *Decision Making.*

15. George and Smoke, *Deterrence,* pp. 291-92, 385-86.

16. The importance of deadlines and the functions they serve has been stressed in the work of a number of specialists on organizational decisionmaking. For a summary of research findings, *see* Lennart A. Arvedson, *Deadlines and Organizational Behavior* (Ph.D. diss., Stanford University, July 1974).

17. As Janis notes (in a personal communication), defensive avoidance is probably rare when different persons at different levels of an organization work independently on a policy problem, insofar as this increases the likelihood that flimsy rationalizations entertained by any one person or group will be challenged by others. The absence of such conditions, on the other hand, is likely to increase the incidence of defensive avoidance. For a fuller discussion, *see* Janis and Mann, *Decision Making.*

18. Janis and Mann also discuss a third type of defensive avoidance — the familiar practice of "buck-passing" (*Decision Making,* pp. 58, 312-14).

19. Bolstering also occurs when the decisionmaker resorts to consistency-striving devices to avoid value trade-off problems; the present discussion focuses on its use in dealing with uncertainty, as defined here.

20. This is still something of a controversial issue among social psychologists, with some of those associated with cognitive dissonance theory holding that bolstering or dissonance reduction occurs only *after* a decision is made. However, Janis and Mann present evidence that under certain conditions bolstering occurs *before* a decision is made.

21. I am indebted for the last point to Lincoln Bloomfield (personal communication).

22. This seventh type of rationalization is suggested by Jervis, *Perception and*

Misperception, p. 135, who gives as an example the argument of the type made by McGeorge Bundy in February 1965 for the bombing of North Vietnam.

23. The following discussion draws upon and elaborates the ideas presented earlier in George, "Adaptation to Stress."

24. This simple (and widely used) distinction between seeking a satisfactory (i.e., sufficient and good enough) as against an optimal outcome was made by Herbert A. Simon, "A Behavioral Model of Rational Choice," *Quarterly Journal of Economics* 69 (February 1955). *See also* James G. March and Herbert A. Simon, *Organizations* (New York: Wiley, 1958), pp. 140-41; and Richard M. Cyert and James G. March, *A Behavioral Theory of the Firm* (Englewood Cliffs, N.J.: Prentice-Hall, 1964).

25. Charles E. Lindblom is perhaps the foremost expositer and exponent of incremental decisionmaking. *See* "The Science of 'Muddling Through'," which appeared originally in *Public Administration Review* 29 (1959):79-88 and has been widely reprinted. For a fuller development of his views, in which he doubted that incrementalism was an appropriate strategy in foreign policy, *see* C. E. Lindblom and D. Braybrooke, *A Strategy of Decision* (New York: Free Press, 1963), and C. E. Lindblom, *The Policy-making Process* (Englewood Cliffs, N.J.: Prentice-Hall, 1968). For an important reformulation of incrementalism, *see* Steinbruner, *Cybernetic Paradigm,* Chapter 3.

26. George and Smoke, *Deterrence,* chapter 7.

27. This section draws upon A. L. George, "Problem-oriented Forecasting," in Nazli Choucri and Thomas W. Robinson, eds., *Forecasting in International Relations* (San Francisco: W.H. Freeman & Co., 1978), pp. 329-36.

28. *See,* for example, the discussion of uncertainties in Edward Quade and Wayne Boucher, eds., *Systems Analysis and Policy Planning* (New York: American Elsevier Co., 1968), pp. 39-40, 312, 355-57, 371-72, 384-85. *See also* Edward Quade, ed., *Analysis for Military Decisions* (Santa Monica: The Rand Corporation, 1964), pp. 136, 170-72, 228ff, 232, 235.

29. The emphasis of this strategy on creating options and maintaining policy flexibility encounters other criticisms as well, among them that there are often hidden costs to avoiding clear-cut and timely policy commitments. *See,* for example, Thomas L. Hughes, "Relativity in Foreign Policy," *Foreign Affairs,* July 1967.

30. Davis Bobrow, "The Chinese Communist Conflict System," *Orbis* 9 (winter 1966):931. *See also* Jervis, *Perception and Misperception,* chapter 6.

31. Ernest May, "The Relevance of Diplomatic History to the Practice of International Relations" (Paper given at the annual meeting of the American Political Science Association, September 1965).

32. For a useful discussion, *see* Ernest R. May, *"Lessons" of the Past: The Uses and Misuses of History in American Foreign Policy* (New York: Oxford University Press, 1972), p. 161.

33. A. F. Lowenthal, *The Dominican Intervention* (Cambridge, Mass.: Harvard University Press, 1972), p. 161.

34. Cordell Hull, *Memoirs* (New York: Macmillan, 1948), vol. 1, p. 173.

35. Arthur Schlesinger, "The Roosevelt Era: Stimson and Hull," *The Nation*

(June 5, 1948). As Schlesinger's essay indicates, historians often employ cognitive psychology to interpret the behavior of historical actors. Available historical materials contain considerable data relevant for such analysis, but they are seldom studied systematically and with a more explicit theoretical framework.

36. The following paragraphs draw upon Nathan Leites, *A Study of Bolshevism* (New York: Free Press, 1953), and Alexander L. George, "The 'Operational Code': A Neglected Approach to the Study of Political Leaders and Decision-Making," *International Studies Quarterly* 13 (1969).

37. Pioneering research of a systematic kind on the stress-inducing effects of international crises on decisionmaking has been done by Charles F. Hermann in *Crises in Foreign Policy: A Simulation Analysis* (Indianapolis: Bobbs-Merrill, 1969) and in a later book which he edited: *International Crises: Insights from Behavioral Research* (New York: Free Press, 1972). Important pioneering work on the effects of stress on policymakers during the events leading to World War I was undertaken by Robert North and his associates at Stanford University; the fullest account is Ole R. Holsti, *Crisis, Escalation, War* (Montreal and London: McGill-Queen's University Press, 1972).

An important synthesis of the effects of crisis-induced stress on foreign-policy decisionmaking, together with suggestions for monitoring and dealing with these effects, was presented by Margaret G. Hermann and Charles F. Hermann, "Maintaining the Quality of Decision-making in Foreign Policy Crises: A Proposal," in A. L. George et al., *Towards A More Soundly Based Foreign Policy: Making Better Use of Information,* vol. 2, Appendices, Commission on the Organization of the Government for the Conduct of Foreign Policy, June 1975 (Washington, D.C.: U.S. Government Printing Office, 1976). A broader summary of research findings of the effects of stress from a variety of sources, including crises, was presented by Ole R. Holsti and Alexander L. George, "The Effects of Stress on the Performance of Foreign Policy-makers," in Cornelius P. Cotter, ed., *Political Science Annual,* vol. 6, 1975 (Indianapolis: Bobbs-Merrill, 1976), pp. 255-319.

38. Robert F. Kennedy, *Thirteen Days* (New York: W. W. Norton & Co., 1969), p. 22.

39. Theodore C. Sorensen, *Decision-Making in the White House* (New York: Columbia University Press, 1964), p. 76.

3
The Importance of
Beliefs and Images

While the subject of foreign policy generates many disagreements, most thoughtful observers of international affairs nonetheless do agree upon the overriding importance of some of its fundamental characteristics.[1] Thus, sophisticated policymakers and academic scholars alike agree that relations among states are shaped by the way in which leaders view each other and, more generally, by their beliefs about the nature of conflict within the international system. The importance of such beliefs and images is emphasized, for example, by a former State Department planner, Louis Halle, who reminds us that the foreign policy of a nation addresses itself not to the external world, as is commonly stated, but rather to "the *image* of the external world" that is in the minds of those who make foreign policy. "In the degree that the image is false," Halle warns, "no technicians, however efficient, can make the policy that is based on it sound."[2]

The same point is increasingly emphasized in the work of academic scholars who, influenced by psychological theories of cognition, have been struck by the role that the subjective beliefs, perceptions, and misperceptions of foreign-policymakers play in their decisionmaking.[3]

It is useful at the outset, therefore, to remind ourselves of some of the basic tenets of cognitive psychology and to take note of some recent developments in this field that have considerable relevance for the study of decisionmaking.

For at least a decade now there has been among social psychologists "an epidemic of critical self-evaluation and debate about the current status of the field's theory, research strategy, practical contributions, and prospects for the future."[4] Of particular interest to political scientists and others engaged in research on political decisionmaking is the fact that these developments in psychology have produced a major paradigm shift referred to by some as "a cognitive revolution" in psychology. Recent developments in cognitive balance and dissonance theories, attribution theory, attitude theory, social learning theory, and personality theory are moving or already have moved each of them into an information-processing framework.[5]

The convergence of so many important subfields of psychology into a common information-processing framework promises not only to produce a more fruitful synthesis of psychological theories relevant to the study of decisionmaking; we are on the threshold—indeed already beyond it—of a new wave of research in psychology that promises to be even more relevant and useful for study of political decision-making than these subfields, individually and collectively, have been in the past.

Two important aspects of this paradigm shift should be noted. First is the shift in the fundamental "model of man" assumption away from the conception of man as a passive agent who merely responds to environmental stimuli back to a conception of man as selectively responding to and actively shaping his environment.[6] Second, within the conceptualization of man as an active agent, an additional shift has occurred away from the fundamental premise of earlier cognitive balance theories that viewed man as a "consistency seeker" to the different premise of recent attribution theory (and other psychological theories as well), which views man as a "problem solver."

This recent emphasis on viewing man as a problem solver does not mean that it is no longer fruitful to view man also as a consistency seeker in certain contexts. What it does is to overcome the narrowness of the earlier model of man as a mere consistency seeker and to substitute a broader framework that encompasses man's effort to function as a rational problem solver in dealing with his environment. We shall discuss in more detail the implications for decisionmaking of both models—man as a problem solver and man as a consistency seeker. But first it will be useful to state briefly the major tenets of cognitive psychology that are pertinent for the information-processing paradigm.

Information Processing Viewed from the Perspective of Cognitive Psychology

The fundamental tenets of cognitive psychology that are directly pertinent for this study can be listed briefly, since, once stated, they are readily recognizable in everyday experience.[7]

First, the mind can be fruitfully viewed as an information-processing system. Individuals orient themselves to their surroundings by acquiring, storing, appraising, and utilizing information about the physical and social environment.

Second, in order to function, every individual acquires during the course of his development a set of beliefs and personal constructs about the physical and social environment. These beliefs provide him with a relatively coherent way of organizing and making sense of what would otherwise be a confusing and overwhelming array of signals and cues picked up from the environment by his senses.

Third, these beliefs and constructs necessarily simplify and structure the external world. That such beliefs are indispensable was emphasized many years ago by the philosopher, Joseph Jastrow, in the striking observation that the mind is essentially "a belief-seeking rather than a fact-seeking apparatus."

Fourth, much of an individual's behavior is shaped by the particular ways in which he perceives, evaluates, and interprets incoming information about events in his environment.

Fifth, information processing is selective and subject to bias; the individual's existing beliefs and his "attention-set" at any given time are active agents in determining what he attends to and how he evaluates it.

Sixth, there is considerable variation among individuals in the richness-complexity as well as the validity of their beliefs and constructs regarding any given portion of the environment. (These differences are evident also in the way in which different individuals view the international arena and can be of considerable significance in the conduct of foreign policy.)

Seventh, while such beliefs can change, what is noteworthy is that they tend to be relatively stable. They are not easily subject to disconfirmation and to change in response to new information that seems to challenge them. Instead, individuals (including decisionmakers) tend to downgrade discrepant new information of this kind or interpret it in ways that reduce its inconsistency with their prevailing beliefs, images, and theories of the physical, social, and political world.

Eighth, and notwithstanding the preceding tenet, individuals are capable of perceiving the utility of discrepant information and adopting an attitude of open-mindedness with regard to new information that significantly goes counter to their current beliefs.

Knowledge of cognitive psychology is indispensable for understanding some of the fundamental constraints on processing of information in foreign-policymaking. While these tenets apply in the first instance to the individual qua individual, they have their analogues also in the constraints that apply to information processing in small groups and organizations. There are, of course, additional sources of impediments to information processing in policymaking; some of them will be discussed later in this report.

Attributional Biases: The Policymaker as "Naive Scientist"

We noted developments in social psychology that have elevated man's status from that of a mere "consistency seeker" to that of a "problem solver." No longer are those social psychologists who are engaged in developing theories about human behavior content to work within the narrow confines of the premise that man has a drive to seek consistency (or "balance") in his cognitive beliefs. The new emphasis on man as a "problem solver" shifts attention to three types of activities in which man engages in order to understand and exercise some control over the environment and the outcomes of social situations. Thus, as a problem solver man seeks (1) to discern the attributes of other actors and social phenomena; (2) to infer the causes of salient events; and (3) to predict historical trends and the behavior of other persons.

Hence, there is an emphasis on man as a would-be scientist, one who is engaged in acquiring knowledge and theories by means of which to explain, predict, and control. But at the same time, as attribution theory reminds us, man often performs these tasks as a "naive" scientist. That is, instead of employing scientific epistemology to perfection in attempting to discern the attributes of other actors, to explain, and to predict, man often lapses into the use of "naive epistemology," which betrays various flaws, biases, and errors.

A political scientist who reads the descriptions of the "naive scientist" and the systematic, documented accounts of the "naive scientist's" flawed epistemology that attribution theorists have recently provided is immediately struck by the fact that these are apt descriptions also of the way in which policymakers and, indeed the policymaking system as a whole, often perform![8] One can go further and fruitfully define the task of designing and managing policymaking and advisory systems as that of avoiding or at least correcting flaws, errors, and biases of the kind that the policymakers' lapse into naive epistemology otherwise introduces into the information processing associated with decisionmaking.

Attribution theorists have been engaged in identifying the various types of errors and biases that characterize naive epistemology. A brief listing and discussion of some of them will suffice to indicate their relevance to a study of the various sources of impediments in policymaking.

The "fundamental" attribution error, as described in this literature, is the tendency to overemphasize *situational* variables when explaining one's own behavior and, conversely, when explaining the behavior of others to emphasize *dispositional* variables in their makeup. The tendency to explain another person's behavior in terms of his dispositions is enhanced when the observer dislikes the other person and regards his action as blameworthy. A Norwegian political scientist, Daniel Heradstveit, has applied this hypothesized attribution tendency in his study of the mutual perceptions of Arab and Israeli opinion leaders and the role that they play in accentuating the Middle East conflict.[9] His interview materials provide considerable support not for the original hypothesized attribution tendency, but for a refinement and reformulation of it that takes into account the type of situation and the respondent's evaluation of the behavior being explained. Thus, Heradstveit finds that:

1. When observing one's own "*good*" behavior, the tendency of both Arabs and Israelis is to explain it in dispositional terms.
2. But when observing the behavior of one's own side of which the respondent disapproves, the tendency is to explain it in situational terms—i.e., one's own side is forced by the situation to behave badly. However, these relationships are reversed when the individual respondent observes and explains the opponent's behavior.
3. Thus, when the opponent admittedly behaves well in a particular instance, the tendency of both Arab and Israeli respondents is to explain it in situational terms.
4. In contrast, when the opponent is seen as behaving badly in a particular situation, the explanation offered is in terms of his dispositions.

As Heradstveit notes, this attributional pattern is of considerable significance for understanding some of the psychological obstacles to negotiation and resolution of the Arab-Israeli conflict. Each side tends to believe that any "good" behavior by the opponent has been forced on him by situational factors and that the opponent's "bad" behavior toward the respondent's side springs from the opponent's negative dispositions, not situational factors. Given this kind of attributional pattern, it becomes particularly difficult for either side to show good faith and to overcome the opponent's distrust. Psychological de-escalation of the conflict becomes difficult, for neither side tends to give the opponent credit for good behavior. Evidence to the contrary is explained away as forced on the opponent by circumstances; and when the opponent is forced by circumstances to act in an unfriendly manner, it is interpreted as reflecting his hostile, immoral dispositions, and this reinforces the existing negative stereotype of the opponent.

Another attributional bias is the tendency when making inferences about other people or explaining situations to overlook the evidentiary value of nonoccurrences. As Sherlock Holmes pointed out to Dr. Watson on one occasion, it was the fact that the dog did *not* bark during the night in question that provided a clue as to the identity of the intruder. The distinguished diplomatic historian, Ernest May, calls attention to the fact that when Truman and his advisers were drawing general conclusions about the nature of the Soviet opponent and Soviet foreign policy from the evidence of the hard position that the Soviets were taking on Poland, Rumania, and Bulgaria, they ignored or dismissed the fact that Stalin's behavior elsewhere was more moderate. Thus, Stalin did not object to a non-Communist regime in Finland so long as the government gave meaningful asssurances of nonhostility toward the Soviet Union. In Czechoslovakia, the Soviets were tolerating a coalition government in which the Communists were a minority. In Hungary, the Soviets did not interfere in the elections, which strongly favored the non-Communist parties. (The Soviets did not pressure Hungary into becoming a full satellite until 1947, after the Truman Doctrine was proclaimed.)[10]

Another type of attributional bias often creeps into a person's explanation of outcomes. When the outcome is favorable for the actor, he tends to attribute decisive importance to his role in bringing it about.[11] Conversely, when the outcome is unfavorable, the actor tends to find the explanation in factors outside his own behavior or control. These attributional biases, of course, impede efforts to draw valid inferences from one's own experiences.

Finally, attribution theorists have noted various biases that creep into the intuitive predictions of the naive scientist. D. Kahneman and A. Tversky have demonstrated that the intuitive predictions and judgments made by social observers and even those made by trained social scientists often deviate markedly from the canons of statistics. Rather, these observers seem to be employing a limited number of "heuristics" or rules-of-thumb to simplify the task of estimating probabilities.

One of these is the "availability" heuristic, which describes a tendency for predicting the outcome that is most easily remembered or imagined on the basis of past experience. Another is the "representativeness" heuristic, which refers to the tendency to predict the outcome that appears to be the most representative of the salient features of the type of situation or person in question.

The use of such rules-of-thumb in making predictions ignores conventional statistical criteria such as the reliability, validity, and amount of available evidence, or the prior baseline probabilities associated with the relevant outcomes. Hence, use of the "availability" and "representativeness" heuristics may lead to serious errors in prediction.

Related to the "availability"–"representativeness" heuristics is the tendency to place more reliance on concrete information than abstract information in making predictions. Connected with this is the policymaker's well-known tendency, already noted in Chapter 2, to rely on a concrete historical analogy—the "lessons" of an earlier case—in diagnosing a new situation and in predicting the consequences of alternative ways of dealing with it. Recent or highly salient events are generally more readily retrieved from memory. The policymaker typically turns most readily to relatively recent historical cases that had a profound impact on him and his peers, which he experienced personally or vicariously through contact with persons influential in his development.

Another type of bias in making predictions occurs when a person confuses the conceivability of an outcome with its probability. This difficulty is likely to arise particularly when policymakers have to consider the likelihood of developments for which there is very little relevant historical experience. This is a familiar problem in policy planning when one must judge the credibility of various scenarios. It may be possible to identify the conditions under which a development or outcome is conceivable; the scenario, then, may be said to be plausible. But the probability of the scenario's outcome, subject as it is to the likelihood that all the conditions, interactions, and sequences depicted in the scenario will occur together, is another matter.

The use of heuristics and rules-of-thumb of this kind is inevitable, since they simplify and make possible the handling of otherwise enormously complex, difficult tasks of prediction. Nor does their use necessarily lead to serious informational biases in all instances. Awareness of that possibility, however, is useful, and institutional provisions are needed for vigilant monitoring and correction of the flaws that such heuristics can introduce into information processing.

Dissonance-Reduction Biases:
The Policymaker as "Consistency Seeker"

While much of man's behavior can best be understood by viewing him as a problem solver, nonetheless, in processing information he also displays a strong tendency to see what he expects to see and to assimilate incoming information to the images, hypotheses, and theories that he has already formed. It is not inappropriate, therefore, to regard man as, among other things, a "consistency seeker." To be sure, this penchant for consistency seeking may hamper him in his role as problem solver. This is true not only for individual decisionmakers but also for small decisionmaking groups and organizations. In this section of the chapter we will consider the impact that "consistency striving" can have on the quality of information processed for policymaking purposes.

We must recognize at the outset that there is no easy solution to this problem, for, it cannot be emphasized too strongly, a pronounced tendency toward consistency striving is inherent in human behavior. Thus, perception and interpretation of new information would hardly be possible unless it were filtered through existing beliefs and frames of reference. One must be careful, therefore, not to apply the labels of "closed-mindedness," "cognitive distortion," and "irrationality" in too facile a manner. For under many circumstances it is quite natural for an individual to strive to maintain his beliefs in the face of seemingly discrepant information that challenges them and, additionally, to attempt to maintain some degree of consistency among his beliefs. Organizations as well as individuals typically attempt to incorporate new information in ways that render it comprehensible within existing cognitive frameworks on which they rely to organize new experience and to orient the organization effectively to the environment in which it exists.

Besides, we must recognize that the mind is called upon to interpret inherently vague or conflicting data. It is often quite inappropriate to refer to the resulting perceptions and judgments as being "rational" or "irrational." We must be careful, in other words, not to confuse error with irrationality, not to infer from post hoc observations that an error or oversimplification that occurred in policymaking was due to some form of irrational perception or judgment. It seems advisable, therefore, to avoid using the term "irrational" (which has the general connotation that a person has abandoned reality-testing, is totally lacking in sense, behaves impulsively or mindlessly, etc.) in referring to instances of consistency striving of the kind discussed here.

At the same time, however, to accept the fact that consistency striving is pervasive does not require us to take a deterministic and fatalistic view of the matter. That some manifestations of an individual's consistency striving are excessive and possibly harmful in policymaking is something that he, or certainly other participants in policymaking, are capable of recognizing and possibly correcting. This way of approaching the phenomenon of consistency striving has the merit of drawing attention to the practical question of how to design and manage the policymaking process in order to avoid the occurrence of those forms of consistency striving that are likely to severely narrow, distort, or curtail information processing and appraisal.

While it will be difficult sometimes even with the benefit of hindsight to ascertain whether a given instance of consistency striving was excessive and inadequately scrutinized, a number of criteria or indicators can be identified as relevant and useful for this purpose. The individual's striving for consistency need not arouse concern when his interpretation of new information is not clearly illogical and when the preexisting beliefs he relies upon are adequately grounded in previous experience. On the other hand, the striving for consistency becomes suspect and demands greater vigilance in information processing

(a) when the beliefs preserved thereby are not well-grounded to begin with; or

(b) when the individual (or organization) relies upon inappropriate beliefs or irrelevant rationalizations in order to ward off incoming information; or

(c) when the assimilation of the new information into preexisting beliefs involves violations of generally accepted rules for treating evidence; or

(d) when the individual fails to notice events of obvious importance that contradict his beliefs or theories; or

(e) when he displays unwillingness to look for evidence that is readily available which would pose challenges to existing policy beliefs; or

(f) when he refuses to address the arguments of those who disagree with his interpretation of events; or

(g) when he repeatedly shifts rationales on behalf of his policy in response to new facts.

From a practical standpoint these criteria are useful in and of themselves even though they will not always enable a historian to make confident *post facto* judgments as to whether consistency striving in any particular instance was excessive. Thus, awareness of the criteria among policymakers should alert participants to the possibility that the natural tendency to consistency striving may be leading them or their colleagues into narrowing or distorting their processing and appraisal of information about the situation.

For the policymaker to discount a single item of information that challenges existing beliefs may not constitute very good evidence of harmful consistency striving. But when a whole series of such items is discounted in an ad hoc, piecemeal way, there is a higher probability that the policymaker is engaged in excessive consistency striving that is likely to result in biased information processing. For one way to avoid the burden of a substantial amount of discrepant information is to refute it on an item-by-item basis, as such information becomes available over a period of time, rather than to face the implications of examining the larger body of relevant data in toto.

Let us turn now to some historical cases in which consistency striving appears to have impeded the search for and processing of information.

Evidence of this phenomenon can be seen in the events leading to the American intervention in the Dominican crisis of April 1965. In his detailed, scholarly account of this crisis Abraham Lowenthal emphasizes the extent to which the administration's fear of another Castro in the Caribbean distorted information processing:

> From the very outset, both Washington officials and those in Santo Domingo keyed their questions and reports to the need to avoid a 'second Cuba.' Because American intelligence agencies were geared to produce lots of data on Communist activities but were unprepared to assess correctly the configurations of non-Communist Dominicans in this confused period, the picture they presented was bound to be unbalanced and wrong. . . . There was a tendency throughout the week (as previously) to err on the side of magnifying the Communist risk, by reporting on all the possible connections of other Dominican actors in the crisis and by passing on to Washington all reports of presumed Communist plans and intensions.[12]

As a result, all dissimilarities of the internal Dominican situation with that of Cuba prior to Castro's takeover were ignored. Thus, that a skillful and attractive political leader like Castro was missing in the Dominican situation; that a popularly based guerrilla movement was absent in the Dominican Republic; that the Dominican Communists were weak, divided, and totally lacking in support in the rural areas, etc. – "all these facts were forgotten, or probably not known. . . ."[13]

Excessive consistency striving on the part of British leaders at the outset of the Suez crisis in 1956 appears to have impeded the search for and processing of readily available information. When Nasser seized the canal, British leaders quickly adopted the comforting but erroneous view that the Egyptians could not operate the Suez Canal. Since almost all of the pilots who guided ships through the canal were European and were expected to quit, British leaders concluded that the canal would soon have to close. This prospect was so pleasing that they failed to inquire whether much training was required to produce competent pilots which, as a matter of fact, was not the case![14]

The two historical examples cited illustrate distortion of information processing created in the first case by the fears of policymakers and in the second instance by their "wishful thinking." In both instances, policymakers were in fact conscious of entertaining the particular fear or hope in question. What was lacking was sufficient vigilance as to the possibility that their fears or hopes might weaken their receptivity to relevant information. As Jervis reminds us, lack of awareness that one's beliefs can distort receptivity to incoming information can have damaging consequences for policymaking. Thus, what is in fact ambiguous or equivocal information in a given situation can be mistaken by the individual (or by the organization) as firm evidence on behalf of a favored interpretation simply because it is not inconsistent with a preexisting belief. Conversely, new information that is really unambiguous and unequivocal can be mistakenly rejected or down-graded as being inconclusive or implausible because it is inconsistent with preexisting beliefs. Lacking awareness of the critical role his prior beliefs may be playing in evaluating new information, the individual may fail to realize that the incoming information is compatible with other interpretations as well, or that it provides only plausible rather than compelling support for the prior belief he holds.

Distorted information processing of this kind can contribute to an unjustified and dangerous lowering of one's guard—as, for example, when warning indicators of a military attack are rejected as inconsistent with preexisting beliefs. Or, equally, it can lead to an unjustified and costly raising of one's guard—as, for example, when an opponent's failure to cooperate is misread as further evidence in support of a preexisting belief regarding his hostility.

Many historians believe that distorted information processing of this kind contributed to the exacerbation of the Cold War. One instance of this can be seen in the interpretation American decisionmakers placed on the Russian rejection in the late forties of the Baruch Plan for the control of nuclear weapons. Ignoring the possibility that the Soviet Union, whether or not it entertained aggressive aims, would have legitimate reasons for finding this American plan unacceptable, some U.S. leaders regarded rejection of it as evidence of Soviet aggressive and expansionist aims.

Consistency striving plays a role also in enabling opponents in an acute conflict situation such as the Cold War to maintain basic images of each other as hostile and malevolent in the face of seemingly contradictory evidence. When one attributes "inherent bad faith" to the opponent, such an image can easily become self-perpetuating, since the assumption of "inherent bad faith" does not easily admit of evidence that could invalidate it. Thus, when the opponent behaves in a seemingly conciliatory fashion there is a strain toward rendering such discrepant information consistent with one's preexisting negative image of him, and this leads to various strategems for discounting, ignoring, or discrediting that new information.[15]

Psychological tendencies of this kind made it more difficult for both sides in the Cold War to credit indications from time to time that the other side might be inclined to change some of its policies and attitudes in the interest of bringing about a relaxation of tensions and a search for accommodation. Thus, after Stalin's death in 1953, Secretary of State Dulles dismissed the conciliatory gestures of the triumvirate which succeeded him as "rotten apples" intended to beguile the Free World. On this and, as Professor Ole Holsti has shown, on numerous other occasions — such as the signing of the Korean armistice, the Soviet acceptance of the Berlin Foreign Ministers Conference in 1954, the signing of the Austrian State Treaty, the Geneva Summit Conference in 1960 — Dulles interpreted Soviet actions that did not conform to his image of an implacably hostile enemy as having been imposed on Soviet leaders by weakness.[16] Dulles argued that it was the frustration and inability of Soviet leaders to conduct a successful foreign policy that had forced them into less aggressive behavior on these occasions.

Similarly, Dulles' conduct of the Middle East crisis that led to the Suez War in 1956 was influenced by a deeply rooted conviction that the Soviet Union was economically weak. He regarded the Soviet shift to an economic offensive in foreign affairs in 1955-56 as a bluff designed to force the United States into bidding against the Soviet Union and thereby spending itself eventually into bankruptcy. Dulles decided upon Egypt as the place to call the Soviet economic bluff and, partly for this reason, he cancelled the Aswan Dam offer the U.S. had made to Egypt. It was only in his final year in office, 1957-58, that Dulles finally abandoned his view that economics was the "fatal weakness" of the Soviet regime.

Understanding the Opponent's Perspective

Many thoughtful observers of history have been struck by the frequency with which major errors in policy that resulted in avoidable catastrophes or missed opportunities can be traced to the inability of foreign-policymakers to view events from the perspective of their adversaries.[17] This is a difficult task at best. Policymakers often employ the criteria of "national interest" and "rationality" as vehicles for grasping the opponent's perspective and for inferring the way in which he views events and decides what to do about them. To make this task easier for themselves, policymakers also slip into the simplifying assumption that the opponent is a single actor, thereby ignoring the complex organizational dynamics within the opposing government and the play of broader political forces that constrain and shape its foreign-policy actions. However, neither of these two criteria nor the simplifying assumption that often accompanies their use provide a reliable basis for gauging the opponent's perspective.

The Criterion of National Interest

The uses and limitations of the criterion of "national interest" as a guide to American foreign policy will be discussed in detail in Chapter 13. Much of what is said there applies also to the attempt to use the opponent's national interest as a basis for understanding and predicting his behavior. It may be reasonable to assume, as a general first approximation, that all actors in the international system are motivated to protect and advance their national interests. But one must go on to recognize that the concept of national interest is not likely to be so well defined or uniformly interpreted by members of the opposing government as to enable confident predictions of how that government perceives and will pursue its interests in any given situation.

The Criterion of Rationality

Attributing "rationality" to the opponent is hardly more helpful. The assumption that all actors in the arena of world politics can be counted upon to take a rational approach in foreign policy is not without some validity and utility; but it does not offer a sufficient basis for estimating how these other actors view events, calculate their options, and make their choices of action. Additional comment on the assumption of rationality is necessary here since policymakers often rely on it to estimate how other actors will behave, and many scholars use it to explain foreign-policy behavior.

To describe behavior as "rational" is to say little more than that the actor attempts to choose a course of action that he hopes or expects to further his values. But, of course, what the opponent's values are and how they will affect his policymaking and decisions in different kinds of situations remains to be established. Moreover, foreign-policy issues are typically complex in that they raise multiple values and interests that cannot easily be reconciled. Even for the rational actor, therefore, choice is often difficult because he faces a value trade-off problem. How the opponent will resolve that dilemma is not easily foreseen, even by those close to him let alone by those in another country who are attempting to predict his action on the basis of the rationality assumption.

In addition to being complicated by value complexity of this kind, the opponent's attempt at rational decisionmaking is likely to be affected by uncertainties that render problematical his efforts to calculate expected outcomes of various courses of action open to him. These uncertainties stem from inadequate information about the situation and a deficit of the kind of general knowledge of ends-means relationships that is needed to assess the consequences of any particular option. How the opponent will deal with these uncertainties is not easily foreseeable, and once again this limits the ability to predict his behavior by applying the general assumption of rationality to his behavior.

It is clear, therefore, that behavioral models are needed that will characterize in a more discriminating way how each opponent approaches the difficult task of rational calculation in the face of value-complexity and cognitive uncertainty. In other words, the abstract model of rationality has to be supplemented or replaced by an empirically derived theory as to how a particular opponent tends to deal with the various constraints on rationality in his approach to decisionmaking. Ideally, a good model of this kind would also recognize the possibility that genuine changes in the opponent's behavioral style might occur, attempt to postulate conditions under which such changes might occur, and specify appropriate ways for recognizing them in order to modify the initial model.[18]

It is not an easy matter to develop empirical models of this kind and to apply them effectively. We may recall the difficulties that U.S. policymakers encountered during the Cold War in trying to estimate the intentions or expected reactions of the Soviet Union, Communist China, and North Vietnam. The results of this experience strongly reinforce the view that available information for estimating an adversary's behavior in a particular situation rarely speaks for itself but must be interpreted with reference to a valid model of that adversary's general patterns of behavior. Even when such information is plentiful, consistent, and relatively free of "noise," correct appraisal of it requires hypotheses about the way in which that particular adversary typically approaches political conflict, and a theory or model of that adversary's behavioral style and approach to calculation of action.

One's image of the opponent includes an understanding of his ideology, his "operational code," and his mode of calculating utility and assessing risks. An incorrect image of the opponent can distort the appraisal of even good factual information on what he may do. A single familiar historical example will suffice to illustrate this point. Prior to the Nazi attack on the Soviet Union in 1941, Stalin had ample high-quality intelligence of Hitler's military dispositions and plans. The Soviet leader, however, did not believe that Hitler would launch a surprise attack. For Stalin's image of the opponent in this case encouraged him to believe that Hitler would almost certainly present demands and attempt to bargain before deciding on whether he needed to resort to force. Stalin, therefore, misperceived the purpose of the menacing Nazi military buildup on the Soviet border, believing that it was intended to set the stage for serious negotiations and coercive bargaining.[19]

Egregious and fateful miscalculations of an opponent's behavior occurred more than once also in the conduct of American foreign policy in recent decades. During the Korean War rather good information was available for assessing the threat of Chinese Communist intervention in October and November 1950. But that information was rendered equivocal when filtered through the incorrect U.S. image of Chinese Communist leaders. Incoming information on Chinese intentions was systematically misinterpreted and minimized by American decision-makers for reasons that are as simple as they are fundamental. U.S. leaders miscalculated because they failed to understand the frame of reference from which the Chinese Communists were assessing the significance of what the United States was doing in Korea. By failing to comprehend the ideology and complex motivational calculus of the Chinese leaders, U.S. leaders misread Peking's perception of the threat that U.S. behavior in Korea was posing for it.

Washington's estimates of Chinese intentions were based on the faulty premise that Chinese leaders were calculating their interests in much the same way as U.S. leaders perceived Peking's interests. Since Truman and Acheson had convinced themselves that legitimate Chinese national interests were not importantly threatened by the U.S. occupation of North Korea or by plans for unifying it with South Korea, they believed that Peking also saw it in this way or could be persuaded to do so by verbal assurances that the United States harbored only friendship, not hostility, towards China.

As Robert Jervis notes, the U.S. misperception of Peking's intentions in this case illustrates a more general tendency for actors to assume that their intentions, especially if they are basically peaceful, are as clear to others as they are to themselves. This results in an important obstacle to understanding an opponent's perspective in that to do so involves recognizing that he sees you in a less than flattering light.[20]

Similarly, defective U.S. images of North Vietnamese leaders played a role in the miscalculation of Hanoi's vulnerability to coercive military pressure. Underestimating Hanoi's motivation and the strength of its commitment to its objectives, some American leaders assumed that the North Vietnamese would not risk destruction of their new industrial facilities by U.S. bombing.

Even a reasonably good model of the opponent's behavioral style, however, does not insure correct interpretation of his intentions in any given situation. By 1962 U.S. analysts had developed considerable insight into patterns of Soviet behavior; nonetheless, they were taken by surprise by the Soviet deployment of missiles in Cuba. The U.S. failure to give credence to the possibility of a missile deployment can be traced to a number of factors, among them a faulty assessment of the risk calculations that had accompanied the Soviet decision to put missiles in Cuba. American analysts erred in assuming that Soviet leaders would regard such a deployment as a *high-risk* venture and, therefore, would forego it. However, Soviet leaders evidently convinced themselves that the missile deployment was a calculable, controllable, low-risk strategy.

The inability of U.S. leaders to sense correctly the Soviet approach to the calculation and acceptance of risks had been, in fact, a chronic problem from the beginning of the Cold War. In late June of 1948, despite considerable warning, American leaders were taken by surprise by the Soviet blockade of allied ground access to West Berlin. Most American officials had believed that Soviet leaders would surely recognize that a move against West Berlin would constitute a high-risk venture, and hence that Moscow would reject it as posing an unacceptable risk. From the perspective of the Soviets, however, their action was a well-calculated, controllable low risk.

Once the blockade of West Berlin was imposed, Truman displayed considerably more caution than other officials thought necessary. Truman's caution, it may be noted, stemmed partly from his image of the opponent. Unlike some of his advisers, who tended to perceive the Soviet Union as something of a neighborhood bully, full of tough talk and menacing gestures until challenged, Truman and others of his advisers saw the USSR as a wily adversary—deceitful, to be sure, but also unstable and, worst of all, unpredictable! (Secretary of Defense Robert Lovett remarked that the heads of Soviet leaders were "full of bubbles.") Given his image of the opponent, Truman disagreed with "hard-line" advisers who believed that the Soviets would not run any risk of World War III until they were ready for it. For his part, Truman believed that Moscow was willing to "risk a military incident" during the crisis to test U.S. "firmness and patience." In his view it was possible that Soviet leaders might even be looking for a pretext to begin a war. Thus, different images of the Soviet opponent among American policymakers at this time produced divergent perceptions not only of Moscow's intentions and its willingness to accept high risks, but also of the utility and risks of different measures the United States might take to maintain itself in West Berlin.

Divergent images of the Soviet opponent also underlay a major policy disagreement among President Kennedy's advisers during the Berlin crisis in 1961. Dean Acheson's diagnosis of the threat and his recommendations typified the "hard-line" view shared by other important advisers as well. The essence of this position was that the Soviets were engaged in an *offensive* move in Berlin that posed serious dangers to the entire Western position in Europe. For the Western powers to offer to negotiate or to present an image of flexibility in the face of Khrushchev's deadline for concessions, the "hard-line" school argued, was to encourage the Soviets to press for the greatest possible realization of their far-reaching objectives.

Opposed to the firm stand advocated by these advisers was a "soft-line" position advocated by other Kennedy advisers, including Ambassadors Harriman and Thompson. They believed that the Soviets were engaged in an essentially *defensive* operation in Berlin, aimed at consolidating their control over Eastern Europe. These advisers urged Kennedy to undertake active negotiations immediately in order to avoid a dangerous confrontation and also as a means of conveying to Moscow that the West was willing to reduce the irritants which West Berlin no doubt imposed on Soviet interests in East Europe. Fearing that the intransigent position advocated by the "hard-line" school could lead the Soviets to make desperate moves, advocates of the softer line favored immediate negotiations in order to assure the Soviets that their legitimate, minimum-security interests would be respected. To the "soft-line" school it appeared that the expansionist thrust of Soviet foreign policy, if indeed it had been as virulent as had been feared, was moderating, and that Moscow was acting increasingly out of "nationalist" and "defensive" motives.

We have looked at a number of cases in which American policymakers held differing views as to whether and to what extent the adversary was aggressive. Such disagreements, as we have shown, underlie many policy disputes over foreign policy.[21] It should be further noted that participants in these policy debates may not be fully aware of the fact that their specific disagreement over policy rests fundamentally on different images of the opponent. When this is the case, participants in the policy discussion may fail to come to grips with the root issue. Not only may the quality of the policy debate suffer as a result, the decision eventually taken—as by President Kennedy in the Berlin crisis of 1961—may be a muddy compromise that contains internally inconsistent elements reflecting both positions rather than a well-considered hedge against uncertainty as to the true nature of the opponent's motivations.

The Assumption of the Opponent as a "Single Actor"

In the effort to capture the perspective of their adversary, policymakers often "overrationalize" the actions and behavior of the opposing government. That is, they slip into the highly questionable assumption that everything the other side does is the result of unified planning and highly centralized calculation. The other government is reified; its actions are viewed as the product of rational calculations by a superordinate individual. Moreover, personalization of other governments is often accompanied by stereotyping them as friend or foe.[22]

While such a simplification of the image of an adversary lightens the policymaker's task of understanding his perspective, it also creates serious impediments to information processing and appraisal. For to regard the adversary in the image of a single actor desensitizes the policymaker to information that reflects the complexities of the opponent's policymaking process. Clues as to the play of organizational factors, bureaucratic politics, and domestic political pressures on the opposing government's policies are either ignored or reinterpreted to make them consistent with the image of a highly centralized actor. What is actually the result of compromise, bargaining, or uncoordinated actions by different participants in the other government's policymaking system is misperceived as a well-considered action by a single rational actor.

Simplified images of this type are to be found not only in the relationships among staunch opponents like the United States and the Soviet Union. There is disconcerting evidence that the same tendency operates on occasion in relationships between friendly governments. Thus, Richard Neustadt has set forth evidence of a dozen instances of misperception between Washington and London in two major crises: Suez 1956 and Skybolt 1962. "In every instance," Neustadt observes, participants in policymaking on one side "failed to understand the stakes of the players on the other side."[23] Thus, the positions taken by each side at critical junctures in the *inter*-state contest were defined by *intra*-state bureaucratic politics and domestic politics. Preoccupied with the complexities of their own policymaking, decisionmakers on each side failed to consider that officials in the other government were also constrained in what they perceived and would do by the exigencies of their own bureaucratic and domestic politics. Instead, each side engaged in wishful thinking as to how its ally perceived unfolding developments. "Each hopeful estimate of friends abroad," Neustadt observes, "was grown at home; . . . in effect, these men saw what they had to see if what they felt they had to do stood any chance to work. . . ."[24]

The Problem of Receptivity to Warning of Emerging Threats to Foreign-Policy Interests

The trauma of Pearl Harbor sank deeply into the American consciousness and led to emotional efforts to pin the blame for failure to heed warning of the Japanese attack on scapegoats or knaves. In time there emerged a more dispassionate understanding of the circumstances that had enabled the Japanese to achieve surprise despite the availability to U.S. policymakers of what seemed, in retrospect particularly, to be ample warning of the forthcoming attack. Objective analysts of Pearl Harbor and of other instances of surprise have pointed to ways in which this type of danger can be reduced; but, at the same time, they have drawn the sober conclusion that the possibility of surprise is inherent in the nature of the problem and can never be reliably excluded.[25] They have identified various mechanisms imbedded in individual psychology, the dynamics of group behavior, the ways in which organizations function, and the play of governmental politics that can hamper receptivity to and proper evaluation of warning. Only a brief discussion of some of the factors which can impede receptivity to warning can be presented here.[26]

Laboratory studies of difficulties in perception of stimuli provide useful analogies to the problem of receptivity to warning of emerging threats in the international arena. The results of perception experiments, however, do not encourage hopes for easy or complete solutions to this problem. Studies of a person's ability to recognize a stimulus that is imbedded in a stream of other stimuli have shown at least three factors to be important:

1. The "signal-to-noise" ratio—i.e., the strength of the signal relative to the strength of the confusing or distracting background stimuli;
2. The expectations of the observers; and
3. The rewards and costs associated with recognizing and correctly appraising the signal.

One might assume that the stronger the signal and the less the background "noise," the easier it should be to detect the signal. However, the task of correct signal detection is more complicated than this even in the laboratory and even more so in international affairs. Thus, the results of perceptual experiments that deal with relatively simple psychophysical auditory or visual stimuli indicate that detection of a signal is not simply a function of its strength relative to background "noise." Rather, the effect of a signal's strength on the person's ability to identify it can be cancelled out by the impact of the second and third variables mentioned above.

In foreign-policy situations, too, the decisionmaker's expectations or "set" and the rewards and costs associated with his recognition of the signal may be more important in determining his receptivity to, and correct appraisal of, incoming information that points to an emerging threat. Not only the individual, but small policy-making groups and organizations as well, are capable of engaging in various psychological strategems for diluting or discrediting information that challenges the structure of existing expectations, preferences, habits, or convenience. It is well known that discrepant information of this kind is often required, in effect, to meet higher standards of evidence and to pass stricter tests of admissibility than new information that supports existing expectations and hypotheses. As a result, it is disconcertingly easy at times for policymakers and their intelligence specialists to discount discrepant information or to interpret it in such a way as to "save" a preferred hypothesis or policy.

The "reward-cost" aspect of correct signal detection can sharply reduce the policymaker's receptivity to information of emerging threats. For to take available warning seriously may require the policymaker to make new decisions of a difficult or unpalatable character; anticipation of this can lower his receptivity to that information. The policy background at the time can further strengthen the tendency to ignore or downgrade incoming information that challenges existing beliefs or exacerbates decisional dilemmas. Thus, as is well known, once policies have been made within the government, they tend to acquire a momentum of their own and the support of vested interests. Top-level decisionmakers are often reluctant to reopen policy matters that were decided earlier with great difficulty; for to do so, they fear, can easily plunge the government once again into the turmoil of decisionmaking.

Psychological mechanisms of this kind have contributed to a number of important intelligence and policy failures. Among them was the Truman administration's pronounced lack of receptivity to available warning in the spring of 1950 of the forthcoming North Korean attack on South Korea. Had the warning been taken more seriously, the attack would not have come as a surprise. The time made available by the warning might have been used to weigh more carefully whether what was at stake in Korea warranted U.S. military intervention. If an affirmative answer to this fundamental question had emerged, then the administration might have utilized the warning before the attack took place to undertake to deter the North Korean move. As it was, the North Koreans acted as they did on the mistaken notion that the United States would not intervene militarily on behalf of South Korea. Thus, the Korean War, with all of its fateful consequences, qualifies as a genuine example of war-through-miscalculation. It was clearly a war that might have been avoided had Washington been more receptive to available warning and acted upon it.

Instead, information processing within the U.S. policymaking system was impeded and distorted both by the existing expectations or "set" of the administration and by the costs associated with greater receptivity to incoming information of the emerging threat.[27] Taking available warning seriously always carries the penalty of deciding what to do about it. In this case, it would have required Truman and Acheson to reconsider the earlier decision they had taken in 1949 to draw a line defining U.S. security interests in the Far East to exclude Formosa, South Korea, and Indochina. The exclusion of Nationalist-held Formosa was part of the administration's policy of disengaging from the Chinese Nationalists. This was a far more controversial decision within the administration and with the public than the exclusion of South Korea. So much so that a reversal of the existing policy of no military commitment to South Korea in response to the warning of a possible North Korean attack would have been politically inconceivable unless Truman and Acheson had also been willing—which they were not, *prior* to the North Korean attack—to extend a new commitment to the Chinese Nationalist regime on Formosa as well.

As this case and others show, the policy background at the time that warning becomes available may subtly erode the policymaker's receptivity to it. A similar misfortune occurred later in the Korean War. During September and early October 1950 the administration eased itself into a commitment to occupy North Korea and to unify it with South Korea. But then, when repeated warnings that this would trigger Communist Chinese military intervention came in, the administration found itself so locked into its more ambitious war policy that it was disposed to dismiss the warnings as bluff. For to have given credence to the worrisome indications of a forthcoming Communist Chinese intervention carried with it the cost of reconsidering and abandoning the war policy that had given rise to that danger. In this critical situation the administration's wishful thinking encouraged grossly defective information processing. The result was that, once again, Washington was taken by surprise when the Communist Chinese launched their massive offensive in late November. A new war resulted that neither side had wanted, one that could have been avoided had Washington not misperceived and misjudged the evidence of Chinese intentions.

Similarly, in the spring of 1948, most American policymakers refused to take seriously the possibility of a Soviet blockade of West Berlin despite mounting tension and the fact that only recently, in March, had the Soviets imposed a temporary blockade of Western ground access to the city. Some of the same psychological dynamics that interfered with optimal processing of incoming information in the cases already described can be seen here, too. For U.S. policymakers to have taken available warning of a possible Soviet blockade of West Berlin seriously would have carried with it the "cost" of having then to face up to and resolve difficult, controversial policy problems. At the time an American commitment to West Berlin did not yet exist. Officials within the administration were badly divided over the wisdom of attempting to defend the Western outpost that lay deep in Soviet-occupied East Germany. Under these circumstances, it was easier to believe that the Soviets would not undertake serious action against West Berlin than to decide beforehand what the American response should be to such an eventuality. In this case, fortunately, while American policymakers were taken by surprise by the Soviet blockade, Truman managed to deal with the crisis without backing down or going to war.

While this discussion of receptivity to warning has been necessarily brief, it should suffice to indicate that the impediments are numerous and that they cannot be easily eliminated. For this reason, most specialists have urged that the problem of securing warning should be linked closely with the problem of deciding what responses are appropriate and useful in the light of the available warning, however equivocal or ambiguous it may be. While high-confidence warning is desirable, often it is not available. But neither is high-confidence warning always necessary for making useful responses to the possibility of an emerging crisis. Recognizing that the responses a policymaker can make to warning often entail costs and risks of their own, and indeed that some responses can be quite harmful, this approach to the problem emphasizes the need to search for responses to warning that are useful in the situation without posing unacceptable costs. Even ambiguous warning, for example, gives policymakers more time to consider what to do, to step up efforts to acquire more information about the developing situation, to rehearse the decision problem they would face if the warning proves to be correct, to spell out the likely consequences if the low probability warning proves to be genuine, to review their commitments and contingency plans, and — not least in importance — to seize the opportunity to avert a possibly dangerous crisis. Thus, even ambiguous warning provides an opportunity to deal with the conflict situation and/or the misperceptions associated with it before it leads to a military conflict.

Finally, we should note that this discussion of receptivity to warning of emerging threats applies also to information about favorable developments elsewhere in the world that offer *opportunities* for foreign-policymakers to advance positive goals. For many purposes, policymakers do not need high-confidence forecasts of emerging opportunities in order to take some sensible measures to facilitate such opportunities and to turn them to account. Thus, for example, following the Soviet invasion of Czechoslovakia in 1968 and the enunciation at that time of the Brezhnev Doctrine, policymakers in Washington (as well as other observers) speculated that these events may have heightened Peking's anxiety regarding a future Soviet move against Communist China. Was Peking's anxiety over the possibility, which its border conflict with the Soviet Union could only have heightened, sufficient to make it interested in a détente with the United States? The point that deserves emphasis here is that it did not require a forecast that could confidently predict Peking's readiness for a détente to make it worthwhile for Washington to discretely explore and encourage the possibility. Sensible steps could be taken to reinforce and activate any disposition for a détente on Peking's part. From the standpoint of U.S. policy, the matter of a possible détente was "actionable" even in the face of considerable uncertainty as to Peking's readiness and conditional willingness to reorient its policy towards the United States.[28]

This chapter and the preceding one have identified psychological impediments to information processing that spring from the responses individuals make to the challenge of making difficult decisions. It is useful to be aware of the nature of these psychological mechanisms and the fact that they are pervasive. At the same time, it would be naive and misleading to suggest that if only our knowledge of these impediments to information processing could be perfected we could then hope to eliminate their occurrence. Rather, as we have sought to convey, the very processes of perception, cognition, calculation, and choice are subject to inherent limits. The mind cannot perform without structuring reality, thereby often oversimplifying or distorting it. Nor, as cognitive psychologists have emphasized, can the mind function without a consistency principle. Even if there were no other constraints on creative, adaptive policymaking, the operation of the consistency principle by itself would necessarily limit the flexibility and ingenuity with which an individual can recognize and deal with the novel and complex features of foreign-policy problems.

• • •

As emphasized in this and the preceding chapter, error in the individual's perception and judgment is to be expected; the very cognitive processes and psychological mechanisms that allow the individual to make decisions at all also help to produce error! At the same time, however, knowledge of the sources of error and, in particular, of the *symptoms* of inadequate information processing to which these psychological mechanisms give rise can be helpful. Such knowledge should serve to sensitize both those who participate in policymaking and those who address the challenging task of developing better information-processing systems. This should be of practical value in enabling them to design, manage, and operate the policymaking system in ways that are likely to reduce tendencies toward narrowing and distorting of information processing. Possibilities of this kind will be taken up in Part Two of this report. But first we have to consider additional sources of impediments to information processing that can arise from certain dynamics of behavior in small policymaking groups and in the larger organization.

Notes

1. All scholars who have addressed the questions taken up in this chapter are indebted to the seminal discussion provided a decade ago by Dean G. Pruitt, "Definition of the Situation as a Determinant of International Action," in Herbert C. Kelman, ed., *International Behavior* (New York: Holt, Rinehart & Winston, 1965).

2. Louis Halle, *American Foreign Policy* (London: G. Allen, 1960), pp. 316-18.

3. A number of policy-oriented scholars—in particular Lincoln Bloomfield—have emphasized the value of political-military-diplomatic games as a means of seeing political reality through the perspectives of other actors.

4. Lee Ross, "The Intuitive Psychologist and His Shortcomings: Distortions in the Attribution Process," in L. Berkowitz, ed., *Advances in Experimental Social Psychology* (New York: Academic Press), p. 212.

5. For assistance in monitoring these developments I am indebted to my Ph.D. student, Deborah Larson, whose forthcoming dissertation on the origins of the Cold War utilizes some recent developments in attribution theory. The interested reader may wish to consult Ross, "Intuitive Psychologist"; Robert Abelson, "Script Processing in Attitude Formation and Decision-making," in J. S. Carroll and J. W. Payne, eds., *Cognition and Social Behavior,* (Hillsdale, N.J.: Lawrence Erlbaum Associates, 1976); Kenneth Bowers, "Situationism in Psychology," *Psychological Review* (Sept. 1973); Walter Mischel, "On the Future of Personality Assessment," *American Psychologist* (April 1977); and Richard Anderson, Rand J. Spiro, and William Montague, *Schooling and the Acquisition of Knowledge* (Hillsdale, N.J.: Lawrence Erlbaum Associates, 1977).

6. For a reflection of this controversy, *see* Bowers, "Situationism."

7. For a useful explication of developments in cognitive theory, see Robert B. Zajonc, "Cognitive Theories in Social Psychology," in G. Lindzey and E. Aronson, eds., *Handbook of Social Psychology,* 2d ed., vol. 1 (Reading, Mass.: Addison-Wesley Co., 1968).

8. *See,* for example, the summaries provided by Ross, "Intuitive Psychologist."

9. Daniel Heradstveit, *The Arab-Israeli Conflict: Psychological Obstacles to*

Peace (Oslo: Universitetsforlaget, 1979).

10. Ernest R. May, *"Lessons" of the Past: The Use and Misuse of History in American Foreign Policy* (New York: Oxford University Press, 1973), pp. 44-45.

11. Jervis, *Perception and Misperception,* p. 343ff.

12. A. F. Lowenthal, *The Dominican Intervention* (Cambridge, Mass.: Harvard University Press, 1972), p. 154. Robert Jervis (personal communication) calls attention to the possibility that a "magnification effect" of President Johnson's own preferences and fears may have occurred in this situation as a result of the way in which the intelligence process worked. Thus, because members of the foreign-policy organization knew of Johnson's beliefs and preferences, they may have gone out of their way to make sure that they did not miss any signs of Communist strength.

13. Lowenthal, *Dominican Intervention,* pp. 154-55.

14. Example cited by Jervis, *Perception and Misperception,* p. 174, from Terence Robertson, *Crisis: The Inside Story of the Suez Conspiracy* (New York: Atheneum, 1965), pp. 94-95, 109.

15. Perhaps it should also be noted that one can become the victim of one's "inherent good faith" image of an ally. "Good faith" images may be less durable than "bad faith" images, but they also can impede information processing (Ole Holsti, personal communication).

16. Ole R. Holsti, "Cognitive Dynamics and Images of the Enemy: Dulles and Russia," in D. J. Finlay, O. R. Holsti, and R. R. Fagen, eds., *Enemies in Politics* (Chicago: Rand McNally, 1967).

17. This section and the next draw upon George and Smoke, *Deterrence.*

18. This position is consistent, I believe, with the more general position advanced by John Steinbruner, who argues that if one wants better behavioral models, one ought first to recognize the severe limits on what can be effectively modeled and then attempt to build models informed by cybernetic and cognitive logic.

19. For an analysis of Stalin's miscalculation of Hitler's intentions, *see* Barton Whaley, *Codeword Barbarossa* (Cambridge, Mass.: M.I.T. Press, 1973).

20. For a more detailed discussion, *see* Jervis, *Perception and Misperception,* p. 71.

21. Jervis also emphasizes this point and gives historical examples from the policymaking of a number of countries.

22. For a useful discussion, *see* "Perceptions of Centralization," in Jervis, *Perception and Misperception.*

23. Richard E. Neustadt, *Alliance Politics* (New York: Columbia University Press, 1970), p. 115.

24. Ibid., p. 62. The role of bureaucratic politics in the failure of the U.S. government to notify the British about the forthcoming cancellation of the Skybolt missile is discussed in Chapter 5.

25. Roberta Wohlstetter, *Pearl Harbor: Warning and Decision* (Stanford, Cal.: Stanford University Press, 1962).

26. For a more detailed discussion, *see* George and Smoke, *Deterrence,* chapter 20.

27. For example, American global security planning at the time did not envisage what has come to be known as "limited war." The expectation, rather, was that the next war would resemble World War II and that the Soviets would not be ready to start a war with the United States for at least five more years. These expectations and other factors, only some of which are discussed here, are all part of the explanation for the "surprise" that U.S. policymakers experienced over the North Korean attack.

28. As we now know, beginning in 1969 the Nixon administration in fact did engage in a series of signals and probes to explore and encourage Peking's interest in a détente. For a detailed account, *see* Marvin Kalb and Bernard Kalb, *Kissinger* (Boston: Little, Brown & Co., 1974).

4

The President and His Advisers: Structure, Internal Processes, and Management of Small Groups

Many high-level foreign-policy decisions are made in the setting of a small group in which the president interacts in some way with leading officials and advisers.[1] While interest in the role of "adviser to the prince" is of long standing,[2] surprisingly little systematic research has been done on executive-adviser relations or advisory systems.[3] The problem has been defined and approached in various ways. For our purposes it is best to begin by recognizing that a president may meet and consult with advisers for different reasons. At least four such purposes can be identified in order to develop a better understanding of the role that executive-adviser relationships can play in foreign-policymaking.

First, the president may turn to advisers for information and advice; hence, they may help him to satisfy his *cognitive needs* prior to making decisions. Second, the chief executive may interact with advisers in order to obtain the *emotional support* needed to cope with the strains of making difficult, possibly fateful, decisions. Third, consultation with leading foreign-policy officials of his administration may be useful to the president for gaining their *understanding and support* for whatever decision he makes, since his advisers then at least have the satisfaction of knowing that their views were solicited and considered. Finally, since it is expected that a president will consult and take advice from properly constituted officials who share responsibility in foreign-policy and national security matters, he will want to do so in order to gain greater *political legitimacy* in the eyes of Congress and the public for his policies and decisions. Of course, a president's incentives for consulting may include more than one of these objectives, and his purposes in doing so may vary from one situation to another.

In this chapter we shall be concerned mainly with the first of these reasons for consultation — the president's need for information and advice before making a decision. We shall also consider the president's reliance on advisers for emotional support in coping with the strains of decisionmaking, giving particular attention to the possibility that this can impede information processing. Together, a president and his advisers can be said to form a group (or groups) in the sense that they engage in continuing, at least partly structured, task-oriented relationships with each other. Information processing will be affected, among other things, by the *structure, internal processes,* and *management* of these group tasks and relationships.

It is well to recognize at the outset that relationships within small groups can be structured in a variety of ways and that markedly different interaction patterns are possible. Depending on the form they take, group processes can have either a positive or negative impact on the search for effective decisions. This point, long emphasized by social psychologists, has been made with particular reference to political decisionmaking by Professor Irving L. Janis:

> A group whose members have properly defined roles, with traditions and standard operating procedures that facilitate critical inquiry, is probably capable of making better decisions than any individual in the group who works on the problem alone. And yet the advantages of having decisions made by groups are often lost because of psychological pressures that arise when the members work closely together, share the same values, and above all face a crisis situation in which everybody is subjected to stresses that generate a strong need for affiliation.

As Janis implies, members of the small group interact not only in order to deal with the substantive tasks of policymaking; their interactions also include efforts to deal with the emotional needs and stresses that can be aroused by the value-complexity and uncertainty which, as was noted at length in Chapter 2, are often associated with foreign-policy decisionmaking.

In this chapter we shall consider some of the ways in which structural variables, internal processes, and management of small groups can impede — or facilitate — information processing. For this purpose we shall draw, necessarily selectively, from the vast theoretical and empirical literature bearing upon this problem that has emerged mainly from the disciplines of social psychology and sociology. Despite its limitations, this literature is highly suggestive; it serves as an important source of insights and hypotheses for those concerned with the behavior of foreign-policymaking groups. Used with caution, it can sensitize and assist both those who study policymaking and those who participate in it.

First, however, we must recognize that laboratory groups, with whom much of the systematic experimental research has been conducted, differ in some important respects from real-world decisionmaking groups. The emotions aroused among real-world decisionmakers stem from the perceived consequences of the difficult and often distressing choices they must make which may affect themselves and their own individual career prospects as well as the lives of many other people; indeed, in foreign-policymaking, the peace of the world may be at stake. Decisions made in laboratory experiments, on the other hand, tend to mean much less to the participating subjects and to be objectively much less consequential in other ways. Moreover, laboratory studies usually employ groups of strangers brought together for meetings of limited duration. The members of such groups have approximate equality and, though leaders often do emerge or are designated by the experimenter, they usually have little formal or institutional authority. A presidential advisory group, by contrast, is comprised of members who have prior associations, and it meets over long periods of time under a leader who possesses great authority, both formal and informal.

Finally, the laboratory environment tends to be somewhat artificial, with extraneous influences eliminated and coping options severely cur-tailed. In short, although experimental studies sometimes do possess great verisimilitude for the subjects upon whose responses they rely, ex-perimenters can never be absolutely sure either whether they are measur-ing what they intend to measure or whether the variables they choose to manipulate are the most important ones affecting the particular kind of behavior in which they are interested. Only when experimental findings coincide with further independent observations of behavior in natural settings, as indeed they often do, can we be reasonably confident that they possess sufficient validity and, therefore, that they are potentially useful in suggesting sources of impediments to information processing in actual policymaking groups.

In this chapter we will examine a number of ways in which group deci-sionmaking behavior can be influenced by such social-structure variables as group size, membership composition, internal role structure, group cohesion and conformity, the nature of the tasks involved, decision rules and group norms, and leadership and management styles.

Size, Membership Composition, and Role Structure

Most real-world decisionmaking groups tend to be quite small—be-tween two and seven members according to one study—and their size tends to be reduced at times of crisis, or when "crucial choices" have to be made.[4] This is true, for instance, of the foreign-policy groups within the U.S. government that developed plans in several recent crises, in-cluding Korea (1950), Indochina (1954), Cuba (1962), Vietnam (1965), Cambodia (1970), and the Arab-Israeli conflict of October 1973.

There are various reasons why the size of the group becomes smaller when important decisions are being made, which we need not take up here. Let us turn instead to a quick review of some of the factors that affect the internal structure and interaction patterns in committees. The work at Harvard of Robert Bales (and others employing his research approach) suggests that committees whose members are focused upon a decision task form informal power-prestige orderings.[5] That is, members evaluate each other's early contributions (or lack of contributions) to the discussion and form expectations based on these evaluations about the relative worth of each other's future contributions. On the basis of these expectations, opportunities to participate in the discussion are differentially allocated by the members to each other. Thus, after a time, the members tend to be stably ranked in terms of their relative frequency of contribution to the discussion; and a member's position in that rank tends to be related to other measures of influence and informal power in the group. For example, high participators interrupt others but are not likely to be interrupted by others; they tend to get agreed with more often than others and they have more control over the interaction process itself than lower participators. Thus, the members are functionally differentiated from each other both in terms of frequency of contributions and by the character of those contributions.

It is important, therefore, to understand the formation of such role systems and to relate them to successful committee interaction. Approximate equality of interaction frequencies among the members is very rare and does not seem to be associated with committee success, as measured by either membership satisfaction or the quality of the decision.[6] What does seem to be important is that some notion of "adequate representation" obtain, so that all members have an equal *right* to voice positive or negative reactions, to ask questions, and to make a suggestion which will receive appropriate reactions. It is difficult, of course, to know exactly what "adequate" representation means; the members themselves may well not know. Research suggests that successful committees tend to strike a 50/50 balance between the amount of interaction in the form of questions and the amount in the form of answers and reactions. They also tend to have a ratio of positive to negative reactions of about two to one. Not only are too many negative reactions expressed by individuals within the group symptomatic of difficulties encountered in the process of deliberation, but too many positive ones also appear to indicate difficulties. A very high ratio of positive to negative reactions may mean either a lack of involvement or that the members are afraid to risk disagreement. In short, successful communication tends to be associated with the development of a functionally differentiated role system that produces a widely distributed (but not equally distributed) frequency of suggestions, reactions, and questions, and a certain amount of disagreement as well as agreement. What these findings suggest is that improving the quality of committee decisions may require that less emphasis be placed on issues of leadership and more on identifying the composition and interaction process of the group as a whole.

Bales recommends choosing members who will tend to fall "naturally" into a moderate gradient of participation by virtue of their characteristic frequency of interaction in committee settings. Groups composed of all high participators may suffer from competition, and groups composed of all low interactors may find themselves short on ideas.[7] He further suggests that the optimum size of a committee is four to seven, with five being the optimum number. Below seven, each person in the group says at least something to each other person; in groups over seven, the low participators tend to stop talking to each other and center their infrequent communications on the few top-ranked men. This increases the centralization of communication and influence. Committees as small as two or three are also problematic, especially if there is a power problem among the members. In a two-person group, no majority short of unanimity can form; each person can exercise veto power over the other. In a three-person group, the tendency of two to form a combination against the third seems fairly strong; thus it is hard for a three-person group to have an optimum amount of disagreement because the structure is too sensitive to disagreement and tends to an all-or-none extreme in its decision.

Turning now to other possible consequences of having decisions made in small-group settings, it should be noted that smaller groups tend to have simpler role structures—that is, less differentiation of tasks, less division of labor and specialization within the group, and less formalized modes of procedure. As a result, there is less need of coordinating the activities of participants in small decisionmaking groups than would be the case for larger, more complex policymaking units. Accordingly, more of the time and energy of the small group can be focussed directly on the problem-solving task. But the fact that relatively few individuals comprise the decisionmaking group may also mean that fewer policy options will be considered insofar as a smaller range of values, beliefs, and attitudes and a reduced amount of knowledge and analytical skills are then represented or are available to the group. To enhance the performance of small decisionmaking groups, therefore, it is often critical not only that a flow of relevant and timely information and advice be provided to the group from sources outside the group itself, but that the members of the group remain open and receptive to it.

Smallness can be beneficial if it means that the values invoked during the decision period are more consistent; hence, in this sense, the choice of action is likely to be more "efficient" in furthering those particular values. However, while value-consistency within the group facilitates choice of action, as was noted in Chapter 2, this may be at the expense of ignoring other values relevant to the problem. The quality of the decision may suffer under these circumstances.

We should recognize, too, that in constituting small decisionmaking groups executives often prefer individuals who operate with a broader, less parochial view of the values at stake. The advantage of forming the group in this way is that such advisers are less likely to engage in bargaining in order to protect the narrow bureaucratic interests of subunits of the organization. When decisionmaking is in the hands of a small group, it is probably easier for individual members to convince each other or to change their own minds than it is in larger, more formal groups in which each high official is identified as representing his own department or agency. As a result, small informal groups may produce more examples of genuine persuasion and, because the participants know that persuasion is possible, the arguments may be better (*see also* Chapter 12).

But while the broad perspective of top-level officials may serve to improve the quality of decisions in this respect, the smallness and hierarchical position of such groups may lead to new constraints on effective problem solving. For when decision evolves to the top of an organization, there is some risk that harassed senior officials will lose contact with sources of information and experts at lower levels, and thus lack information and expertise relevant to the policy problems they are deciding.[8]

A related danger is that of "uncertainty absorption" as communication flows upward in large, complex organizations characterized by hierarchy, specialization, and centralization. Specialists on organizational behavior have noted a marked tendency for the critical uncertainties identified in policy analyses provided by experts at lower levels of the organization to be left out, deemphasized, or presented in an oversimplified or one-sided manner when summaries of these analyses are transmitted upwards to top-level officials.[9] The inadequacies of such summaries can easily reinforce rather than counterbalance the psychological tendency of policymakers to deal with complex issues by squeezing them into preexisting but perhaps inappropriate cognitive categories and repertoires of action.

To safeguard against these possibilities, the executive may be well advised to assign the role of "expert's advocate" (comparable to, but more specific than a "devil's advocate") to someone in the small decisionmaking group who is indeed well qualified to appreciate the complexities of the expert's reports and whose function it is to make sure that the group does not oversimplify the analytical summaries obtained from specialists from elsewhere in the organization. Similarly, the executive could encourage members of the small policymaking group to check their understanding of critical facts, assumptions, and uncertainties with experts in their own agencies while the group is still deliberating and before the final decision is made.[10]

The smallness of a decision group can be harmful also if it leads to increased pressure for conformity. Small groups are likely to be more cohesive because they provide fewer opportunities for subgrouping and the intragroup conflicts associated with it. But cohesion implies conformity insofar as the members of a small group are inclined to reject dissident members who persist in taking deviant positions. At the same time, as will be emphasized later in this chapter, this danger can be mitigated in a small group in which the leader adopts nondirective or nonpromotional practices with respect to the substantive content of the decisions that are being made.

It was noted earlier that the differentiated role system described in Bales's work has the character of being a power-prestige ordering and that this can have important consequences for the degree of conformity within committees. The probability of conformity is likely to be increased when the ordering is affected by evaluations based on criteria not relevant to the decision and therefore not relevant to an accurate judgment about the relative worth of the members' contributions. The evidence indicates that irrelevant status characteristics may importantly influence the internal role structure and interaction patterns within the group. Thus, members' evaluations of each other's general status characteristics (e.g., sex, race, age, education, occupation) may affect the evaluative expectations formed by the members and the resulting power-prestige ordering. Strodbeck et al. have shown that this is likely to happen in jury deliberations[11] and the work of Berger et al. indicates that this process is quite general whenever the members are strangers to each other and thus have no previous judgments about their relative competence with respect to the issues relevant to the committee decision.[12] In this way, irrelevant status characteristics can indirectly affect the quality of the decisional outcome. Members who enjoy high prestige by virtue of status considerations are likely also to be the high-ranking members in the group's role system. Low-status members are likely also to be low participators and low on influence within the group. When such effects are undesirable, care should be taken to establish the relevant expertise of each member, thus improving the possibility that expectations will be based on relevant evaluations.

Torrance[13] studied decision committees composed of members of the military who held different ranks. The findings suggest that the military rank of each member very heavily affected the formation of the power-prestige order in the committees. High-ranking officers systematically held high positions in the group's role structure and low ranking officers held low ones. Low-ranking officers gave public agreement to decisions without privately necessarily believing in their accuracy and were more likely to be dissatisfied with the committee. The influence attempts made by low-ranking officers were less frequently successful than those of other members, even when they had the right answer. This suggests that when committees are formed from members of a formal authority structure (such as a government), the members' ranks in the larger system may well affect their rank in the committee in a way which is not beneficial to the decision.

By implication, whenever status or position in an external authority system affects the formation of a role system in a committee, then those factors are likely to affect the decisional content. Low-ranking members may withhold important facts, suggestions, or negative reactions; and they may agree to a decision about the merit of which they are not privately convinced. In effect, then, the quality of the decision will be about the same as if the top-ranking member or two had made the decision independently.

While conformity pressures are most likely to occur in very small groups, smallness per se is not necessarily disruptive of optimal information processing. Indeed, at times of crisis or when urgent deadlines must be met, it is virtually inevitable that the size of the decisionmaking group will shrink. This may be desirable as well as necessary, *so long as the norms operating within the group emphasize the necessity for considering a reasonably wide range of options, for making reality-based estimates of potential dangers and opportunities, and for avoiding the hazards of conformity pressures that may lead to a premature stifling of diverse viewpoints.* We shall return to the importance of norms that regulate the group's problem-solving activities and to the related topic of leadership practices, but first it is necessary to differentiate among two types of conformity tendencies in small policy groups.

Two Patterns of Conformity

Until recently, following the lead of the eminent social psychologist Kurt Lewin, students of small-group behavior have tended to emphasize the benefits of group cohesion. "Cohesion" refers to the members' positive valuation of the group and their motivation to continue to belong to it. When group cohesiveness is high, the members experience and express solidarity, mutual liking, and positive feelings toward participating in group tasks. Highly cohesive groups provide members with a sense of security, with solace and support against anxiety or distress, and help them to maintain self-esteem.

As a result, not surprisingly, the dominant view of specialists on group behavior has been that high cohesiveness improves group performance. Thus, when present in policymaking groups, cohesiveness provides an atmosphere in which the clash of parochial and bureaucratic viewpoints can be minimized and in which consensus can be reached without excessive interpersonal friction and rivalry that tend to be disruptive of group performance as well as distressing to its members.

It is increasingly recognized, however, that *highly cohesive groups are not necessarily high-performance groups.* This is particularly so when, as in foreign-policymaking, the group is under pressure to deal with situations in which a great deal may be at stake. In these circumstances members of the group may begin to see maintaining group cohesion and well-being as the overriding goal to the detriment of task-oriented activities. The policy consensus arrived at under these conditions may be more than simply the convergence of individual opinions on a particular issue; rather, it may also express fundamental individual needs and group values that transcend normal canons of objectivity, and it may reflect a tacit agreement within the group to agree unquestioningly upon whatever course of action causes least interpersonal strife.

Recent emphasis on the hazards of group cohesion has led to the delineation of two dynamically different patterns of conformity: first, the long familiar pattern of group pressure on individual members which leads them to quell vague doubts or stronger misgivings out of fear of recrimination or anxieties about presenting a disloyal self-image; and second, a less obvious pattern, labeled "Groupthink" by Irving Janis, in which conformity springs from strong group cohesion brought about or accentuated by a threatening, stressful environmnt. The first pattern of conformity has received most attention from experimental social psychologists, partly because it is much easier to study systematically. We shall consider each of these dynamic patterns in turn, keeping in mind, however, that elements of both may be present in the way in which a group responds to a difficult situation.

Conformity from Group Pressure on the Individual

Most policymaking groups are composed of individuals with somewhat different value systems and beliefs. Foreign-policy problems often activate the conflicting as well as the shared values and beliefs within the group. In these circumstances, arriving at a preference ordering of the salient values within the group and reaching agreement on the evaluation of options is difficult, if not logically impossible. Therefore, some kind of bargaining process is likely to operate within the group, even if members are unaware of it. This process may be less overt and, therefore, less readily observable in smaller groups.

Typically, this bargaining process works in the direction of conformity, with group members interacting to reduce variances in behavior and to crystallize attitudes and beliefs. The individual who deviates from the emerging consensus or dominant view of the group becomes the center of attention as members address themselves to him in efforts to force him to conform. If these efforts fail, the dissident individual may be isolated by the group, being placed in the distressing position of having either to maintain his unpopular stand without support or to withdraw into silence and inactivity. In extreme cases the deviant member may be rejected altogether by the group. This type of rejection has been produced experimentally by Stanley Schachter,[14] and the classical experiments by Solomon Asch demonstrated convincingly that many people will distort reality in the interests of maintaining a conformist position rather than face isolation or rejection.[15]

Conformity pressures operate in natural settings as well as in the laboratory. In politics these pressures are especially strong, not only because there is "safety in numbers" for elected officials, but also because of the need to present a united front to the outside world. Particularly in foreign policy there is pressure for executive advisory groups to agree in order to allow the president to act, or seem to act, decisively toward other international actors.

There is a danger, therefore, that advisors holding unpopular policy views will be silenced or ineffectual when subjected to pressure for conformity by the group or the executive. Numerous participant-observers in policymaking groups have noted this phenomenon. "Even the most distinguished and forthright adviser," Theodore Sorensen notes, "is usually reluctant to stand alone. If he fears his persistence in a meeting will earn him the disapprobation of his colleagues, a rebuff by the President . . . he may quickly seek the safety of greater numbers."[16] Moreover, the mere anticipation of disapproval either by the leader or other prestigious members of the group may lead to self-censorship by an adviser who holds unpopular views. This danger is particularly acute in political decisionmaking groups in which there is typically a great disparity in power and status between the leader on the one hand and other group members on the other. Extreme instances of kowtowing to the whims of leaders are found, of course, among advisers to Hitler, Stalin, and other dictators. But similar tendencies appear even in democratic political systems. Not only does the formal authority and prestige of the democratic executive give him great "idiosyncrasy credit" with other members of his policymaking group; in addition, their reluctance to challenge his views or to give him unwelcome advice is often reinforced by fear of incurring his displeasure.

The articulation of dissenting opinions by an adviser may lead to his isolation or expulsion from the policymaking group. In his memoirs, George Kennan gives numerous examples of difficulties he experienced in playing the devil's advocate role in the State Department.[17] In his account of the Cuban missile crisis, Robert F. Kennedy recalled: "I had frequently observed efforts being made to exclude certain individuals from participating in a meeting with the President because they held a different point of view. . . ."[18] According to Townsend Hoopes, Vice-President Humphrey's last-ditch attempt in February 1965 to prevent the bombing of North Vietnam was received at the White House "with particular coldness, and he was banished from the inner councils for some months thereafter, until he decided to 'get back on the team.'"[19]

Rejection of a dissident, however, is only the extreme outcome of pressure for conformity. Attitudes towards dissenters may be more complex than this particular outcome implies. Both in real-world settings and in some experimental laboratory groups, countervailing considerations are often present, or can be introduced, that make it undesirable or unnecessary to squelch or reject a dissenter. For one thing, persons with power or status within the group may have "idiosyncrasy credit" to deviate from the group consensus without being squelched.[20] Moreover, the possibility that a dissenter is likely to increase malaise over policy within the rest of the group is often accepted and legitimized by group norms in the expectation that divergent views and disagreement, up to a point, will strengthen the capabilities of the group to cope with its difficult tasks. Still another possibility, noted particularly in real-world groups, is that dissidents may be controlled and neutralized and even used in subtle ways (*see* Chapter 8).

It is interesting to note that pressures *against* conformity in policymaking groups often arise from motives inspired by bureaucratic politics and the institutional loyalties of individual members rather than on the basis of the objective merits of a particular proposal. In these circumstances what matters most is who makes the proposal and who opposes it. When this is the case, disagreement tends to be person-centered rather than task-oriented, and this type of conflict is likely to decrease the quality of policy decisions unless it can be disciplined by analytical procedures and some form of balanced multiple advocacy[21] (*see* Chapters 10 and 11).

There is some reason to believe that personality variables partly account for individual differences in susceptibility to conformity pressures. But the relationship between personality characteristics and susceptibility to social influence has proven to be difficult to test experimentally, since it is usually mediated by intervening variables.[22] As a matter of fact, freedom to deviate from the group majority has been associated with nonpersonality variables such as the presence of a permissive discussion leader, the perception within the group that it is composed of persons different in interest and knowledge, the emergence of role differentiation within the group, and the fact that an individual is a member of more than one group.[23] Not all conformity, in other words, springs from the same motivations, and while there appear to be some consistent individual differences in certain aspects of persuasibility, it is not clear whether and to what extent either conformity or "deviation" are identifiable personal propensities that some people possess to a significantly greater extent than others.

A distinction between "conformity" and "uniformity" may be useful at this point. Cohesive or homogeneous groups may produce pressures for conformity on members, but this does not imply that members hold uniform opinions on all policy positions; nor does it imply that decisions are made only when the group has reached a position of unanimous approval for a particular course of action. This depends upon both the *norms* and the *decision-rules* prevailing in the group. Thus, as Cartwright and Lippitt have argued, "A group might have a value that everyone should be as different from everyone else as possible. Conformity to *this* value, then, would result not in uniformity of behavior but in non-uniformity." But these authors also concede that "the pressure to uniformity which arises from the need for 'social reality'" and the necessity for the group to act cannot "simply be obliterated by invoking a group standard of tolerance."[24] There may be times when excessive tolerance is counterproductive, especially if dissent is used as a bargaining tool as, for example, when a member dissents on a trivial point but, after a long argument, agrees to concede hoping that his opponents will make a return concession on another point that is, in reality, more important to him.

Thus, the introduction by the leader of a simple group norm of "tolerance" for dissident opinions, while helpful, will generally not suffice to create an optimal problem-solving culture within the group.[25] For this, the general instrumental task in which the group is engaged needs to be differentiated into a set of interrelated subtasks. Specific norms and "rules of the game" need to be established to govern each of the various subtasks of policymaking.

Conformity from Stress-Induced Cohesion

In his book, *Victims of Groupthink,* Irving Janis, a social psychologist who has long been preoccupied with problems of real-world decision-making, identifies another pattern of group dynamics that is distinct from group pressures on the dissident individual for conformity. Quite apart from such pressures, Janis notes, the very fact that a small group of decisionmakers experiences strong group cohesion, induced or reinforced by having to cope with a stressful environment, may lead to an erosion of their critical intellectual capacities. Janis suggests that, under conditions of stress-induced cohesion, a group begins to take on the characteristics of an embattled primary group. "Concurrence-seeking" within the group tends to replace reality-based estimates of the efficacy and morality of policy options being considered.[26]

Janis sees in concurrence-seeking within small groups "a form of striving for mutual support based on a powerful motivation in all group members to cope with the stresses of decision-making."[27] This striving for support is helpful to group members insofar as it alleviates stressful emotions, feelings of insecurity or anxiety about risks or errors, and conflicts between humanitarian ideals and utilitarian (but perhaps unethical) courses of action.

Clearly, this pattern of conformity is a much more subtle and insidious thing than pressure to conform exerted against dissident members of a policymaking group. Its danger to high-quality information processing lies not so much in the fact that critical opinions are being suppressed as in the fact that group members do not realize that this suppression is occurring, since overt pressure for conformity is rare, if not entirely absent. In view of this, it is hardly surprising that what Janis calls the Groupthink pattern of conformity has been less well articulated and studied than the first conformity pattern. Hard evidence to support the Groupthink hypothesis is more difficult to obtain since it is difficult, though not impossible, to simulate in a laboratory the kind of real-life conditions in which Groupthink occurs.

If the dynamic processes that underlie Groupthink are themselves difficult to observe directly, they produce a number of behavioral symptoms that are more readily noted. Janis lists a number of symptoms of Groupthink: illusions of invulnerability and of unanimity held by members of the group, euphoria and overoptimism, risk-taking and aggression, shared stereotypes of opponents, sloganistic thinking, beliefs in the inherent morality of the group, direct and indirect pressures for conformity, and poor information processing.

Leaving aside the question whether these behaviors are produced only by Groupthink, most of them have been observed in natural groups experiencing emotional stress in difficult situations. While careful not to overstate his thesis or to claim proof for his hypotheses, Professor Janis has found plausible support for his theory in the historical materials available on high-level foreign-policymaking in a number of crisis situations: in particular, in the Bay of Pigs fiasco but also to some extent in the Pearl Harbor case, the Korean War, and the Vietnam escalation.

Sensitized by Janis's theory, no one who reads the accounts of U.S. high-level policy deliberations in the Bay of Pigs case can fail to be impressed by the evidence of Groupthink symptoms and by the plausibility of Janis's interpretation that this pattern of conformity played a role in distorting information processing and appraisal within Kennedy's policymaking group.[28] Janis cites Arthur Schlesinger's recollection that the dominant mood in the White House in the first few months of Kennedy's administration was one of "buoyant optimism" and notes its resemblance to the Groupthink illusion of invulnerability. As Schlesinger puts it: "Euphoria reigned; we thought for a moment that the world was plastic and the future unlimited." Janis believes that this mood might well have encouraged the group to adhere to a number of highly questionable beliefs that underlay its acceptance of the Bay of Pigs plan — i.e., that the U.S. role in the invasion could be effectively masked, that the Cuban airforce was so ineffectual that it would be knocked out completely by the few obsolete B-26s at the disposal of the Cuban exile force, that Castro's army was so weak that the small Cuban exiles' brigade would be able to establish a beachhead, that the invasion would touch off a strong uprising against Castro, etc.

Evidence of the Groupthink illusion of unanimity is also available. "Our meetings," Schlesinger recalls, "took place in a curious atmosphere of assumed consensus." His additional comments show that this illusion could be maintained only because the major participants did not reveal their possible reservations. From conversations held later with men in the State Department and in the White House, Sorensen concluded that they had entertained doubts about the invasion plan which they had not expressed, "partly out of a fear of being labelled 'soft' or undaring in the eyes of their colleagues."[29]

A broader perspective on the Groupthink phenomenon can be gained by observing that under certain conditions a small decisionmaking group may take on the characteristics of an embattled "primary group." The special kinds of mutual identification and emotional ties that bind members of a primary group have been emphasized by sociologists and psychologists who have noted the remarkable cohesiveness that develops sometimes in small military combat groups. Group ties support and sustain individual members of the group in coping with the stresses of combat.[30]

While it may seem farfetched to invoke the analogy of a combat group, nonetheless the members of a small decisionmaking group, too, can develop primary group ties and rely upon them as a means of adapting to decisional task environments of prolonged or periodically acute stress. From membership in a small intimate group the individual may secure some of the psychological support—supplies of esteem, respect, affection, protection—needed to sustain him in his efforts to cope with the cognitive complexity, the uncertainty and risks, and the criticism of outsiders that are an inevitable part of political decisionmaking.

Indeed, on more than one occasion in recent history high-level policymaking groups have taken on some of the characteristics of just such an embattled group. Historian Henry Graff, who had occasion to conduct private interviews with President Johnson and his principal foreign-policy advisers on four different occasions between mid-1965 and the end of 1968, noted that as these advisers "felt increasingly beleaguered, they turned toward one another for reassurance" and became "natural friends" of their chief.[31] Graff was impressed with the repeated emphasis on unanimity expressed by members of Johnson's "Tuesday Lunch Group," as this group of policy advisers was called. Graff's impression of the group was that it was highly cohesive: "The men of the Tuesday Cabinet were loyal to each other, with a devotion compounded of mutual respect and common adversity. They soon learned, as all congenial committeemen learn, to listen selectively and to talk harmoniously even when in disagreement. . . ."[32]

Bill Moyers not only supports Graff's impression that Johnson's inner circle was highly cohesive but adds that the concurrence-seeking tendency within this group and other policymaking groups is part of the explanation for its lack of critical debate of Vietnam War policy: ". . . One of the significant problems in the Kennedy and Johnson administrations was that the men who handled national security affairs became too close, too personally fond of each other. They tended to conduct the affairs of state almost as if they were a gentlemen's club. . . ."[33]

Cohesiveness within the top decisionmaking group may also indirectly restrict information processing. Subordinates outside the group may perceive that its members do not welcome discrepant information and advice and adjust their own behavior accordingly. Thus, subordinates may censor information flowing upwards into the top policy-making group in the light of the anticipated rejection of it.

Stress-induced cohesiveness may emerge not only at the highest levels of decisionmaking but also within tightly knit factions that pursue a highly valued policy against odds and in the face of great and persistent difficulties. In "fanaticized" policy cliques of this kind a tacit understanding may develop among members against arousing each other's doubts concerning the correctness of the group's position and tactics. The critical and moral capacities of individual members are impaired not so much because of their strong commitment to the policy in question but as a result of group dynamics that encourage tendencies towards regressive forms of thinking (as well as regressive emotional states). Members of such groups tend to adopt a simplified cognitive view of the external world and of other political actors; they employ dichotomized modes of thought and oversimplified notions of causality; they tend to lose a sense of proportion and to confuse means with ends. Supported by other members of the cohesive faction, the individual may indulge in a degree of intellectual arrogance, rigidity, and amoral behavior that he would be incapable of sustaining by himself.

The source of Groupthink resides neither in the individual nor in the organizational setting, but in the cohesive group itself. However, high group cohesion does not lead automatically to Groupthink; it must be accompanied by at least two additional factors: insulation of the policymaking group from outside influences and assertively directive leadership practices. Thus, once again, we must observe the crucial importance of group norms in determining the quality of small-group decisionmaking: if the group boundaries are permeable and its members are accessible to dissenting opinions from outgroups to which they are attached, and if the group leader avoids the trap of promoting his own views at an early stage in the decisionmaking process, taking care to insure that differences of opinion are fully and fairly considered, then high or moderate levels of group cohesion may be acceptable, or even desirable, at the information-processing stage of decisionmaking.[34]

Group vs. Individual: Quality of Decisions and Risk-Taking

The preceding discussion has emphasized that if the potential advantages of a small group or committee are to be realized, it requires—among other things—that (1) a differentiated role structure develop within the group which is based upon judgments of relevant contributions that different members can make to the decisionmaking tasks at hand, and that (2) the processes of reaction, questioning, and suggestion making within the group not be inhibited. Whether groups or individuals perform better depends on other factors as well—for example, the nature of the task undertaken.[35] Groups appear to perform better than individuals in remembering information; they also do better when the task places a premium on duplication of effort or on a division of labor. Groups usually perform better on very complex problems, except on tasks requiring a great deal of interpersonal organization within the group.[36]

Without allowing ourselves to be drawn into the complexity of this issue and the voluminous, if not always consistent, findings that have been reported, it suffices to note that both groups and individuals appear to have relative advantages and disadvantages for dealing with complex cognitive tasks associated with policymaking. It appears desirable, therefore, to search for mixed procedures that will enable an executive to benefit from both collective and individual insights into policies under consideration.

We turn now to a central task in foreign-policy decisionmaking: the calculation and acceptance of risks. On this critical issue, the social psychological research of some years ago seemed to support the view that groups are on balance inclined to take greater risks than individuals. But recent critiques have called this finding into question, and no conclusion can be drawn.[37] Widely different interpretations have been made on the basis of similar evidence in this area of research. One popular early explanation for the apparent shift to risk in small-group decisionmaking held that the shift, if it occurred at all, resulted from a diffusion of responsibility among group members: a special form of continuous buck passing. Speculations abound on this subject and are almost as numerous as studies undertaken, but no simple and definitive conclusions can be reached in spite of the vast research resources expended. More recently, the risky-shift hypothesis has been assimilated into the broader category of "choice shifts," leaving it open whether groups are more risky or more conservative than individual members.[38]

It seems likely that investigators will be forced to develop more discriminating hypotheses regarding the different conditions under which *groups* are and are not likely to choose riskier options than would be chosen by the individuals comprising the group. More attention needs to be directed, too, at the idiosyncratic characteristics of the individual who fills an executive position and the effects of exposure to different kinds of group processes on his risk-taking behavior in different types of situations. Finally, whether or not the group picks riskier choices than the individual, the question remains whether the riskier choice in that situation constitutes a poorer decision or, in fact, a better one. Acceptance of a riskier option may reflect defective judgment or, conversely, a more adequate analysis of the requirements of the situation.

It should be noted in this connection that Janis's Groupthink hypothesis that was discussed earlier in this chapter is an attempt to present a rather precise variant of the risky-shift argument. Thus, Janis identifies a special set of conditions under which the task performance of highly cohesive groups deteriorates, and he details a wide range of factors that may operate to encourage excessive risk taking by such groups of which they are unaware. But, as Janis emphasizes, these are factors against which can be marshalled a number of ingenious managerial techniques designed to avoid or reduce the likelihood of distorted information processing and excessive risk taking.[39]

Group Norms and Decision Rules

That the decisionmaking culture within the small group exercises an important effect upon the quality of information processing already has been emphasized. We will content ourselves here with explicating what is meant by "decisionmaking culture," which refers to the norms that regulate different aspects of the process by means of which an advisory system operates.

It is well known that executives vary substantially in their cognitive styles, i.e., the way in which they seek to organize information processing and to benefit from advice. Executives who find personal contact with too many advisers inefficient or wearing, or who find exposure to the rough-and-tumble of vigorous debate within the advisory group incompatible with their habitual or preferred mode of decisionmaking, will seek to limit their direct involvement with others in the search and evaluation phases of policymaking that precede final choice of action. The type of communication network that an executive develops around him will reflect not only his cognitive style but also his conception of the role he should play in the management structure and in the decisionmaking process. Some executives prefer to restrict their role to making the final choice of action; others prefer to involve themselves more actively in the search and evaluation activities that precede the final phase of decisionmaking.[40] But all executives rely to some extent on a relatively small number of advisers and staff to ferret out information, make suggestions, develop and appraise policy options, and to monitor the implementation of decisions taken.

The way in which advisers and staff perform these tasks is influenced by the expectations that develop regarding how they are to interact together for this purpose. These expectations, in turn, are shaped by the preferences of the executive or his surrogates — that is, by the norms that he or they introduce into the advisory system to define, guide, and regulate the roles and behavior of the participants. Thus, for example, some executives favor debates among advisers that go to the heart of crucial assumptions and premises that divide the group; other executives prefer to limit the discussion to the advantages and disadvantages of specific options. The importance of the group norms that an executive introduces into the policymaking group is better grasped if we specify in some detail the various subtasks of policymaking to which they apply. Thus, norms will be needed to cover questions of the following kind which arise in any advisory system:

1. Who will constitute the policymaking group for different kinds of issues?
2. How will policy alternatives be identified, discussed, and evaluated within the policymaking group?
3. How will participants in the group satisfy their needs for information and analysis?
4. Will general advice or specialized inputs to the policymaking task be expected from each participant?
5. What process will be followed in attempting to form consensus within the group on behalf of the policy that is chosen?
6. What "rules" will govern the expression of disagreement, the regulation of competition among participants to influence the leader's choice, and the scope of bargaining and compromise during different phases of policymaking?
7. How will the task of synthesizing the various elements of complex policy problems be handled?
8. In arriving at a decision, what relative weight will be given by the executive to arriving at the technically best alternative as against one that commands the desired kind and magnitude of consensus within the group?
9. What degree of support, however expressed, will be expected of the participants once a decision has been made by the executive?
10. What "rules" will govern reconsideration of a past decision or policy?

There is relatively little systematic research on the nature and consequences of different norms covering these questions either in laboratory or real-world decisionmaking groups.[41] We are forced, therefore, to rely largely upon impressionistic material in order to discuss their importance. It is clear, to begin with, that the style and preferences of the executive tend to define the norms that will be followed in addressing these tasks. However, some executives assert themselves more forcefully than others in introducing norms of this kind into the advisory system. Norms covering these subtasks are not always well defined, comprehensive, and shared by all participants. Nor is an executive necessarily consistent in his setting of norms and in his enforcement of them.

This matter is of interest here because it is quite likely that contradictory, inconsistent, or ambiguous norms represent an important impediment to information processing. Unless group norms are well defined and comprehensive, an executive may find his advisers filling the vacuum in their own way to enhance their own interests, often competing with each other in ways that create misunderstandings and counterproductive frictions.

This is not to say that an executive should make explicit all of the criteria he employs in making his choices of policy. The weight he gives to different considerations or to the judgment of particular advisers in arriving at his final decision may well be a matter that is better left unclarified in many situations. Similarly, requiring his advisers to engage in explicit voting before he makes or announces his decision may degrade the quality of the advice he receives; it may also serve to promote rivalries as well as strengthen pressures for conformity.

The decision rule that a leader chooses to follow may importantly affect the quality of the information processing and appraisal that takes place and, hence, the policy outcome. If he is perceived by his advisers as having a preference for unanimity, for example, the result may be counterproductive bargaining leading to a unanimous recommendation offered by his advisers that represents a hodgepodge of inconsistent values or a delicately structured system of compromises which satisfies most interests partly, none wholly, and which may turn out to be quite inappropriate to the problem at hand. A decision rule of unanimity may also tend to result in minimum action, since a person who feels compelled to please those who are against him as well as those who are for him may end up doing as little as possible.

An explicit majority decision rule, on the other hand, does not avoid the problem of compromise and may create a win-lose fighting stance among group members. Bitterness and hostility among defeated minority may be the result.

High-level political decisions, however, usually involve a third decision rule: authoritative choice by the executive, after consultation. While in this case the executive is not bound to seek either unanimous or majority support for the action he decides to take, nonetheless, the nature of his consultation becomes a critical factor in determining the quality of the search and evaluation provided him by the advisory system. His consultation practices will also be highly germane for developing consensus within the group (and, through its members, outside the immediate group as well) on behalf of his decisions.

Leaders vary in the degree to which they deliberately use their authority to block or hamper consideration of certain policy alternatives and to achieve agreement within the group for their own preferred course of action. But, as is well known, this can occur even when it is not the executive's intention or desire to curtail full consideration of alternatives. Some members of the group may develop a sensitivity to what the leader is thinking and may wish to please him by channeling their advice in the same direction. Or they may feel pressure not to pursue a line of thought to which the leader is obviously opposed.

A corollary danger is that an assertive leader may promote a feeling among group members that they are only fact-gatherers and expediters and that all value questions are his sole prerogative. This may lead not merely to a diffusion of responsibility but to its displacement upon the executive; thus, members may vest their consciences in the leader, ignoring the moral or ethical considerations pertinent to the policy options being discussed.[42] The executive may have to take special precautions to prevent his authority from hampering free communication and unfettered discussion of policy alternatives, and he may have to make explicit his desire for value judgments from group members.

Leadership

Since control over the process of deliberation and decisionmaking within the group is likely to be exerted particularly by members possessing greater power and prestige, the issue of leadership is raised. It is more useful to look at the importance of leadership in this respect in terms of the special tasks or functions that need to be performed rather than in terms of personality style or skills.

Successful committees are also associated with leaders who, although highly differentiated in terms of the previously mentioned behaviors, do not control heavily on *content* issues. Content suggestions and evaluations should be broadly (though not equally) distributed among the other members. If a leader overcontrols on content, he is likely to produce conflict or superficial agreement and inhibition. Successful committees also tend to have a relatively high-ranking member (second or third in the ordering) who functions as a socioemotional leader. That is, he provides support for other members, tension release in times of disagreement, and so on.[43] Finally, special leadership skills (beyond the behavioral requirements already discussed) may not be necessary.[44]

Leaders relate differently to the groups with which they work. One dimension of this difference concerns the quality of "distance" or aloofness maintained by a leader. Fred Fiedler has presented evidence from which he concludes that good leadership is contingent upon the leader having a moderate distance between himself and his key associates.[45] But his evidence is not completely consistent, which suggests that the value of leadership "distance" may depend both on the nature of the task and the personality of the leader himself.

At times of crisis, as has been demonstrated experimentally, group members are more willing to accept directive leadership, and this may be because they require more emotional support from the leader at such times.[46] A boost in morale may help the group out of the trough of depression and pessimism so that it can concentrate on the task of meeting the crisis more realistically. Planning a military intervention may require a more distant leader than, for example, preparing for a goodwill tour of a friendly nation. Someone like Harry Truman might habitually feel that people who did not think as he did were basically different from him and, therefore, he would have no trouble remaining aloof from them. Someone like Dwight Eisenhower might habitually assume that there was one truth that all men of goodwill could get together and, therefore, have some difficulty in maintaining emotional distance in his interpersonal relations. If a moderate degree of distance were required for a particular task, a man like Truman might deal more effectively with a group of sympathetic friends, while a man like Eisenhower would be more effective among a group of strangers or opponents.

Leaders differ, too, in terms of how they perform the instrumental and affective facets of leadership: Richard Nixon apparently felt uncomfortable in groups (though not with certain individuals, particularly Haldeman, on whom he was apparently highly dependent) and tended to be operationally vague, preferring to make his decision in solitude and then leave it to one of his advisers to carry it out. Fearing he might concede unwisely in the heat of an emotional argument, he preferred to maintain a rigid control over his own emotions and to surround himself with severe, unemotional technocrats. Since these were the men who substituted for him in many group meetings, we may assume that their performance of the affective side of leadership was also deficient in some respects; e.g., their unsympathetic manner might lead to less free discussion of policy options.[47] A leader who is not very good at the affective, morale-boosting aspects of leadership might find it beneficial to employ someone else to perform these tasks in his policymaking groups.

The behavior of groups often differs markedly under different leadership conditions. The classic experiments of Ronald Lippitt and Ralph White, employing three different leadership styles—authoritarian, laissez-faire, and democratic—among adults in charge of boys' clubs, showed that a democratic style was both more preferred by group members and more productive in terms of work.[48] This style was characterized by high levels of participation in policymaking by group members and the use of "guiding suggestions" rather than orders, i.e., indirect guidance that takes into account the purposes of the group member rather than direct expression of what the leader wants to do. Democratic leaders were also careful to outline procedures in advance, in contrast to the authoritarian leaders who dictated procedures one at a time so that future steps remained uncertain and members could not seize the initiative. Laissez-faire leaders left groups alone to determine their own policies, supplying information only on request. The autocratically led groups showed a large amount of either aggressive or submissive behavior, lacked spontaneity, engaged in scapegoating activities, and had the highest dropout rate. The groups with laissez-faire leaders performed little work, largely of poor quality, and spent most of their time playing. Under democratic leadership, more work was done, though less time was spent on it than under autocratic conditions and the work accomplished was more original and spontaneous, continuing even in the absence of the leader. More mutual praise occurred, and there was more use of the word "we" and a greater readiness to share property.

Generalizations from these findings must be made cautiously, however, since there was little potential for serious conflict between leader and followers in this special experimental situation. In a foreign-policy group we would expect sharp differences of opinion occasionally with which a democratic-style leader might have some trouble coping, but the Lippitt and White experiments do at least suggest that the extreme styles of autocratic or laissez-faire leadership may have important dysfunctional consequences for information processing by small groups. A more moderate and flexible style that explicitly encourages task-oriented participation by group members, confers praise and criticism in an impersonal manner, and limits the boundaries of desired behavior in advance, may be optimally functional under most circumstances. Note also that the *appearance* of democratic leadership can be illusory: it may be employed with a certain amount of deviousness as a means of manipulating the group into thinking that it has made a decision which it has not, in fact, made. But such manipulation is not always successful; most individuals feel some psychological pressure to resist perceived manipulation of their attitudes. A leader may have to build up a good deal of "idiosyncracy credit" with his advisers before he can successfully use them in this way without incurring their resentment.[49]

Thus far in the report we have identified possible impediments to information processing that stem either from the behavior of the individual decisionmaker or from the dynamics of small groups to which he belongs. We turn next to the larger organizational context.

Notes

1. Important parts of the chapter were contributed by Professor Joseph Atkinson, University of Otago, New Zealand, and Professor Anne McMahon, then a member of the Sociology Department, Stanford University.

2. For a useful summary and thoughtful commentary on the varied forms of advice and types of advisers to political leaders over the past 3,000 years, *see* Herbert Goldhamer, *The Advisor* (New York: Elsevier, 1978). Goldhamer draws primarily on the writings of those who have served as advisers — some famous (Bacon, Machievelli, Richelieu, Kissinger), some less well known (Han Fei Tzu, Kautilya, Ibn Khaldun, Commynes).

3. Among studies that provide useful data, conceptualizations, and hypotheses about the relationships between presidents and their advisers, *see* the following: Lester G. Seligman, "Presidential Leadership: The Inner Circle and Institutionalization," *Journal of Politics* 18 (August 1956); Thomas E. Cronin and Sanford D. Greenberg, eds., *The Presidential Advisory System* (New York: Harper & Row, 1969); Richard F. Fenno, *The President's Cabinet* (New York: Knopf, 1959); Victor H. Vroom and Philip W. Yetton, *Leadership and Decision-making* (Pittsburgh: University of Pittsburgh Press, 1973); Anthony Downs, *Inside Bureaucracy* (Boston: Little, Brown & Co., 1967), chapters 8 and 9; Joseph de Rivera, *The Psychological Dimension of Foreign Policy* (Columbus: Charles E. Merrill, 1968), chapters 6, 7, and 8; Irving L. Janis, *Victims of Groupthink* (Boston: Houghton Mifflin, 1972); John Rogers, "In Pursuit of Survival: Presidential Leadership, Advisory Groups, and Decision-making" (Senior Honors Thesis, Stanford University, June 1976); Joseph B. Atkinson, "President Nixon's Advisory System as a Variant of the Patron-Client Model of Association" (Yale University, April 1974); Patrick Anderson, *The Presidents' Men* (New York: Doubleday, 1969); Richard T. Johnson, *Managing the White House* (New York: Harper & Row, 1974); Louis Koenig, *The Invisible Presidency* (New York: Rinehart, 1960); Theodore Sorensen, *Decision-making in the White House* (New York: Columbia University Press, 1963); George E. Reedy, *The Twilight of the Presidency* (New York: World, 1970); Alan Rush, *How Kings Take Counsel* (tentative title of forthcoming Ph.D. dissertation, Stanford University); Robert J. Sickels, *Presidential Transactions* (Englewood Cliffs, N.J.: Prentice-Hall, 1974), chapter 2; Abraham Zalesnik, *Human Dilemmas of Leadership* (New York: Harper & Row, 1966), chapter 8; Lewis A. Dexter, "Court Politics: Presidential Staff Relations as a Special Case of a General Phenomenon," *Administration & Society* (December 1977); and Alexander L. George and Juliette L. George, *Woodrow Wilson and Colonel House* (New York: John Day Co., 1956; Dover edition, 1964).

4. Richard Snyder and Glenn Paige, "The U.S. Decision to Resist Aggression in Korea: The Application of an Analytical Scheme," *Administrative Science Quarterly* 3 (1958):362; also, J. James, "A Preliminary Study of the Size Determinant in Small Group Interaction," *American Sociological Review* 16 (1951):474-77.

5. R. F. Bales, *Interaction Process Analysis* (Reading, Mass.: Addison-Wesley, 1950).

6. This entire paragraph is based quite heavily upon the summary paper by R. F. Bales, "In Conference," *Harvard Business Review* 32 (1954):44-50.

7. E. F. Borgatta and R. F. Bales, "Interaction of Individuals in Reconstituted Groups," *Sociometry* 14 (1953):302-20. For a detailed discussion of the effects of group size within the range 2-7, see R. F. Bales and E. F. Borgatta, "Size of Group as a Factor in Interaction Profile," in *Small Groups: Studies in Social Interaction*, A. P. Hare, E. F. Borgatta, and R. F. Bales, eds. (New York: A. A. Knopf, Inc., 1966), pp. 495-512.

8. Thus, as James Thomson, Jr., has noted, "The more sensitive the issue, and the higher it rises in the bureaucracy, the more completely the experts are excluded while the harassed senior generalists take over (that is, the secretaries, undersecretaries, and the presidential assistants)" ("How Could Vietnam Have Happened? An Autopsy," *Atlantic Monthly*, [April 1968]:49).

9. On "uncertainty absorption," see James G. March and Herbert A. Simon, *Organizations* (New York: Wiley, 1958), p. 165. See also the discussion of "organizational pathologies" in Harold Wilensky, *Organizational Intelligence* (New York: Basic Books, 1967) and Anthony Downs, *Inside Bureaucracy*.

10. These suggestions were advanced by Irving Janis (personal communication, and chapter 9 of his *Victims of Groupthink*).

11. F. L. Strodbeck, R. M. James, and C. Hawkins, "Social Status in Jury Deliberations," *American Sociological Review* 22 (1957):713-19.

12. J. Berger, B. P. Cohen, and M. Zelditch, Jr., "Status Characteristics and Social Interaction," *Interpersonal Behavior in Small Groups*, R. J. Ofshe, ed., (Englewood Cliffs, N.J.: Prentice-Hall, Inc., 1973), pp. 163-75.

13. This effect was especially pronouced in permanent groups when compared with temporary groups (E. P. Torrance, "Some Consequences of Power Differences in Decision-Making in Permanent and Temporary Three-Man Groups," *Research Studies*, State College of Washington, vol. 22 [1954], pp. 130-40).

14. "Deviation, Rejection, and Communication," in *Group Dynamics*, 2d ed., Dorwin C. Cartwright and A. Zander, eds. (Evanston, Ill.: Row, Peterson, 1960).

15. Solomon Asch, *Social Psychology*, (Englewood Cliffs, N.J.: Prentice-Hall, 1952).

16. Sorensen, *Decision-making*, p. 90; *see also* Chester L. Cooper, *The Lost Crusade* (Greenwich: Fawcett, 1972), pp. 273-74.

17. G. Kennan, *Memoirs, 1925-1950* (Boston: Little, Brown and Co., 1967), pp. 474, 480, 491-96, 499.

18. R. F. Kennedy, *Thirteen Days* (New York: Norton, 1969), p. 117.

19. Townsend Hoopes, *The Limits of Intervention* (New York: David McKay, 1969), p. 31.

20. The term "idiosyncracy credit" is normally applied to subordinates, but it applies to some degree to superordinates as well. See Edward Hollander, "Conformity, Status, and Idiosyncracy Credit," *Psychological Review* 65

(1958):117-27.

21. N.R.F. Maier, *Problem-solving and Creativity in Individuals and Groups* (Belmont, Cal.: Brooks/Coles, 1970), pp. 227, 387, 413; Harold Guetzkow and John Gyr, "An Analysis of Conflict in Decision-Making Groups," *Human Relations* 23 (1970):288-317.

22. William McGuire, "Personality and Susceptibility to Social Influence," in Edgar F. Borgatta and William W. Lambert, eds., *Handbook of Personality Theory and Research* (Chicago: Rand McNally, 1968). McGuire reviews the results of studies that have attempted to account for "conformity" and "uniformity" of views within a group on the basis of individual personality characteristics. The findings that have accumulated in this heavily researched field have turned out to be increasingly complex and inconsistent. A similarly sober conclusion regarding the difficulty of explaining conformity in terms of personality traits has been drawn by political scientists specializing on the personality correlates of political attitudes. See Giuseppe Di Palma and Herbert McClosky, "Personality and Conformity: The Learning of Political Attitudes," *American Political Science Review*, (December 1970):1054-1073.

23. D. C. Cartwright and R. Lippitt, "Group Dynamics and the Individual," *International Journal of Psychotherapy* 7 (January 1957):86-102.

24. Ibid. (Italics supplied.)

25. N.R.F. Maier and A. R. Solem found in an experimental study that the presence of a permissive discussion leader who protected individuals holding minority views from the social pressures of the majority upgraded the quality of the discussion and the problem-solving performance of the group ("The Contribution of a Discussion Leader to the Quality of Group Thinking: The Effective Use of Minority Opinions," *Human Relations* [1952]:277-88).

26. In this respect, Janis echoes an important element in Leon Festinger's theory of informal social communication, which Stanley Schachter later developed in his studies of conformity pressures. Schachter postulated that "on any issue for which there is no empircial referent, the reality of one's own opinion is established by the fact that other people hold similar opinions." In other words, concurrence-seeking is an adaptation to the cognitive constraints on rationality that were noted in Chapter 2. In the face of value-complexity and uncertainty, individuals engage in concurrence-seeking vis-à-vis other members of the group in order to establish thereby the validity of their opinions and judgements.

27. *Victims of Groupthink*, p. 202.

28. Janis's detailed analysis of policymaking in the Bay of Pigs case occupies a full chapter in his book. Only a brief and selective summary of his well-reasoned analysis can be presented here. It is important to note that in focusing upon evidence of Groupthink in this and other cases, Janis does not deny that other factors also played an important role in these fiascos.

29. Cited by Janis, *Victims of Groupthink*, pp. 36, 39, 40. In his book, Janis also presents detailed case studies of the Marshall Plan and the Cuban missile crisis, in both of which he sees evidence of high-quality decisionmaking that avoided the pitfalls of Groupthink.

30. See, for example, Edward S. Shils and Morris Janowitz, "Cohesion and

Disintegration in the Wehrmacht," *Public Opinion Quarterly* 12 (1948):280-315; Samuel A. Stouffer et al., *The American Soldier*, 4 vols. (Princeton, N.J.: Princeton University Press, 1949); Irving L. Janis, "Group Identification Under Conditions of External Danger," *British Journal of Medical Psychology* 36 (1963):227-38.

31. Henry Graff, *The Tuesday Cabinet* (Englewood Cliffs, N.J.: Prentice-Hall, 1970), p. 24; cited by Janis, *Victims of Groupthink*, p. 105.

32. Graff, *Tuesday Cabinet*, p. 6; cited by Janis, *Victims of Groupthink*, p. 105.

33. Quoted in Hugh Sidey, "White House Staff vs. the Cabinet," *Washington Monthly* (February 1969); cited by Janis, *Victims of Groupthink*, p. 106.

34. Janis concludes his study with a detailed discussion of various ways in which Groupthink may be prevented.

35. Victor Vroom, "Industrial Social Psychology," in Gardner Lindzey and Elliot Aronson, eds., *The Handbook of Social Psychology*, 2d ed., vol. 5 (Reading, Mass.: Addison-Wesley, 1969), p. 230.

36. Harold Kelley and John Thibaut, "Group Problem Solving," in Lindzey and Aronson, *Handbook*, pp. 1-101; Barry Collins and Harold Guetzkow, *A Social Psychology of Group Processes for Decision Making* (New York: Wiley, 1964), pp. 15-16.

37. Professor Dorwin Cartwright has incisively criticized the quality of experimental research on the so-called "risky-shift" phenomenon. See his "Risk-Taking by Individuals and Groups: An Assessment of Research Employing Choice Dilemmas," *Journal of Personality and Social Psychology* 20 (1971):361-78. See also the same author's "Determinants of Scientific Progress: The Case of Research on the Risky Shift," *American Psychologist* 28 (1973):222-311.

38. For a summary of recent trends in this research area, *see* Samuel A. Kirkpatrick, "Psychological Views of Decision-Making," in Cornelius Cotter, ed., *Political Science Annual*, vol. 6 (Indianapolis: Bobbs-Merrill, 1975); and S. A. Kirkpatrick, D. F. Davis, and R. D. Robertson, "The Process of Political Decision-Making in Groups: Search Behavior and Choice Shifts," *American Behavioral Scientist*, 20 (September/October 1976).

39. Janis, *Victims of Groupthink*, chapter 9.

40. These observations are developed further in Chapter 10.

41. Two important exceptions may be noted: Victor H. Vroom and Philip W. Yetton, *Leadership and Decision Making*, and Irving L. Janis and L. Mann, *Decision Making: A Psychological Analysis of Conflict, Choice and Commitment* (New York: Free Press, 1977).

42. Stanley Milgram, *Obedience to Authority* (New York: Harper & Row, 1974). *See also* the discussion of factors that make for acceptance or rejection of illicit demands from an authoritative leader in Janis and Mann, *Decision Making*, chapter 10.

43. R. F. Bales, "In Conference," *Harvard Business Review* 32, (1954):44-50.

44. Edgar Borgatta, A. S. Couch, and R. F. Bales, "Some Findings Relevant to the Great Man Theory of Leadership," *American Sociological Review* 19

(1954):755-59.

45. Fred Fiedler, *Leader Attitudes and Group Effectiveness* (Urbana, Ill.: University of Illinois Press, 1958).

46. Robert L. Hamlin, "Leadership and Crises," in Dorwin Cartwright and Alvin Zander, eds., *Group Dynamics*, 3rd ed. (New York: Harper & Row, 1968).

47. See, for a fuller discussion of this point, Joseph B. Atkinson, "President Nixon's Advisory System as a Variant of the Patron-Client Model of Association: A Case Study" (Paper, Yale University, April 1974). See also Atkinson's forthcoming Ph.D. dissertation (untitled), Political Science Department, Yale University.

48. Ralph White and Ronald Lippitt, "Leader Behavior and Member Reaction in Three Social Climates," in Cartwright and Zander, *Group Dynamics*.

49. See further, Hollander, "Conformity."

5
Organizational Behavior and Bureaucratic Politics as Sources of Impediments to Information Processing

Political scientists of an earlier generation were intrigued by the possibility that an overburdened executive might be able to divide his overall responsibilities into a set of more manageable subtasks to be assigned to specialized units of the organization. It was hoped and expected that division of labor and specialization within the organization, coupled with central direction and coordination, would enable the modern executive to achieve the ideal of "rationality" in policymaking. Worth recalling in this connection is that many years ago the concept of "bureaucracy" was synonymous with "rationality." Needless to say, that was before experience with complex bureaucracies gave the term its present invidious connotation.

It is equally interesting that personality theorists of an earlier era who pioneered in studying the disruptive role that emotions and impulses can play in a person's behavior also looked to organizational structures and procedures as providing the means for strengthening an individual's rational capacities. Views of this kind were expressed many years ago by Sigmund Freud and William McDougall and were echoed by W. R. Bion, a specialist on group dynamics who has been associated with the work of the Tavistock Clinic in London. Bion took the position that by relying upon "organization and structure," a work group can prevent the emotional drives of its members from obstructing performance of its tasks.[1] These hopes found strong resonance in the views of some contemporary political scientists who saw in the emerging "scientific" approach to organization and management an opportunity to improve the quality of information processing and appraisal of complex policy issues.

The hopes placed in the potentialities of modern organization by personality theorists and political scientists alike proved to be overly optimistic; certainly they have not been fully realized. Organizations can indeed strongly reinforce the rational, constructive, adaptive sides of an executive's personality, and they can service his need for information, appraisal, and planning. Thereby, organizations also can help to control and counter impediments to information processing introduced into policymaking either by ego defensive maneuvers to which any individual resorts from time to time or by the kinds of group dynamics that, as noted in Chapter 4, can hamper effective reality testing and task performance.

But for various reasons, the potential contribution of organization has proven difficult of realization, and it is clear that earlier expectations were excessively optimistic. For one thing, while executives of organizations do in fact attempt to seek the advantages of internal division of labor and specialization, many policy problems of large scope cannot be neatly divided into separable tasks and dealt with successfully by specialized subunits in isolation from the rest of the organization.[2] Then, too, as political sociologist Harold Wilensky has emphasized, the structural characteristics of hierarchy, specialization, and centralization shared by all large-scale organizations themselves encourage chronic pathologies of information processing and advice.[3]

• • •

The task of central coordination and direction of foreign-policymaking within the U.S. government has gotten steadily worse in modern times as the range, scope, and complexity of foreign-policy problems has expanded. As a result, a much larger number of agencies, bureaus, and departments within the executive branch now have a hand in some aspect of foreign policy. Over thirty separate departments, agencies, and bureaus of the federal government in Washington have offices and representatives abroad. In Washington itself few important foreign-policy issues fall exclusively into the domain of any one of these organizations. Although policymakers might like to classify issues as either military or diplomatic or economic, it is rarely possible to make such a simple classification as regards most issues. For example, it has been pointedly observed that the problem of deployment of U.S. troops in Europe is relevant to the U.S. defense posture (Defense Department), to the balance of payments (Treasury Department), and to U.S. relations with both European allies and the Soviet Union (State Department). Moreover, recent years have seen a rapid erosion of the distinction between foreign and domestic policy.

The result of these historical developments is that many issues of foreign policy—often the most important ones—cut across jurisdictional lines of competence and responsibility within the executive branch. If it were merely a matter of achieving timely, effective communication among the separate units, the task of coordination would be manageable. But the problem runs deeper than that since the intellectual and analytical difficulties that must be overcome to arrive at sound policy cannot be mastered simply by adding together in a mechanical way the separate inputs of the various specialized departments and bureaus. To emphasize this point, some thoughtful observers of foreign policy have suggested that a "policy question" should be defined as one for which there are no experts per se, but only advocates and referees. For policy problems of this kind, effective problem identification, problem solution, and policy implementation cannot be achieved by subdividing the task and delegating different parts of it to subunits of the organization. Rather, these policy problems must be approached within a broader holistic framework, and provision must be made for intellectual and analytical interaction among a variety of experts and representatives from many different specialized departments and agencies.

The difficulties of achieving coordination and intellectual interaction are further compounded by virtue of the fact that subunits within an organization typically develop interests and goals of their own; often these are in sharp variance with organizational goals and value priorities as seen from the perspective of the top executive. The executive's task of policy control, policy analysis, coordination, and implementation is jeopardized, moreover, by competition and conflict among the various subunits. The internal politics of policymaking within the organization are the source of a number of stubborn impediments to optimal information processing. These are described and richly illustrated in the literature on organizational behavior and "bureaucratic politics," and need only be briefly recapitulated here.[4]

The adverse impact on foreign policy of the standard, routine behavior of individual departments and bureaus within the executive branch and the "bureaucratic politics" that often takes place among them emerges more clearly if we differentiate four types of effects:

1. effects on information-processing tasks;
2. effects on the content and quality of the decisions taken;
3. effects on diplomatic negotiations and communications; and
4. effects on implementation of presidential policy.

Effects on Information-Processing Tasks

We can describe the effects on information processing more incisively by recalling the five critical procedural tasks generally regarded as important to the efficacy of a policymaking system. These were discussed in the Introduction and need only be briefly recapitulated here: (1) obtain sufficient information about and good analysis of emerging situations that may require the attention of policymakers in order to provide them with an incisive and valid diagnosis of the situation and policy problem; (2) identify all dimensions of the value complexity imbedded in a decisional problem in order to facilitate careful, balanced consideration of value priorities and to provide a sound basis for trade-off judgments by the policymaker; (3) identify and analyze a reasonably broad, diverse range of option alternatives, giving attention to relevant uncertainties and to the variety of possible costs and risks of each option as well as its presumed benefits; (4) take into account the policy implementation factor in assessing the relative merits of alternative options; and (5) arrange for acquisition and objective analysis of information on how a chosen policy is working and encourage receptivity to feedback.

A variety of studies have called attention to evidence that the performance of the first three of these procedural tasks can be seriously impeded at times by the dynamics of organizational behavior and bureaucratic politics. The findings can be summarized in the following eight propositions:

1. Each organizational unit within the executive branch tends to concentrate on acquiring information about the policy issue that might help to protect or advance its own interests and its own view of the national interest. Each actor tends to supply or withhold information with the same aim. The net result may be that the president fails to get the full, balanced information he needs and, instead, is at the mercy of selective, biased information processing by his subordinates.

2. Each organizational unit's participation in the identification and evaluation of policy options is shaped by its parochial interests and perspectives. Whether cynically or inadvertently, each unit tends to produce "partisan analysis" of the issues and seeks to discredit by fair means or foul the analysis produced by its rivals. As a result, the president may be mislead or confused and may lack balanced, objective analysis of the options from which he must choose.

3. The quality of policy debate in the advisory process is distorted by the tendency of bureaucratic advocates to resort to oversimplification and rhetorical exaggeration. Debasement of debate can easily occur in a highly competitive, pluralistic policymaking system. To gain the executive's attention and to make a striking impression, bureaucratic actors often overstate the expected benefits of the option that they prefer and exaggerate the risks of rival options. Careful, responsible claims and balanced analysis of options tend to be squeezed out.

4. Bureaucratic actors tend to employ whatever bargaining advantages they possess to manipulate the flow of advice in order to influence the executive's choice of policy. Often these bargaining advantages are unevenly distributed among the actors, and there is no assurance that those with superior competence/expertise in the matter being decided can

compete successfully with those having an advantage in other bargaining resources such as power/influence, control over information, skill in persuasion, etc.[5]

5. While the game of bureaucratic politics is generally competitive, the actors sometimes try to restrict competition among themselves in order to protect each other's most important interests. To avoid the risks of policy decisions by the president that might be damaging to their interests or inconsistent with their view of the national interest, they arrange compromises or logrolling deals among themselves. As a result, policy issues may not rise to the presidential level when they should; rather, a perverted form of "lateral coordination" between department and agencies takes place. Also, the policy issue as presented to the president may take the form of a concealed compromise that reflects narrow interests or a parochial view of the "national interest."

6. Contrary to the stereotype of bureaucrats as "empire-builders," bureaucratic actors are not always eager to expand their domains. When their interests require it, they may avoid responsibility for an issue or narrow the range of their participation in policymaking. Additionally, they may be unwilling to get involved in certain policy disputes on behalf of causes that they consider unpromising or potentially costly to themselves. A policy issue may have a low priority from the bureaucratic actor's perspective, though a high priority from the perspective of the president if he were alerted to it. Examples arise in the area of arms control; for example, initiative for the arms control agreement in biological weapons a few years ago had to come from the presidential level.[6]

7. Well-established organizational units tend to rely on policy routines and standard operating procedures that they developed earlier. These routines, however, may be inappropriate for dealing with novel policy problems and yet they often form the basis for the advice furnished the president.

8. Because bureaucratic politics can be enormously time consuming, energy consuming, and attention distracting, it may hamper the ability of policymakers to deal more incisively with foreign-policy issues. Just to keep track of the "game" of bureaucratic politics going on around them and to influence others often requires officials to pay inordinate attention to the internal struggles over policy — thereby limiting the time and energy available for focusing on the overseas situation toward which the policy finally chosen will ostensibly be directed. The phenomenon is succinctly described by Stanley Hoffmann:

> There inevitably occurs a subtle (or not so subtle) shift from the specific foreign-policy issues to be resolved, to the positions, claims, and perspectives of the participants in the policy machine. The demands of the issue

and the merits of alternative choices are subordinated to the demands of the machine and the need to keep it going. *Administrative politics replaces foreign policy.*[7]

Effects on the Nature of Policy Outputs

The central danger, alluded to above, is that policy decision that emerges from the play of intragovernmental politics within the executive branch may be more responsive to the internal dynamics of such a policymaking process than to the requirements of the foreign-policy problem itself. Warner Schilling has provided a useful catalogue of the different types of "distorted" policies that can emerge from such a policy-making system.[8]

1. "No policy at all"—i.e., stalemate.
2. "Compromised policy"—when the direction that policy should take is left unclear; or the means for achieving a well-enough-defined objective are left unclarified or unfocused.
3. "Unstable" or "blind policy"—when the internal struggle over policy is not really resolved once and for all (or even for a substantial period of time), with the result that there may be continuing shifts in the power and influence of rival policy coalitions, with similar shifts in the direction and content of the policy (e.g., the internal policy struggles over the Multilateral Force, SALT II).
4. "Contradictory" or "leaderless policy"—when different parts of the executive branch pursue conflicting courses.
5. "Paper policy"—when a policy is officially promulgated but lacks support within the executive branch needed for effective implementation.
6. "Slow policy"—when continuing competition and conflict among the policy actors delay the development of sufficient consensus and cooperation among them.

Effects on Diplomacy

The phenomenon of bureaucratic politics within foreign-policymaking systems is relatively modern. It was relatively unknown or remained of substantially more modest proportions so long as the scope of a government's foreign policy was restricted and so long as the conduct of foreign relations remained the province of a small number of professional diplomats in each government. This is not to say that internal disagreements and conflict over foreign policy were unknown in the era of classical diplomacy as it developed during the eighteenth and nineteenth centuries. But "cabinet politics," as it was then called, reflected disagreements among a relatively few top-level officials. Lacking until modern times was the complex, highly organized substratum of specialized bureaus and units involved in one or another aspect of the vastly expanded range of foreign policy. While contemporary students of foreign policy sometimes erroneously refer to the top-level "cabinet politics" of the earlier era as "bureaucratic politics," the latter is better understood as a phenomenon peculiar to the *middle echelons* of the large, complex organizations required within modern governments for the conduct of foreign policy. To be sure, "cabinet politics" also occurs today, and it is often linked closely with "bureaucratic politics" at the middle echelons of the government, either further stimulating it or being manipulated by it. But at times, cabinet politics at the highest levels may take place relatively independently of bureaucratic politics and the dynamics of behavior in complex organizations have created new impediments to effective diplomacy. Three such impediments can be identified:

1. Policymakers now must formulate and work with much more complicated images of the foreign-policymaking system of other governments with which they must deal. They need much more information about the other government's policy-making process, the various participants in it, how they perceive different issues, and how they resolve differences. Once policymakers recognize the possibility that bureaucratic politics and the other internal dynamics of complex organization may affect an opponents' foreign-policy behavior, they see (or should see) the need to exercise greater caution in appraising available information about an adversary's intentions, his calculations, and expectations. Further, one's own foreign-policy actions must be calculated and chosen with a view to how they will affect the various interacting officials and departments within the opposing government.

2. The ability of modern governments to send and receive diplomatic communications and to conduct negotiations can be adversely affected by the competitive struggle over policy within each government. Leading officials in different departments and agencies may become so preoccupied with the struggle over foreign policy within their own government that they may inadvertently, if not deliberately, give unclear or misleading signals to officials in other countries.

3. When this process occurs simultaneously in both governments, the danger of adverse effects on diplomatic communications between them is compounded. Thus, not only can bureaucratic politics in Country A distort the quality of its diplomatic communications to Country B; but,

in addition, the different policy officials who are contending with each other in Country B may, in turn, receive and interpret the communications, signals, and actions emanating from Country A quite selectively, since they are looking for evidence to support them in their own bureaucratic battles! Bureaucratic politics is thus capable of introducing a great deal of "noise" and distortion into diplomatic communications and negotiations.

The interactive effects of bureaucratic politics in two countries on their foreign relations have only recently caught the attention of foreign-policy research specialists. The pioneering research is Richard Neustadt's study of two major postwar crises in United States–United Kingdom relations: the Suez crisis of 1956 and the Skybolt crisis of 1962-63.[9]

In both the Skybolt and Suez incidents, noteworthy is the almost nonexistent role of the two embassies: the U.S. embassy in the United Kingdom and the U.K. embassy in the United States. They were inadequately informed of what was going on and were not put to constructive use either to avoid, soften, or deal with the crises. These two cases provide particularly striking illustrations of a general problem: as a result of the modern phenomenon of bureaucratic politics, the task of communicating with and influencing governments through established channels of diplomacy is now much more complicated than it was in the era of classical diplomacy.

Effects on Implementation of Presidential Policy

Even when bureaucratic politics does not distort information processing in the early stages of policymaking, it may come into play later during the implementation of a presidential decision and lead to a policy outcome that is quite inconsistent with the original goals and objectives of his policy.

In recent years, specialists on organization behavior and bureaucratic politics have given increasing attention to the problem of policy implementation. Emphasis has shifted from the task of identifying organizational arrangements and policymaking procedures for achieving high-quality decisions to devising ways of ensuring faithful and effective implementation by middle-level officials of the policies upon which the president has decided.

In his report to the Commission on the Organization of the Governments for the Conduct of Foreign Policy, Graham Allison emphasized that "implementation is at least half the problem in most important government decisions and actions." It may be true that when the president and his associates are sufficiently attentive, they can neutralize the play of bureaucratic politics and exert predominant influence themselves over the selection of policy, but once the decision is made, "the predominant influence over the character of the action taken shifts to the implementor, in most instances, units of the Permanent Government." And so, "bureaucracies dominate implementation."[10]

Various factors contribute to this "gap" between policy enunciation and implementation. The president and other high officials typically are preoccupied with formulating and enacting policy, mobilizing support for it, and issuing policy statements. But getting policies implemented by the appropriate departments and offices within the executive branch usually is a more difficult matter than formulating the policies. There are a number of reasons for this. Policy decisions and high-level policy statements often are very broad and include multiple, sometimes conflicting, objectives. As a result, in order for the president's policies to be implemented at all, they necessarily must be interpreted by middle-level officials.

As previously noted, the policy that emerges from the play of intragovernmental politics is often "compromised," "unstable," "contradictory," or only a "paper policy." The competing values and interests engaged by a policy issue and the controversies that these engender are often not fully resolved once and for all by the president's decision. The way is open, therefore, for a continuation of the struggle over policy during the implementation phase. The president's decision may leave important trade-offs among different objectives embraced by his policy unresolved; they are then left to be settled by others during the implementation phase. Or his decision may leave unsettled the level of costs and risks to be regarded as acceptable in attempting to achieve his policy objectives. So the fact that presidential policy decisions are often only partly successful in dealing with complex issues itself contributes to the so-called "implementation problem."

But, in addition, personnel in departments and bureaus with responsibility for implementing a particular policy decision have perceptions, objectives, and constraints of their own that may differ quite markedly from those of the president and other high officials. It does not require deliberate, conscious "sabotage" of the president's will and his directives for middle-level officials, given their different perception of the matter, to significantly alter his policy in implementing it.

This is all the more likely when, as is often the case, the president exercises his prerogative to choose among alternative policies without the benefit of a good "implementation analysis"—i.e., a sophisticated analysis of the feasibility, the ease or difficulty, of implementing effectively each of the options before him. It is—or should be—well known that organizations tend to implement decisions on the basis of existing standard operating procedures (SOP's), the repetoire of action responses that they have developed over time to deal with different situations. But the president may have chosen a policy that would be distorted in implementation if the organization were to respond on the basis of any of its existing SOP's. In other words, the president's unusual decision may require a novel, creative implementation response by the organization that may not be forthcoming.

We shall turn in the next chapter to a closer look at the implications of these organizational and bureaucratic factors for the functioning of the policymaking system.

Notes

1. W. R. Bion, "Group Dynamics: A Review," *International Journal of Psychoanalysis* 33 (1952):235-47.

2. Robert Axelrod, *Conflict of Interest: A Theory of Divergent Goals with Applications to Politics* (Chicago: Markham, 1970), pp. 122ff.

3. Wilensky, *Organizational Intelligence* (New York: Basic Books, 1967).

4. A useful synthesis and explication of these materials is provided in Graham T. Allison, *Essence of Decision* (Boston: Little, Brown and Co., 1971). On organizational politics, see also the publications of Morton Halperin, particularly his *Bureaucratic Politics and Foreign Policy* (Washington, D.C.: Brookings Institution, 1974); I. M. Destler, *Presidents, Bureaucrats, and Foreign Policy* (Princeton, N.J.: Princeton University Press, 1972); Graham T. Allison, ed., *Adequacy of Current Organization: Defense and Arms Control*, vol. 4, Appendices, Commission on the Organization of the Government for the Conduct of Foreign Policy, June 1975 (Washington, D.C.: U.S. Government Printing Office, 1976); and Anthony Downs, *Inside Bureaucracy* (Boston: Little, Brown and Co., 1967). A number of critical commentaries on the bureaucratic politics model have been published; they are discussed in the review essay by Dan Caldwell, "Bureaucratic Foreign Policy-Making," *American Behavioral Scientist* (September-October 1977).

5. The most important "bargaining advantages," as noted by I. M. Destler, include: "formal authority or responsibility on an issue; the backing of constituents outside the executive branch; recognized expertise; involvement in regular 'action processes' (such as budget review or cable clearance); access to or control over information; the ability to produce good, relevant staff work; and the personal confidence of the president and of other influential officials" ("Country Expertise and U.S. Foreign Policymaking: The Case of Japan," *Pacific Community: An Asian Quarterly Review* [July 1964]:549-50). For a fuller discussion, see Chapter 1.

6. See Forest R. Frank, "CBW: 1962-67; 1967-68; 1969-72," in *Report of the*

Commission on the Organization of the Government for the Conduct of Foreign Policy, vol. 4, Appendices (Washington, D.C.: U.S. Government Printing Office, 1975).

7. Stanley Hoffmann, *Gulliver's Troubles* (New York: McGraw-Hill, 1968), p. 277 (italics supplied).

8. See his "Politics of National Defense: Fiscal 1950," in W. Schilling, P. Hammond, and G. Snyder, *Strategy, Politics, and Defense Budgets* (New York: Columbia University Press, 1962). Schilling's typology is summarized in Destler, *Presidents, Bureaucrats, and Foreign Policy*, p. 74, and, with some changes, by Allison, *Essence of Decision*, p. 155.

9. Richard Neustadt, *Alliance Politics* (New York: Columbia University Press, 1970). An incisive analytical summary of the Skybolt case is provided in Graham Allison, *Adequacy of Current Organization*, pp. 259-65. Somewhat different accounts of the Skybolt case appear in Morton Halperin's "Why Bureaucrats Play Games," *Foreign Policy* (Spring 1971); and Henry Brandon, "Skybolt," *London Sunday Times*, Dec. 8, 1963; reprinted in M. H. Halperin and A. Kanter, eds., *Readings in American Foreign Policy* (Boston: Little, Brown and Co., 1973). Other case studies of the role of bureaucratic politics in confounding U.S.-Japanese diplomatic relations can be found in I. M. Destler et al., *Managing An Alliance: The Politics of U.S.-Japanese Relations* (Washington, D.C.: The Brookings Institution, 1976).

10. Allison, *Adequacy of Current Organization*, p. 45. The following paragraphs draw upon the excellent discussion in this volume; see, particularly, pp. 43-46, 232-34. Examples of implementation problems can be found in the case studies presented in this volume.

6
Some Possible (and Possibly Dangerous) Malfunctions of the Advisory Process

It is not easy to predict what impact the parochialism of subunits described in the preceding chapter will have on the executive's ability to comprehend policy problems, exercise intelligent choice of action, and arrange for effective implementation. This will depend upon a variety of factors, among them the steps the executive takes to protect himself and the advisory system around him from the maneuvers of subunit actors. Besides, we should recognize that conflict over policy within the executive branch may in fact help illuminate issues and improve information search and appraisal. (This possibility will be taken up in Part 2.)

Relevant to this is the way in which the executive attempts to organize foreign-policymaking procedures within the executive branch—i.e., whether the organizational model he establishes is a highly centralized, White House–oriented system, a State-centered system, or a looser decentralized system.[1] Each of these models attempts to cope with the dynamics of organizational behavior and bureaucratic politics in somewhat different ways. Each model requires a somewhat different set of procedures and strategies for curbing and damaging effects of the parochial viewpoints and policy maneuvers in which subunits engage.

The present report confines itself to identifying a number of *general "malfunctions"* of the advisory process that can occur under *any* of these alternative organizational models. It is important to clarify the reasons for doing so. While structural reorganization can aid in the quest for effective policy, there appears to be no single organizational model by means of which the chief executive and his staff can convert the functional expertise and diverse viewpoints of the many subunits within the executive branch into consistently effective decisions and policies. Impediments to information processing will occur under any of the organizational models that are being considered. The dynamics of organizational behavior and bureaucratic politics that create these impediments are stubborn; they will not be eliminated by any of the organizational models under consideration.

It follows from this that efforts to improve the foreign-policymaking system should not stop with structural reorganization along the lines of one or another of the organizational models under consideration. In addition, whichever model is adopted must also include provisions for timely identification and correction of possible malfunctions in the advisory system.[2] Provision must be made for *monitoring* the day-to-day workings of the policymaking system, and strategies for *preventive intervention* must be available within that system.

As defined here, "malfunction" refers to the ways in which a policymaking process fails to achieve one or another of the features of an effective procedure. It is conceded that a procedural malfunction does not always result in a major policy error; nor can it be argued that a better policy will always be chosen if procedural malfunctions do not occur. Rather, the premise on which this report rests is that procedural malfunctions *can* have damaging consequences for policy choices, not that they necessarily will.[3] Nine malfunctions of the advisory process have been identified as having occurred at the presidential level in various historical cases; they will be listed and briefly discussed here. (The reader is asked to keep in mind that malfunctions of this kind are not confined to presidential decisionmaking in the foreign-policy sphere; such malfunctions can occur at any level of decisionmaking, for other kinds of policy issues, and in other kinds of organizations.)

When the president and his advisers agree too readily on the nature of the problem facing them and on a response to it.

Paradoxically, while it is often difficult for an executive to achieve sufficient consensus within the decisionmaking group on behalf of a wise policy without diluting its ingredients, to achieve consensus too quickly and too easily is also likely to degrade the quality of the decision. An experienced executive will regard a readily achieved consensus within the policy-making group as a reason for *postponing* rather than taking action. Alfred P. Sloan, former chairman of General Motors, is reported to have said at a meeting of one of his top policy committees: "Gentlemen, I take it we are all in complete agreement on the decision here. . . . Then I propose we postpone further discussion of this matter until our next meeting to give ourselves time to develop disagreement and perhaps gain some understanding of what the decision is all about."[4]

Deferring action is more difficult, of course, when the situation seems to require it or when the chief executive himself is disposed to take immediate action. In certain types of international crisis a kind of spontaneous consensus may quickly emerge among members of the policymaking group on behalf of the "need for action" to prevent damage to U.S. interests – a consensus which may prevent adequate consideration of the magnitude of the expected damage and how much cost and risk one should undertake in order to prevent it. It is particularly when everyone seems to agree on the need for some action to prevent expected damage that the most dangerous mistakes in the calculation of risk and utility are likely to be committed. The typical error under these circumstances is a gross underestimation of the costs and risks of the action taken. Conversely, *disagreement* within the decisionmaking group on the proper objectives, the proper means, and the kinds and level of risk present in the situation is likely to improve the analytical process and the advice that precedes the final choice of policy that the president makes.

This type of malfunction of the policymaking process can be vividly seen in the events leading to President Johnson's decision to send U.S. military forces into the Dominican Republic in the spring of 1965. As Philip Geyelin (a reporter for *The Wall Street Journal* at the time) put it in his excellent review of this crisis: "If Lyndon Johnson had acted much differently than he did in the early, decisive days of the Dominican crisis, he would have had to invent his own alternatives and ignore the counsel of his principal advisers."[5] There is nothing in the available record to indicate that the Special Assistant for National Security Affairs, McGeorge Bundy, attempted to preserve the president's options in this case.

Indeed, all available accounts of the crisis indicate that consensus on the need for U.S. military intervention developed quickly, easily, and without challenge within the decisionmaking group. Geyelin notes that Johnson "was remarkably at the mercy of the advice and activities of his subordinates on the scene" – who speedily concluded that a rebel victory carried with it the risk of an eventual communist regime. This definition of the situation emerged almost at once in the field and was immediately accepted without question in Washington because everyone's perception of the crisis in the Dominican Republic was shaped by a strong policy predisposition that antedated the crisis. This was the belief that the Dominican Republic should not be allowed to become another Cuba. A distorted, exaggerated perception of the threat in Santo Domingo emerged when available information on the rebels was viewed through the prism of the "Cuban syndrome." No attempt was made until well after the United States was committed to intervention to check the U.S. embassy's definition of the situation and of the policies most appropriate for meeting it.[6]

But decisional premises of this kind do not always paralyze the ability

of decisionmakers to make a reasoned calculation of the utility of intervention. Vigorous multiple advocacy within the Eisenhower administration in the Indochina crisis of 1954 helped to control the effect
that ideologically reinforced decisional premises were allowed to have on
the final decision. The policymaking process worked much better in the
1954 crisis than in the Dominican crisis.

**When advisers and advocates take different positions and debate them
before the president but their disagreements do not cover the full range
of relevant hypotheses and alternative options.**

There is no assurance that on any given policy problem each of the
relevant options will find an advocate within the policymaking group.
Some options may fail to get serious consideration because it is felt that
the president has excluded them or would reject them or because they are
not in the interest of any agency and no once wants to pay the
bureaucratic cost of asking the president to adopt them. Thus, the option
of not giving direct military assistance to South Korea when it was attacked by North Korea in June 1950 was never really considered by
Truman's advisers, in part because the president had made it clear at the
outset that the United States would not allow the attack to succeed. (A
fuller account of this case is given below.)

Other options may fail to get consideration because policymaking officials serving under the chief executive are uninterested in them. There
are various ways of reducing the executive's freedom of action even while
seemingly providing him with multiple options. As Robert H. Johnson
notes: "One of the chief problems with attempts to lay out major policy
alternatives is the strong temptation to load the dice. A typical procedure
is to set up a straw-man alternative on either side of a middle course of
action which quickly becomes the logical choice over the more 'extemist'
options."[7]

When there is no advocate for an unpopular policy option.

In the Vietnam escalation case there was, at least, an advocate for the
unpopular option of withdrawal in the person of George Ball. In the
Korean case, by contrast, the policymaking group assembled by President Truman on the first day of the North Korean invasion quickly
developed a consensus on the need for action to prevent the expected
damage to U.S. interests. While members of the group were by no means
uniformly enthusiastic at the prospect of U.S. military involvement, the
consensus to act was at no time subjected to challenge. This was not

because of any previously agreed upon contingency plans which had only to be put into operation. Indeed, no such plans existed. The North Korean attack came as an unexpected shock. It was this rude reality, not the availability of preexisting plans, that helped produce consensus within the policymaking group. Critical in this respect, too, was the president's initial definition of the situation as one in which too much was at stake to permit the United States to acquiesce.[8] The ingredients for bureaucratic politics and multiple advocacy were present in the long-standing policy and personal conflicts between Secretary of State Dean Acheson and Secretary of Defense Louis Johnson, but their expression was muted by the president's attitude, the atmosphere of crisis, and Acheson's reversal of administration policy on Formosa in the direction that Johnson had advocated.

During the first few days of the conflict, at a time when U.S. assistance was still limited to air and naval support, several of Truman's advisers expressed their reluctance to see U.S. ground troops committed to combat in South Korea. Indeed, the president's own hesitation in the matter was also noticeable. There was some discussion of the disadvantages and hazards of this course of action before the need for U.S. combat troops became evident. Once the deteriorating battlefield situation made it imperative, however, no adviser questioned the introduction of American combat forces except George Kennan, who hesitated on the grounds that it would increase the likelihood of Soviet counterintervention. Neither Kennan nor military advisers who were unenthusiastic about being drawn into a land war on the Asian continent were given any encouragement to play a more vigorous advocate's role in the policy discussions.[9]

Later in the Korean War, when the decision was being made to send the U.S. and U.N. forces across the thirty-eighth parallel to pursue the defeated North Korean army and to unite the two parts of the country, the threat of Chinese Communist intervention became a factor. Important officials in Truman's circle of policy advisers (Secretary of the Air Force Thomas Finletter and Chief of Naval Operations Admiral Forrest Sherman, as well as George Kennan) were disturbed by the risks of Chinese intervention.[10] Once again, however, Truman's structuring and management of the policymaking process discouraged those with reservations about the drift of policy from playing the role of more articulate devil's advocates. Indeed, such a role was not generally congenial to President Truman. He preferred to structure the policy-forming process in terms of functional expertise. Each agency head was expected to provide his considered view of that aspect of the problem for which he was responsible. Within each department, second- and third-level officials contributed their advice to their department head, and deviations from this hierarchically organized flow of advice within each department were discouraged. Kennan's advice on this and other occasions when it differed from Acheson's was overshadowed and controlled by the advice of the secretary of state.[11]

When advisers to the president thrash out their own disagreements over policy without the president's knowledge and confront him with a unanimous recommendation.

In this variant of the workings of bureaucratic politics, the other actors in effect "gang up" on the chief executive and try to sell him the policy they have worked out among themselves. Clark Clifford gives a succinct, authoritative account of this practice in an interview describing his role as assistant to President Truman on domestic affairs:

> The idea was that the six or eight of us would try to come to an understanding among ourselves on what directions we would like the president to take on any given issue. And then, quietly and unobtrusively, each in his own way, we would try to steer the president in that direction. . . . Well, it was two forces fighting for the mind of the president, that's really what it was. It was completely unpublicized, and I don't think Mr. Truman ever realized it was going on. . . .[12]

In this case, as Clifford's account makes clear, two coalitions of advisers were competing for influence over policy. A more dangerous situation arises when all major advisers on a policy issue reach an agreement among themselves before going to the executive. This type of malfunction of the process almost occurred in the late autumn of 1964 when President Johnson was confronted with a solid lineup of advisers recommending that he proceed with the Multilateral Force (MLF) for NATO. The MLF was a strategic force to be composed of surface ships manned by mixed crews drawn from a number of NATO countries. For several years a small but strong group of MLF partisans within the administration had pushed this idea as a way of knitting the alliance together. An opportunity for final U.S. approval of the plan and its implementation arose in connection with Prime Minister Harold Wilson's visit to Washington for discussions with the president. The advocates of the MLF within the administration succeeded in coordinating with all of the president's chief advisers a position paper that would finally have committed the United States firmly to the MLF. Hence, on the eve of his critical meeting with the British prime minister, Johnson "was confronted with a spirited, consecrated, nearly united bureaucracy. . . ."[13]

Now, it is extremely difficult for a president to act contrary to the unanimous advice of all his national security advisers. It is well to regard this variant of the bureaucratic politics process as a possible malfunction, for its occurrence threatens to deprive the chief executive of an adequate evaluation of available options. The president does not benefit adequately from multiple advocacy when the actors thrash out or compromise their differences *privately* and confront him with a unified recommendation.

In the MLF case the special assistant for national security affairs, McGeorge Bundy, did act in time to prevent the emerging malfunction from narrowing the president's information and options. Geyelin states that Bundy's position as "guardian of options and protector of the President was perhaps never more effectively displayed than in the episode of the MLF. Bundy had sensed trouble building up earlier in the year. With the MLF partisans in full cry, the President's position was uncertain. . . ."[14] Sensing the development of the type of malfunction we have been discussing, Bundy intervened to restore some semblance of multiple advocacy to the system. He quietly called upon Richard Neustadt, a part-time consultant to the White House, to make an independent appraisal, for the president's benefit of the MLF issue in Europe as well as in Washington. Armed with this and other information which Bundy assembled, the president entered the final briefing conferences with his foreign-policy advisers prepared to challenge the decisional premises, information, and recommendation of their position paper on the MLF. "In the course of the protracted conferences in preparation for the Wilson visit," Geyelin reports, "Johnson assailed the men around him, questioning their competence as well as their counsel. . . ."[15]

In emphasizing the importance of Bundy's intervention in this case, we do not ignore that other factors also worked against Johnson's adherence to the MLF. There was by no means a clear consensus on its behalf, let alone enthusiasm, within NATO; and senior members of Congress as well as many officials in the executive branch were not enthusiastic supporters of the MLF. What Bundy's timely intervention accomplished was to bring these factors into greater prominence for the president's benefit.

When advisers agree privately among themselves that the president should face up to a difficult decision, but no one is willing to alert him to the need for doing so.

In direct contrast to the malfunction just discussed, in which his advisers privately agree upon a policy which they then attempt to get the president to adopt, this malfunction refers to the unusual and dangerous situation in which a private consensus on the need for presidential action emerges among his advisers but is not communicated to the president. This highlights once again the critical importance of presidential-level participation and sensitivity to policymaking discussions within the system.

In the MLF case, monitoring of these discussions by the special assistant for national security affairs alerted the president in time. But in a different crisis under Truman in November 1950, failure to alert the president resulted in a classic example of this kind of breakdown in the advisory system. By early November, large numbers of Chinese Communist forces had already intervened in the Korean War and had subjected U.S. and South Korean forces to sharp tactical combat; but they had not yet launched an all-out offensive against U.S. and U.N. forces. Nonetheless, Truman's chief civilian and military advisers in Washington were acutely concerned over the risks associated with the maldeployment of MacArthur's forces in North Korea in the presence of large numbers of Chinese Communist forces. The president's advisers seemingly agreed among themselves that MacArthur's directives should be changed in order to reduce the vulnerability of his forces, but this consensus was not translated into action. According to Richard Neustadt's account, each adviser had his own reasons for not taking the problem to Truman. And each adviser interpreted his official role quite narrowly in order to relieve himself of the obligation to take the initiative.

"No one went to Truman," Neustadt writes, "because everyone thought someone else should go." He continues:

> The military chiefs deferred to State; let Acheson, as guardian of "policy," ask Truman to reverse MacArthur. But Acheson, already under fire from the Capitol, was treading warily between the Pentagon and that inveterate idealist about generals, Harry Truman. In immediate terms the risk was "military"; if it justified reversing the commander in the field, then the joint Chiefs must make the judgment and tell Truman. So Acheson is said to have insisted, understandably enough, and there the matter rested.

As for Secretary of Defense George Marshall, who had preceded Acheson at State and had himself been army chief of staff when Bradley (now chairman of the joint chiefs of staff) was subordinate commander, he had "leaned over backwards" since returning to the government shortly before these events took place "not to meddle with the work of his successors in *their* jobs. He had also leaned over backwards not to revive the old Army feud between him and MacArthur. What Acheson and Bradley were not ready to initiate, Marshall evidently felt he could not take upon himself. . . . The President, meanwhile, had little thought of over-riding, on his own, the tactical decisions of a qualified commander."[16]

This was a sorry example, indeed, of narrow bureaucratic role-playing at the highest advisory level. One can only speculate what Truman's response would have been had his advisers shared their concern with him and recommended that MacArthur's directives be changed. If Truman had acted promptly, there would have been time to pull back MacArthur's forces before the Chinese launched their major offensive on November 28. The catastrophe that followed might have been avoided altogether or greatly reduced.[17]

When the president, faced with an important problem to decide, is dependent upon a single channel of information.

A seldom-noted aspect of Khrushchev's behavior during the Cuban missile crisis was that he quickly established multiple channels for securing information on Kennedy's intentions. Too much was at stake for the Soviet government for it to wait passively for Washington to provide deliberate or inadvertent signals regarding the president's intentions. Faced with the need to make important decisions momentarily, the Soviet premier grasped the value of redundancy in information coverage of critical aspects of his opponent's behavior.[18] In striking contrast, U.S. leaders have allowed themselves in several crises to remain dependent on a single channel of information about critical aspects of the situation. Among the many malfunctions of the policymaking process evident in planning the Bay of Pigs fiasco in 1961 was the fact that Kennedy and his advisers, including the JCS, depended on the CIA's estimates of Castro's military and political strength. Both were miscalculated and underestimated by CIA. It was incorrectly estimated that there was a substantial anti-Castro underground, which would lead to an uprising when the invasion by Cuban exiles took place. It was erroneously believed that Castro's air force was weak and vulnerable and that he did not have the air power to defeat the invading force. CIA argued that the invasion should not be delayed since Cuba would soon receive modern air power from the Soviets. As a matter of fact, Castro had already received these modern aircraft.[19]

Although the single channel of information on these and other inputs to policy planning was controlled by CIA, where the chief advocates and planners of the invasion resided, Kennedy's suspicions were not aroused. There was ample time to set up independent channels of information and intelligence evaluation, but the president and his alter egos did not move in this direction. Rather, they allowed CIA to maintain unchallenged its position as dominant advocate, a position which rested partly on its exclusive custodianship of critical information and intelligence inputs.

The type of malfunction we have been discussing occurred again in the Dominican intervention of April 1965. For its picture of developments in the complex internal political situation in the Dominican Republic, Washington was dependent on a single channel of information—this time the U.S. embassy in Santo Domingo. There was no independent source of information on these events.[20] Accordingly, had Johnson (or any of his advisers) wished to act differently in this crisis, as Geyelin puts it, "he would have had to discount the overwhelming weight of intelligence he received from the scene. . . ."[21]

Washington's dependence on a single channel of intelligence cannot be explained on the ground that the crisis developed too swiftly to initiate additional channels. Warning was available that the internal political conflict in the Dominican Republic might get out of hand. But neither the president nor his special assistant for national security affairs, "the guardian of presidential options," utilized the available warning to establish quickly the necessary additional independent sources of information on what was going on in the Dominican Republic.

When the key assumptions and premises of a plan have been evaluated only by the advocates of that option.

A striking example of this type of malfunction occurred in the Bay of Pigs case. Because Kennedy persistently entertained grave doubts about the CIA invasion plan and, moreover, did *not* regard Castro as a direct threat to the United States, it is puzzling that the key premises of the CIA plan were not subjected to thoroughgoing scrutiny. As Irving Janis emphasizes in his study, *Victims of Groupthink*, the answer lies partly in the considerable respect and prestige enjoyed in the new administration by CIA Chief Allen Dulles and Richard Bissell, both carry-overs from the Eisenhower administration, and partly also in Kennedy's wish to have them join his team.

Kennedy's reservations about the invasion plan were never translated into an effective search for an alternative. Instead, a number of partial constraints were imposed on the plan to make it more acceptable to the president.[22] Questions that the president and other policymakers raised from time to time were answered only by those who were preparing the plan and supporting it. As Irving Janis notes, the president let these meetings degenerate into question-and-answer periods. When an occasional skeptic, like Senator Fulbright, who was invited by the president to attend one of the policy meetings, raised questions about the plan,

Kennedy was satisfied to allow the CIA representative to respond. In the last analysis, the key assumptions and premises of the invasion plan were not subjected to thorough independent analysis because the president allowed the CIA to dominate and weaken the multiple advocacy system. The JCS, it is true, was asked to evaluate the CIA plan, but there was no disposition on the part of Kennedy or his leading advisers to ensure that the JCS was sufficiently motivated to give it a properly critical scrutiny, or to look closely at the qualified endorsement the JCS came up with.

In providing consistently reassuring answers, the CIA representatives were not necessarily engaged in conscious deception, though wishful thinking may have been at work in their assessment of uncertainties. Their behavior is not surprising if we keep in mind that the CIA leaders firmly believed that action against Castro was necessary. They had created and trained a Cuban exile force to carry out the invasion; the preparations had already achieved a certain bureaucratic momentum by the time the new president established himself in office and turned some of his attention to reviewing the plan.

When the president asks advisers for their opinions on a preferred course of action but does not request a qualified group to examine more carefully the negative judgment offered by one or more advisers.

We have noted the danger that may arise when no actor in the system is willing to speak up for an unpopular option or to oppose the group's preferred course of action. A different kind of malfunction occurs when advisers who give counsel that runs against the grain suffer from inadequate resources for advocacy in the competitive marketplace of bureaucratic politics. Maldistribution among the actors of informational and analytical resources, of formal status, of informal prestige and reputation, or access to presidential confidence, and so on, can severely weaken the workings of the policymaking system by giving lopsided advantages to some participants.

As a result, the president may "hear" the negative opinion put forward by a dissenting adviser but not be impressed; he may be satisfied all too easily with the seemingly impressive rebuttal of a more powerful and prestigious advocate. This type of malfunction of the policy process was evident in the deliberations leading up to the Bay of Pigs fiasco. On various occasions the CIA plan to invade Cuba was strongly opposed by individual advisers—Chester Bowles, Arthur Schlesinger, and Senator Fulbright. All accounts of Kennedy's management of the policymaking process in this case make clear that, far from seeking opportunities to encourage vigorous multiple advocacy, he was reluctant to see it develop and hoped to satisfy his own doubts about the plan by procedures which did not so directly challenge its advocates and supporters.

Following the president's cue, neither did McGeorge Bundy, his alter ego for national security affairs in the White House, nor Robert Kennedy, nor Secretary of State Rusk, attempt to initiate or encourage an independent evaluation of the plan. When Hilsman suggested that his office do so, Rusk refused on the grounds of secrecy. And at one point, Arthur Schlesinger, who had written two memos opposing the plan, was taken aside by Robert Kennedy and told to "lay off." Those who opposed the invasion were "heard" but given no encouragement to develop the case against it or to form themselves into a group that would look into the issues more thoroughly.

What this case shows, therefore, is that the advice of policy dissidents which remains the mere opinion of the individuals concerned will not suffice to check the momentum of a dominant policy faction that is attempting to control the president's decision.

When the president is impressed by the consensus among his advisers on behalf of a particular policy but fails to ascertain how firm the consensus is, how it was achieved, and whether it is justified.

We spoke earlier of a malfunction (number 4) similar to this one in some respects, in which the other participants in bureaucratic politics thrash out their disagreements on a policy issue privately, without the president's knowledge, and then confront him with a unanimous recommendation. But the chief executive may also be the victim of what Irving Janis calls an "illusory" consensus among his advisers that reflects a rather different working of the policy-forming system. Thus, at the important 4 April 1961 meeting it appeared to President Kennedy that there was no longer any opposition to the Bay of Pigs plan. Evidently he did not realize that the way in which the policy-forming process had been managed had discouraged the emergence of opposition. As Schlesinger recalled it, "Our meetings were taking place in a curious atmosphere of assumed consensus." And, as Sorensen puts it, the advice offered Kennedy "was not so unanimous or so well considered as it seemed."[23]

What this suggests, then, is that a chief executive and his alter egos must not take the consensus among policy advisers at face value. Particularly when the consensus is agreeable to him, the president must force himself to test it in order to establish whether it is complete or obscures important differences and unresolved issues. Similarly, he should ascertain what the consensus is based on and how it was achieved. Is it a well-considered consensus in which actors have done their homework properly and interacted with each other in a joint problem-solving exercise? Or is it a manufactured or synthetic consensus obtained through the dominance of one policy clique, or through bargaining among the actors that resulted in a compromise that papers over difficult problems and shirks the task of identifying and evaluating relevent options?

• • •

The nine malfunctions identified in this chapter do not cover all possible breakdowns in the functioning of information and advisory systems on which an executive is dependent. While the historical illustrations chosen to illustrate these malfunctions are drawn from presidential-level decisionmaking in the sphere of foreign policy, similar malfunctions no doubt occur at lower levels in the organization as well. Nor are such malfunctions confined to the area of foreign policy; they can and no doubt do occur in governmental decisionmaking in other policy areas as well. Finally, malfunctions of this kind can occur in nongovernmental organizations as well. In other words, while this report is concerned with foreign-policymaking, the theory of malfunctions in policymaking presented in this chapter is of general applicability.

Awareness that malfunctions of this kind can occur should sensitize those engaged in policymaking to watch for them and to take timely preventive or corrective actions. We shall return to this possibility particularly in Chapter 11 when we discuss the task of a "custodian-manager" of the policymaking process.

Notes

1. For a discussion of alternative organizational models for dealing with this problem of central coordination of the various actors and units in the policy-making system, see Graham T. Allison, ed., *Adequacy of Current Organization: Defense and Arms Control*, vol. 4, Appendices, Commission on the Organization of the Government for the Conduct of Foreign Policy, June 1975 (Washington, D.C.: U.S. Government Printing Office, 1976), pp. 35-41. See also I. M. Destler, *Presidents, Bureaucrats, and Foreign Policy* (Princeton, N.J.: Princeton University Press, 1972).

2. This point is increasingly emphasized by organization specialists who have been struck by the chronic pathologies of information and advice to which all complex organizations are subject. Harold Wilensky, for example, provides a list of "organizational defenses against informational pathologies" (*Organizational Intelligence*, [New York: Basic Books, 1967], pp. 174-81); and Anthony Downs identifies a number of strategies (such as redundancy, use of counterbases) for reducing or avoiding distortion in hierarchical communication within organiza-

tions (*Inside Bureaucracy* [Boston: Little, Brown & Co., 1967], pp. 118-27).

3. For additional discussion, *see* A. L. George, "The Case for Multiple Advocacy in Making Foreign Policy," *American Political Science Review* (September 1972):765-81.

4. Quoted by Peter F. Drucker, *The Effective Executive* (New York: Harper & Row, 1966), p. 148.

5. Philip Geyelin, *Lyndon B. Johnson and the World* (New York: Praeger, 1966), pp. 244-45.

6. Some of the major accounts on the Dominican intervention, in addition to Geyelin's book, are Abraham F. Lowenthal, *The Dominican Intervention* (Cambridge, Mass.: Harvard University Press, 1972); John Bartlow Martin, *Overtaken by Events* (New York: Doubleday, 1966); Theodore Draper, *The Dominican Revolt* (New York: Commentary, 1968); Tad Szulc, *Dominican Diary* (New York: Delacorte Press, 1965); Rowland Evans and Robert Novak, *Lyndon B. Johnson: The Exercise of Power* (New York: The New American Library, 1966); Dan Kurzman, *Santo Domingo: Revolt of the Damned* (New York: Putnam, 1965); Center for Strategic Studies, Georgetown University, *Dominican Action—1965; Intervention or Cooperation?* (Washington University Press, 1966); Haynes Johnson and Bernard M. Gwertzman, *Fulbright: The Dissenter* (New York: Doubleday, 1968); and Jerome Slater, *Intervention and Negotiation* (New York: Harper & Row, 1970).

7. Robert H. Johnson, "National Security Council," *Orbis* 13 (fall 1969):723. Others who have called attention to the subterfuge of "straw man" options include I. M. Destler, *Presidents, Bureaucrats, and Foreign Policy*; John P. Leacocos, "Kissinger's Apparat," *Foreign Policy* 5 (winter 1971-72):24; and Charles Yost, "On Affairs at State," *New York Times*, 30 May, 1971.

8. Taking note of this, Richard C. Snyder and Glenn D. Paige emphasize that the definition of a situation itself can, in effect, exclude consideration of any but a single course of action. See "The United States Decision to Resist Aggression in Korea," *Adminstrative Science Quarterly* 3 (December 1958):245; Harry S. Truman, *Memoirs: Years of Trial and Hope*, vol. 2 (Garden City: Doubleday & Co., 1956), pp. 332ff; Glenn D. Paige, *The Korean Decision* (New York: The Free Press, 1968), pp. 98-99, 113-15, 124-26, 148-49, 174; Alexander L. George, "American Policy Making and the North Korean Aggression," *World Politics* 7 (January 1955):209-32.

9. Paige, *The Korean Decision*, pp. 136, 164-65, 255, 257, 260-61, 300-301. Kennan's hesitation over use of U.S. ground troops, however, should not be exaggerated into making him, as some revisionist writers have tried to do, into an opponent of U.S. intervention. In his memoirs, Kennan states that from the onset of the Korean crisis he felt that the United States would have to react with all necessary force to repel the attack and to expel North Korean forces from South Korea. He also favored prompt steps to protect Formosa from falling into Communist hands on the ground that "two such reverses coming one on the heel of the other could easily prove disastrous to our prestige and to our entire position in the Far East" (*Memoirs, 1925-1950* [Boston: Little, Brown & Co., 1967] p. 486).

10. Kennan, *Memoirs*, pp. 487-96; also, Trumbull Higgins, *Korea and the Fall*

of MacArthur (New York: Oxford University Press, 1960), pp. 78-79; Robert E. Osgood, *Limited War* (Chicago: University of Chicago Press, 1957), pp. 183-84.

11. In a laudatory account of the way in which Truman organized and managed the process of foreign-policymaking, Dean Acheson credits him with infusing an adversary process into N.S.C. meetings similar to that of the law court. It is clear that what Acheson endorses in this respect is the formal, orderly variant of the adversary process—one which worked to Acheson's advantage because Truman acknowledged and leaned on his special competence in foreign affairs—and not the unstructured and unpredictable variants of multiple advocacy associated with the game of bureaucratic politics. Acheson's distaste for unstructured, informal variants of multiple advocacy—in which he enjoyed less influence—emerges clearly from his critical account of the workings of the ad hoc executive committee of the N.S.C. at the time of the Cuban missile crisis, in which Acheson participated at President Kennedy's invitation (Acheson, *Present at the Creation* [New York: Norton, 1969], pp. 733-37; see also Acheson's review of R. F. Kennedy's *Thirteen Days* in *Esquire* [February 1969]).

12. Patrick Anderson, *The President's Men* (Garden City, New York: Doubleday, 1968), p. 116.

13. Geyelin, *LBJ and the World*, p. 162. A detailed analysis of the workings of the bureaucratic political process leading up to the final confrontation of the MLF advocates with President Johnson, based partly on interviews, is provided in John D. Steinbruner, *The Cybernetic Theory of Decision* (Princeton, N.J.: Princeton University Press, 1974). See also the briefer case study of the MLF by Graham T. Allison and Gregory F. Treverton in Allison et al., *Adequacy of Current Organization*, pp. 266-69.

14. Geyelin, *LBJ*, p. 170. Geyelin's account is generally supported by Steinbruner, *Cybernetic Theory*, who also provides additional details. Other accounts represent McGeorge Bundy intervening not as a neutral watchdog of the president's options but as a concealed advocate against the MLF who had bided his time (Patrick Anderson, *The President's Men*, pp. 271-72; David Halberstam, "The Expensive Education of McGeorge Bundy," *Harper's* [July 1969]:29).

15. Geyelin, *LBJ*, p. 162.

16. Richard Neustadt, *Presidential Power* (New York: Wiley, 1960), p. 145. Neustadt makes use in his account of Martin Lichterman's correspondence and an interview with Acheson, reported in Lichterman, "To the Yalu and Back," in *American Civil-Military Decisions*, Harold Stein, ed., (University, Ala.: University of Alabama Press, 1963), p. 602.

17. Neustadt's and Lichterman's accounts of these events were qualified some years later both by Dean Acheson and General J. Lawton Collins, army chief of staff at the time (Acheson, *Present at the Creation*, pp. 466-68, 754; Collins, *War in Peacetime: The History and Lessons of Korea* [Boston: Houghton Mifflin Co., 1969], pp. 202, 205-17). Neustadt's interpretation was questioned earlier also by David S. McLellan in his "Dean Acheson and the Korean War," *Political Science Quarterly* 83 (March 1968):16-39.

McLellan agrees that Acheson and other top-level advisers did labor under the "dread of Chinese involvement" in *early* November. He notes, however, that at two important policy meetings on 21 November 1950, Acheson displayed relative optimism that MacArthur could accomplish his mission. McLellan is perplexed by this marked change of mood. He fails to see that it can be traced to the Chinese disengagement on the battlefield that took place after the high-point of Washington's (and MacArthur's) anxiety on 9 November. When day after day passed without further combat or major contact with Chinese forces, the acute anxiety that American leaders had felt in early November gradually declined.

18. On this general point, *see also* O. R. Holsti, *Crisis, Escalation, War* (Montreal and London: McGill-Queen's University Press, 1972), p. 21.

19. Theodore C. Sorensen, *Kennedy* (New York: Harper & Row, 1965), p. 302. *See also* the detailed account of flaws in decision making in the Bay of Pigs case in Arthur Schlesinger, Jr., *A Thousand Days: John F. Kennedy in the White House* (New York: Houghton Mifflin, 1965), chapter 10; and Chester Bowles, *Promises to Keep* (New York: Harper & Row, 1971), p. 326. For a critical account of CIA's performance in the case by the then inspector general of CIA, *see* Lyman B. Kirkpatrick, Jr., "Paramilitary Case Study: The Bay of Pigs," *Naval War College Review*, (November-December 1972).

20. A conscious attempt by Washington to develop an alternative source of information on events in the Dominican Republic was undertaken finally on 29 April *after* the U.S. decision to intervene overtly had been made and was being implemented. This was the presidential mission of John Bartlow Martin.

21. Geyelin, *LBJ*, pp. 244-45.

22. Sorensen, *Kennedy*, pp. 304, 306; Schlesinger, *A Thousand Days*, chapter 10.

23. Schlesinger, *A Thousands Days*, pp. 250, 255; Sorensen, *Kennedy*, p. 305.

Part Two
Ways of Reducing Impediments
to Information Processing

7

Introduction to Part Two

Every president faces the task of deciding how to organize and manage foreign-policymaking in his administration. Chapter 8 discusses three management models that past presidents have employed for this purpose: the formalistic, competitive, and collegial models. A new president may be advised by management specialists to select a particular organizational blueprint, but in the last analysis his choice and the way in which he utilizes any particular model will be shaped by preferences of his own that stem from previous experience in executive positions, the extent to which he regards himself as knowledgeable and competent in matters of foreign policy and national security, and certain of his personality characteristics.

Study of the management styles and performance of past presidents suggests that three personality factors are likely to be important in this respect: (1) the president's "cognitive style" (i.e., the way in which he defines his informational needs for purposes of making decisions and his preferred ways of acquiring and using information and advice); (2) his sense of efficacy as it relates to management and decisionmaking tasks; and (3) his personal orientation to the give-and-take of politics and his ability to tolerate conflicts among his advisers.

Viewed from this standpoint, the formalistic, competitive, and collegial management models offer executives different ways of adapting their personalities and past experience to the task of making important political decisions. In Chapter 8 we illustrate the "fit" between Franklin Roosevelt's personality and his use of the competitive model, John F. Kennedy's preference for the somewhat different collegial model, and interestingly different variants of the formalistic model that appealed to Truman, Eisenhower, and Nixon.

The major distinguishing characteristics of these three models are noted and schematized. Each has certain advantages and potential drawbacks, which are noted. General suggestions for improving the performance of each of these management models also are noted, but the conclusion is drawn that we must search for more discriminating ways of improving information processing within presidential policymaking systems.

Accordingly, in the next three chapters we discuss three procedural tools—the "devil's advocate," the "formal options" system, and "multiple advocacy"—that are often recommended and, on occasion, have been employed in an effort to widen the range of information, options, and judgment before decisions are made. The uses and limitations of each of these three procedural devices are evaluated on the basis of available information on past experience with them.

Though the devil's advocate (Chapter 9) is not without value, it appears that this relatively simple device, even if effectively implemented, cannot possibly satisfy all the requirements for designing an effective policymaking system. Clearly, more comprehensive prescriptive theories or models of policymaking are needed. Hence, we proceed in Chapter 10 to a detailed examination of the rationale and modus operandi of the "formal options" system and to an evaluation of the experience gained during its employment on President Nixon's behalf by Henry Kissinger during his service as special assistant for national security affairs.

The reality of the way in which a policymaking system operates is always more opaque and inconsistent than the clarity of the theoretical model that inspired its creation. For this reason it is particularly important to evaluate the performance of such a system in order to understand better its special requirements and vulnerabilities. In this way additional steps may be taken to improve performance. This is done in Chapter 10 for the "formal options" system and in Chapter 11 for "multiple advocacy," which in important respects provides an alternative or supplement to the formal options system.

As outlined in this report, multiple advocacy is not a decentralized policymaking system. Rather, it requires considerable executive initiative and centralized coordination of some of the activities of participants in policy making. The multiple advocacy model accepts the fact that disagreement over policy in one form or another is inevitable. The solution it strives for is not only to ensure that there will be multiple advocates but to do what can be done to provide each of them with at least the minimally necessary analytical and bureaucratic resources required for effective advocacy. These and other requirements for effective multiple advocacy are not easily met. As with the devil's advocate and formal options, multiple advocacy cannot be regarded as a panacea. It, too, has practical limits and costs attached to it, which are discussed in Chapter 11.

No president can effectively oversee the flow of security and foreign-policy issues without major staff assistance. One of the most important developments in the organization of the government for foreign-policymaking was the introduction of the National Security Council (NSC) in 1947. Chapter 11 examines in detail the evolution of the role of the special assistant for national security affairs in successive administrations and the considerable augmentation of his tasks and responsibilities. A detailed description is provided of the steadily expanded "job description" of the special assistant. In addition to exercising responsibility for the role of "custodian-manager" of NSC procedures, the special assistant has acquired and performed five other important roles: policy adviser-advocate; policy spokesman-defender; political watchdog for the president's power stakes; enforcer of policy decisions; and administrative operator.

These various responsibilities are not easily harmonized; the acquisition of so many important tasks has placed the special assistant not only in a powerful position but one in which his performance is bound to be affected by competing demands and, hence, by role conflict. What is of particular concern is that his ability to perform the basic custodial responsibility for maintaining adequate procedures, preventing impediments to information processing, and ensuring balanced and dispassionate appraisal of options can be undermined by his effort to combine this role with that of policy adviser or policy advocate, policy spokesman and defender, watchdog for the president's political interests, or administrative-operator for conduct and/or implementation of policy.

Fortunately, "formal options," "multiple advocacy," and the "devil's advocate" do not exhaust the devices available to a chief executive for broadening the perspective of departmental and agency officials and ameliorating the impediments to information processing that can easily flow from this. Chapter 12 discusses how the executive can restructure and redefine the roles of his departmental advisers in order to broaden the perspective with which they view policy problems. For various reasons, a more loosely structured and not overly formal milieu makes it easier for participants in such a group to free themselves from the constraints of organizational doctrines and from the tendency to overprotect the special interests of their subunits and constituencies. Chapter 12 also discusses ways in which a collegial group can be managed to strengthen the analytic component of policymaking as against the influence of bargaining considerations.

Part 2 turns next to two other ways for reducing impediments to information processing and improving the quality of foreign-policy decisions. Chapter 13 discusses the contribution that a refinement of the concept of "national interest" might make in this respect. As was emphasized in Chapter 2, foreign policy problems typically engage a multiplicity of competing values and interests, so much so that policymakers often encounter great difficulty in reducing them to a single criterion or yardstick by means of which to judge which course of action is "best" in a given situation. In principle, the criterion of "national interest," which occupies a time-honored and revered place in the theory and practice of foreign policy, should assist decisionmakers to cut through much of this value complexity and help improve judgments regarding the proper ends and goals of foreign policy. In practice, however, "national interest" has become elastic and ambiguous, and its role as a criterion in foreign-policymaking obscure, problematical, and controversial.

Most thoughtful observers of foreign policy would readily agree that the "national interest" concept lends itself much more readily to being used as political rhetoric for legitimizing decisions and actions already taken than as an exact, well-defined criterion for determining what these policies should be. One reason for this difficulty is that "national interest," like "general welfare" and "public interest," constitutes what decision theorists refer to as a "nonoperational goal"—that is, it does not provide a measuring rod for comparing alternative policies. Such concepts can be related to specific choices of action only through consideration of the subgoals to which they are presumably related.

Accordingly, we distinguish different types of national interests in order to clarify the concept and indicate how it might be employed more usefully. We believe that a strict notion of "irreducible" (or "vital") interests (referring to the three fundamental national values implied by the terms "physical survival," "liberty," and "economic subsistence") is necessary in order to introduce discipline and restraint into the formulation of foreign policy. Even the criterion of "irreducible national interests" is not easily applied in practice, as a review of the foreign policy of successive administrations since World War II suggests. The chapter also discusses other types of national interests and suggests procedures for applying them in the determination of foreign policy.

Another way in which some of the impediments discussed in Part 1 may be avoided or minimized is by improving the quality and relevance of knowledge available to policymakers about the various substantive activities such as deterrence, crisis management, alliance management, conciliation, etc. that comprise the means of furthering foreign-policy goals. The lack of better knowledge and theory about these matters creates a vacuum, as it were, which gives impediments to information processing freer reign. Chapter 14 discusses the nature of policy-applicable knowledge and theory and suggests how it might be helpful at different stages in the decisionmaking process.

In contrast to Chapter 13 on the national interest, which is concerned with the value dimensions of policy-making, Chapter 14 focuses on its *analytic* components. Foreign policy must be based on sound analysis of the characteristics and dynamics of the international system, the nature of adversaries, the ways in which various instruments of policy can be appropriately and effectively employed in pursuit of foreign-policy objective, etc. These important *cognitive* requirements of foreign policy are difficult to meet; they require not merely factual information, but theories to help policymakers interpret the available facts, diagnose new situations, and assess alternative courses of action. Lack of adequate theories inevitably gives freer reign to the individual, group, and organizational sources of malfunctioning of the policymaking process that were discussed in Part 1. At the same time, these various impediments to information processing in the policymaking system can be minimized by improving the knowledge and theories available to policymakers about other actors, the forces at work in the international arena, the uses and limitations of various strategies, and instruments of policy that together comprise the available means of furthering their foreign-policy objectives. Thus, for example, the policymaker needs theories about policy instruments such as deterrence, crisis management, coercive diplomacy, alliance management, negotiating strategy, détente, conciliation and accommodation, war termination, etc.

Academic specialists on foreign policy and international relations have an opportunity, therefore, to contribute to the development and refinement of such theories. To contribute more effectively, however, academic scholars need to understand better what kinds of theories the policymaker needs and how he uses them in making decisions. Chapter 14 discusses the two functions performed by such theories in policymaking: the "diagnostic" and the "options-assessment" functions. In this connection, Chapter 14 sets forth the argument that policy-relevant theories of this kind are a necessary safeguard against the policymaker's chronic tendency to misuse the "lessons of history" as an aid to decisionmaking. Finally, four such policy-relevant theories — crisis management, coercive diplomacy, deterrence, and détente — are discussed and illustrated.

8
Presidential Management Styles and Models

Every new president faces the task of deciding how to structure and manage high-level foreign-policymaking in his administration. The task is a formidable one since responsibility for different aspects of national security and foreign policy is distributed over a number of departments and agencies. Relevant information, competence, and influence over policy is widely dispersed within the executive branch as well as outside of it. This imposes on the president and his assistants the task of mobilizing available information, expertise, and analytical resources for effective policymaking. In addition, the president and his closest associates have the responsibility for providing policy initiative and coherence throughout the executive branch.

To discharge these tasks effectively requires internal coordination within the government. Those parts of the executive branch that have some responsibility for and/or contribution to make to a particular policy problem must be encouraged to interact with each other in appropriate ways. Left to themselves, these various agencies, of course, would interact voluntarily and achieve some measure of "lateral coordination" in formulating policy. But it is essential for the president (and each department or agency head) to ensure lateral coordination by institution of various procedures and mechanisms, such as ad hoc or standing interdepartmental committees, policy conferences, liaison arrangements, a system of clearances for policy or position papers, etc.

However important lateral coordination is, it cannot be counted upon to produce the caliber of policy analysis, the level of consensus, and the procedures for implementation required for an effective and coherent foreign policy.

Moreover, lateral coordination may be weakened and distorted by patterns of organizational behavior and the phenomenon of "bureaucratic politics" that create impediments to and malfunctions of the policymaking process. Accordingly, all presidents have found it necessary to impose mechanisms for control and coordination of policy analysis and implementation from above—either from the White House itself or from the NSC—or have fixed responsibility for achieving control and coordination with the State Department; or have adopted a combination of these mechanisms.

The traditional practice for seeking improvement in the performance of the foreign-policymaking system was to undertake *structural reorganization* of the agencies and the mechanisms for achieving their coordination and cooperation. Periodically—indeed, at least once in each presidential administration—the foreign-policymaking system was reorganized.[1] But the results of reorganizations have been so disappointing that the "organizational tinkering" approach has fallen into general disrepute. Instead, greater attention is being given to the *design and management of the processes* of policymaking.

Coupled with this shift in focus from organizational structure to process is a new awareness among specialists in organization and public administration that their past efforts to identify a single standardized model of policymaking that would be optimal for all presidents was misguided. Instead, it is now recognized that each president is likely to define his role in foreign-policymaking somewhat differently and to approach it with a different decisionmaking and management style. Hence, too, he will have a different notion as to the kind of policymaking system that he wishes to create around him, feels comfortable with, and can utilize. In brief, the present emphasis is on designing organizational structures to fit the operating styles of their key individuals rather than attempting to persuade each new top executive to accept and adapt to a standardized organizational model that is considered to be theoretically the best.

As this implies, the first and foremost task that a new president faces is to learn to define his own role in the policymaking system; only then can he structure and manage the roles and relationships within the policymaking system of his secretary of state, the special assistant for national security affairs, the secretary of defense, and other cabinet and agency heads with responsibilities for the formulation and implementation of foreign policy.

The president's basic choice is whether to give his secretary of state the primary role in the foreign-policymaking system or to centralize and manage that system from the White House itself. Still another model is that of a relatively decentralized system that is coordinated from the White House for the president by his special assistant for national security affairs.

A new president may receive advice on these matters from specialists in organization or in foreign policy, but in the last analysis his choices in these matters will be shaped by preferences of his own that stem from previous experience (if any) in executive roles and the extent to which he regards himself as knowledgeable and competent in foreign policy and national security matters. Finally, as all president-watchers have emphasized, the incumbent's personality will shape the formal structure of the policymaking system that he creates around himself and, even more, it will influence the ways in which he encourages and permits that formal structure to operate in practice. As a result, each president is likely to develop a policymaking system and a management style that contain distinctive and idiosyncratic elements.

Detailed comparison of past presidents from this standpoint suggests that a variety of personality characteristics are important, of which three can be briefly noted.[2] The first of these personality dimensions is *"cognitive style."* As noted in Chapter 3, cognitive psychologists have found it useful to view the human mind as a complex system for information processing. Every individual develops ways of storing, retrieving, evaluating, and using information. At the same time the individual develops a set of beliefs about the environment, about the attributes of other actors, and about various presumed causal relationships that help the person to explain and predict, as best he can (correctly or incorrectly), events of interest to him. Beliefs of this kind structure, order, and simplify the individual's world; they serve as models of "reality." Such mental constructs play an important role in the individual's perception of what is occurring in his environment, in the acquisition and interpretation of new information, and in the formulation and evaluation of responses to new situations.

At the same time, individuals differ in their approaches to processing and evaluating information, and this is generally what is meant by "cognitive style." There is as yet no standardized approach to characterizing the dimensions of cognitive style. For present purposes, the term is used to refer to the way in which an executive such as the president defines his informational needs for purposes of making decisions. "Cognitive style" also refers to his preferred ways of acquiring information from those around him and making use of that information, and to his preferences regarding advisers and ways of using them in making his decisions.

Defined in these terms, as we shall note, an individual's cognitive style plays an important role in his preference for one management model as against others. Cognitive styles do vary among presidents, and it simply will not work to try to impose on a new president a policymaking system or a management model that is uncongenial to his cognitive style.[3]

A second personality dimension that influences a president's choice of a policymaking system is *his sense of efficacy and competence* as it relates to management and decisionmaking tasks. In other words, the types of skills that he possesses and the types of tasks that he feels particularly adept at doing and those that he feels poorly equipped to do will influence the way in which he defines his executive role.

A third personality dimension that will influence the president's selection of a policymaking model is his general *orientation toward political conflict* and, related to this, toward interpersonal conflict over policy among his advisers. Individuals occupying the White House have varied on this personality dimension, too. Thus, we find that some chief executives have viewed politics as a necessary, useful, and perhaps even enjoyable game while other presidents have regarded it as a dirty business that must be discouraged or at least ignored. The personal attitude toward conflict that a president brings into office is likely to determine his orientation to the phenomena of "cabinet politics" and "bureaucratic politics" within his administration as well as to the larger, often interlinked game of politics surrounding the executive branch. Individuals with a pronounced distaste for "dirty politics" and for being exposed to face-to-face disagreements among advisers are likely to favor policymaking systems that attempt to curb these phenomena or at least shield them from direct exposure. They also are likely to prefer staff and advisory sytems in which teamwork or formal analytical procedures are emphasized in lieu of partisan advocacy and debate.

Cognitive style, sense of efficacy, and orientation toward conflict (and of course, as noted earlier, the nature of any prior experience in executive roles and the level of personal competence and interest in foreign policy and national security affairs) — all these combine to determine how a new president will structure the policymaking system around him and how he will define his own role and that of others in it.

Three management models have been identified that characterize at least in general terms the approaches displayed by different presidents in recent times.[4] These are the "formalistic," "competitive," and "collegial" models. The formalistic model is characterized by an orderly policymaking structure, one that provides well-defined procedures, hierarchical lines of communication, and a structured staff system. While the formalistic model seeks to benefit from the diverse views and judgments of participants in policymaking, it also discourages open conflict and bargaining among them.

The competitive model, in contrast, places a premium on encouraging a more open and uninhibited expression of diverse opinions, analysis, and advice. To this end the competitive model not only tolerates but may actually encourage organizational ambiguity, overlapping jurisdictions, and multiple channels of communication to and from the president.

The collegial model, in turn, attempts to achieve the essential advantages of each of the other two while avoiding their pitfalls. To this end, the president attempts to create a team of staff members and advisers who will work together to identify, analyze, and solve policy problems in ways that will incorporate and synthesize as much as possible divergent points of view. The collegial model attempts to benefit from diversity and competition within the policymaking system, but it also attempts to avoid narrow parochialism by encouraging cabinet officers and advisers to identify at least partly with the presidential perspective. And by encouraging collegial participation in group problem-solving efforts, this approach attempts to avoid the worst excesses of infighting, bargaining, and compromise associated with the competitive model.

Truman, Eisenhower, and Nixon employed one or another variant of the formalistic approach. Franklin D. Roosevelt employed the competitive model, and John F. Kennedy the collegial one. As for Lyndon B. Johnson, he began by trying to emulate Franklin Roosevelt's style and gradually moved toward a formalistic approach but one that exhibited idiosyncratic features.

Let us begin with Franklin D. Roosevelt, whose unusual policymaking system is the prototype for the competitive management model. A dominant feature of FDR's personality was his strong sense of political efficacy. He felt entirely at home in the presidency, acting in the belief that there was close to a perfect fit between his competence and skills and some of the most demanding role requirements of the office. Then, too, FDR viewed politics and the games that go with it as a useful and enjoyable game and not, as others before him (for example, Taft and Hoover) as an unsavory, distasteful business to be discouraged or avoided. FDR not only felt comfortable in the presence of conflict and disagreement around him; he saw that, properly managed, it could serve his informational and political needs. Instead of trying, as his predecessor had, to take the politics out of the policymaking process, Roosevelt deliberately exacerbated the competitive and conflicting aspects of cabinet politics and bureaucratic politics. He sought to increase both structural and functional ambiguities within the executive branch in order to better preside over it. For Roosevelt, exposure to conflict among advisers and cabinet heads did not stir up anxiety or depression; nor did he perceive it as threatening in a personal or political sense. Not only did he live comfortably with the political conflict and, at times, near-chaos around him, he manipulated the structure of relationships among subordinates in order to control and profit from their competition. What is noteworthy is that Roosevelt did not attempt to create a formal, centralized model of the policymaking process (as advocated, for example, in later Hoover Commission proposals for reorganization of governmental agencies); rather, he deliberately created "fuzzy lines of responsibility, no clear chains of command, overlapping jurisdictions" in order to promote "'stimulating' inter-departmental conflict which could and did eventually land in his own lap."[5]

At the risk of simplification, it is possible to delineate some features of the distinctive communication network or patterns associated with FDR's competitive model[6] (see Figure 2).

Characteristic features of the competitive model (FDR): (1) the president deliberately encourages competition and conflict among advisers and cabinet heads by giving them overlapping assignments and ambiguous, conflicting jurisdictions in given policy areas; (2) relatively little communication or collaboration among advisers; (3) the president reaches down on occasion to communicate directly with subordinates of cabinet heads to get independent advice and information; (4) relevant information on important policy problems is forced up through the network to the president himself; competing advisers are forced to bring important policy problems to the president for resolution and decision; but (5) the president avoids risk of becoming overloaded or involved by operating this system selectively; on occassions (not depicted on the chart), he encourages and insists that subordinate officials settle things themselves and refuses to become identified with their policies or pet projects.

Harry Truman adopted a different strategy for coping with the com-

Figure 2. The Competitive Model (FDR)

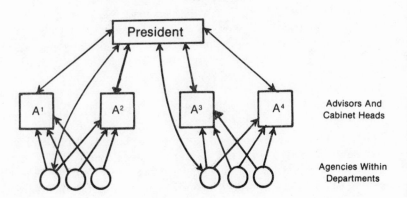

Advisors And
Cabinet Heads

Agencies Within
Departments

plex morass that governmental structure had become as a result of Roosevelt's style and administrative practices and the wartime expansion of agencies. Initially, Truman tried to tidy up the mess by clarifying and dividing up the jurisdictions. He also established the NSC in 1947 as a vehicle for providing orderly, balanced participation in foreign-policymaking deliberations. Truman tried to weaken the game of bureaucratic politics by strengthening each department head's control over his particular domain and by delegating presidential responsibility to him. New in the office, Truman took special pride in his ability to delegate responsibility and to back up those he trusted. He learned through experience, however, that to delegate too much or to delegate responsibility without providing clear guidance was to jeopardize the performance of his own responsibilities.

When faced with larger policy issues that required the participation of heads of several departments, Truman attempted to deal with them by playing the role of chairman of the board, hearing sundry expert opinions on each aspect of the problem, then making a synthesis of them and announcing the decision. Truman not only accepted the responsibility of making difficult decisions, he liked doing so for it enabled him to satisfy himself—and, he hoped, others—that he had the personal qualities needed in the presidency. His sense of efficacy expressed itself in a willingness to make difficult decisions without experiencing undue stress. A modest man in many ways, Truman adjusted to the awesome responsibilities of the presidency suddenly thrust upon him by respecting the office and determining to become a good role player. By honoring the office and doing credit to it, he would do credit to himself. Included in this role conception was Truman's desire to put aside personal and political considerations as much as possible in the search for quality decisions that were in the national interest. He was willing to accept the political costs both to himself and to his party entailed in making controversial decisions, such as his policy of disengaging the United States from the Chinese Nationalists in 1949, his refusal to escalate the Korean War after the Chinese Communist intervention, his firing of General MacArthur, and his refusal to dismiss his loyal secretary of state, Dean Acheson, when he came under continuing attack.

Truman's variant of the formalistic model may be depicted, again in simplified terms, as in Figure 3.

Characteristic features of the formalistic model (Truman): (1) specialized information and advice flows to the president from each of his cabinet heads and advisers; (2) the president tends to define the role of each cabinet head as a functional expert on some aspect of national security or foreign policy; each official briefs the president authoritative-

Figure 3. The Formalistic Model (Truman)

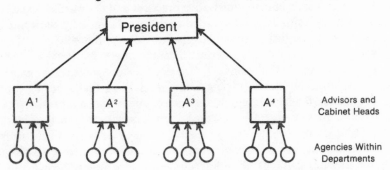

ly on that aspect of a policy problem for which he has jurisdiction; (3) each adviser receives information and advice from his subordinate units; (4) the president does not encourage his advisers to communicate with each other or to engage in joint efforts at policy analysis and problem solving; (5) the president sticks to channels and seldom reaches down to bypass a cabinet head to get independent information/advice from one of his subordinates; and (6) the president takes responsibility for intellectual synthesis of specialized inputs on a policy problem received from his advisers.

Dwight D. Eisenhower avoided personal involvement as much as possible in the bureaucratic politics aspects of policymaking within the executive branch and in less savory aspects of politics generally. At the same time, however, Eisenhower recognized that conflict and politics are inevitable and adapted to them by defining his own role as that of someone who could stand "above politics," moderate conflict, and promote unity. In doing so, Eisenhower expressed his special sense of efficacy that led him (and others) to believe that he could make a distinctive and unique contribution by seeming to remain "above politics" and by emphasizing the shared values and virtues that should guide governmental affairs. This did not prevent Eisenhower, however, from engaging in political maneuvers of his own when he perceived that his interests required it.[7]

Eisenhower did not attempt (as Nixon was to later) to depoliticize and rationalize the formal policymaking process completely. Rather, Eisenhower's variant of the formalistic model encompassed advocacy and disagreement at lower levels of the policymaking system, even though he wanted subordinates eventually to achieve agreement, if possible, on recommendations for his consideration. Moreover, formal meetings of the large NSC were often preceded by less formal "warm-up" sessions with a smaller group of advisers that provided opportunities for genuine policy debate. The conventional depiction of Eisenhower's NSC system as an unimaginative, bureaucratic body laden with the preparation and presentation of cautiously formulated positions, therefore, is not justified.[8]

What these observations about Eisenhower's policy system reveal is that a formalistic management model need not be highly bureaucratized. Examples of the formalistic management model, which always seem bureaucratized on the surface, need to be examined much more closely in order to determine how they actually function. As is well known, policymaking in complex organizations usually proceeds on *two* tracks: the formal, visible, official track and the informal, less visible track. Even the most formalistic of policymaking systems is accompanied by some kind of informal track that is utilized by the participants — including sometimes the president himself — in an attempt to "work with" or "work around" the formal procedures.

In particular, a president's use of surrogates as "chiefs of staff" in a formalistic management model needs close examination to determine to what extent he actually restricts his own involvement in policymaking and remains unaware or disinterested in the important preliminaries of information processing. Thus, in Eisenhower's case, recent archival research reveals that two of his "chiefs of staff" — Governor Sherman Adams and Secretary of State John Foster Dulles — were by no means as powerful as has been thought. "Adams was not the all powerful domestic policy gate-guard he is said to have been. He did not keep important information from Eisenhower's attention, nor did he make important decisions solo. . . . In the case of Dulles . . . not even the most obsequious Lyndon Johnson courtier could have been more assiduous about testing the waters. . . . Dulles was in touch with the president daily, and was consistently responsive to Eisenhower's directives."[9]

With these important caveats in mind, we can proceed to examine how the visible structure of his formalistic model differed from Truman's. This can be seen by comparing the chart for Truman's system with that presented here of Eisenhower's (see Figure 4).

Characteristic features of the formalistic model (Eisenhower): similar to Truman's variant of the formalistic model with two important exceptions: (1) a "chief of staff" position is created to be utilized, when the president wishes, as a buffer between himself and cabinet heads and to arrange for preparation of formal recommendations to the president (Sherman Adams performed this role for Eisenhower on domestic policy matters; in practice, Secretary of State John Foster Dulles came to assume a similar, though informal, role for Eisenhower in foreign policy,

Figure 4. The Formalistic Model (Eisenhower)

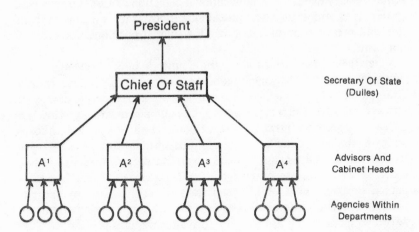

though not in defense matters); and (2) again, unlike Truman's version of the formalistic model, in this one the president attempts to protect himself from being overloaded by urging advisers/cabinet heads to analyze problems and resolve policy differences wherever possible at lower levels.

Richard Nixon, too, strongly favored a formalistic model. As a number of observers have noted, several of Nixon's well-defined personality characteristics shaped his management style and approach to decisionmaking. During his earlier years, Nixon had developed a cognitive style that enabled him to cope with deeply rooted personal insecurities by adopting an extremely conscientious approach to decisionmaking. As described so well in his book, *Six Crises*, the whole business of acquiring information, weighing alternatives, and deciding among them was experienced by him as extremely stressful, requiring great self-control, hard work, and reliance upon himself. Dealing with difficult situations posed the necessity but also offered an opportunity for Nixon to prove himself over and over again. He experienced his greatest sense of self and of his efficacy when he had to confront and master difficult situations in which a great deal was at stake.[10]

Nixon's pronounced sense of aloneness and privacy, his thin-skinned sensitivity and vulnerability were not conducive to developing the kind of interpersonal relationships associated with a collegial model of management. Rather, as Richard T. Johnson notes, "Nixon, the private man with a preference for working alone, wanted machinery to staff out the options but provide plenty of time for reflection. . . . " Similarly, "with his penchant for order," Nixon inevitably "favored men who offered order," who acceded to his demand for loyalty and shared his sense of banding together to help him cope with a hostile environment.[11]

Nixon's preference for a highly formalistic system was reinforced by other personality characteristics. He was an extreme "conflict avoider"; somewhat paradoxically, although quite at home with political conflict in the broader public arena, Nixon had a pronounced distaste for being exposed to it face-to-face. Early in his administration, Nixon tried a version of multiple advocacy in which leading advisers would debate issues in his presence. But he quickly abandoned the experiment and turned to structuring his staff to avoid overt manifestations of disagreement and to avoid being personally drawn into the squabbles of his staff.[12] Hence, Nixon's need for a few staff aides immediately around him who were to serve as buffers and enable him to distance himself from the wear and tear of policymaking.

It is interesting that Eisenhower's "chief of staff" concept was carried much farther in Nixon's variant of the formalistic model. The foreign-policymaking system that Kissinger, the special assistant for national security affairs, developed during the first year of Nixon's administration is generally regarded as by far the most centralized and highly structured model yet employed by any president.[13] Nixon was determined even more than Eisenhower had been to abolish bureaucratic and cabinet politics as completely as possible; but, more so than Eisenhower, Nixon also wanted to enhance and protect his personal control over high policy. To this end, a novel system of six special committees was set up operating out of the NSC, each of which was chaired by Kissinger. These included the Vietnam Special Studies Group, the Washington Special Actions Group (to deal with international crises), the Defense Programs Review Committee, the Verification Panel (to deal with strategic arms talks), the 40 Committee (to deal with covert actions), and the Senior Review Group (which dealt with all other types of policy issues).

Reporting to the Senior Review Group were six lower-level interdepartmental groups that were set up on a regional basis (Middle East, Far East, Latin America, Africa, Europe, and Political-Military Affairs), each of which was headed by an assistant secretary of state. In addition, Kissinger could set up ad hoc working groups composed of specialists from various agencies and run by his own top staff aides.

Thus, not only did Kissinger's committee structure reach down into the departments and agencies, absorbing key personnel into various committees controlled by Kissinger or his staff aides, but other committees created on an interdepartmental basis, though chaired by assistant secretaries of state, were given their assignments by Kissinger and

Figure 5. The Formalistic Model (Nixon)

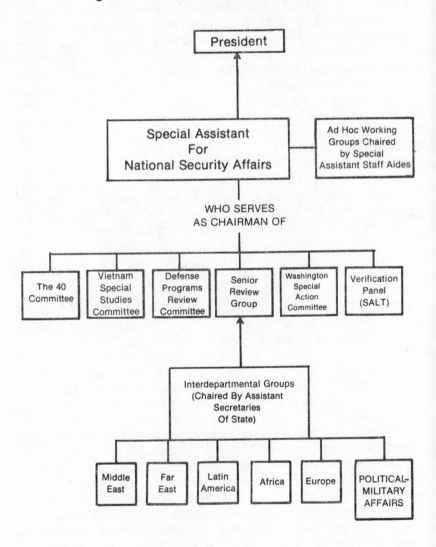

reported to the Senior Review Group chaired by Kissinger. As a result, a novel, unconventional policymaking structure was created and superimposed upon the departments and largely superseded the traditional hierarchical policymaking system. Striking differences with Eisenhower's formalistic model can be noted (see Figure 5).

A further description and evaluation of the workings of Nixon's variant of the formalistic model is provided in Chapter 10.

John F. Kennedy felt much more at ease with the conflictual aspects of politics and policymaking than his predecessor; his sense of efficacy included confidence in his ability to manage and shape the interpersonal relations of those around him in a constructive fashion, and his cognitive style led him to participate much more actively and directly in the policymaking process than Eisenhower had or Nixon would later on. These personality characteristics contributed to forging a collegial style of policymaking based on teamwork and shared responsibility among talented advisers. Kennedy recognized the value of diversity and give-and-take among advisers, and he encouraged it. But Kennedy stopped well short of the extreme measures for stimulating competition that Roosevelt had employed. Rather than risk introducing disorder and strife into the policymaking system, Kennedy used other strategies for keeping himself informed, properly advised, and "on top." He did not find personally congenial the highly formal procedures, the large meetings, and the relatively aloof presidential role characteristic of Eisenhower's system. Particularly after the Bay of Pigs fiasco, Kennedy employed a variety of devices for counteracting the narrowness of perspective of leading members of individual departments and agencies and for protecting himself from the risks of bureaucratic politics. Noteworthy is Kennedy's effort to restructure the roles and broaden the perspectives of top department and agency officials and to introduce a new set of norms to guide their participation in policymaking.

The kind of teamwork and group approach to problem solving that Kennedy strove to create—and achieved with notable success in the Cuban missile crisis at least—is often referred to as the "collegial" model to distinguish it both from the more competitive and more formal system of his predecessors. The sharp contrasts between Kennedy's collegial system and the competitive and formalistic models emerge by comparing Figure 6 with Figures 2-5.

Characteristic features of the collegial model (JFK): (1) president is at the center of a wheel with spokes connecting to individual advisers/cabinet heads; (2) advisers form a "collegial team" and engage in group problem-solving; (3) information flows into the collegial team from various points lower in the bureaucracy; (4) advisers do not perform as individual filters to the president; rather, the group of advisers functions as

Figure 6. The Collegial Model (JFK)

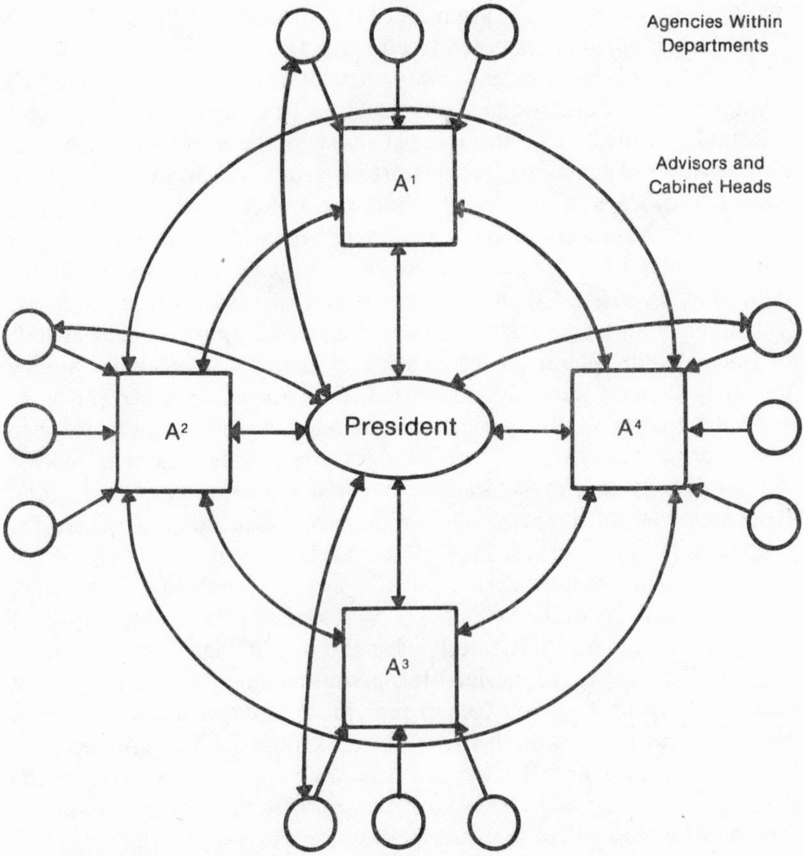

a "debate team" that considers information and policy options from the multiple, conflicting perspectives of the group members in an effort to obtain cross-fertilization and creative problem solving; (5) advisers are encouraged to act as generalists, concerned with all aspects of the policy problem, rather than as experts or functional specialists on only part of the policy problem; (6) discussion procedures are kept informal enough to encourage frank expression of views and judgments and to avoid impediments to information processing generated by status and power differences among members; and (7) the president occasionally gives overlapping assignments and occasionally reaches down to communicate directly with subordinates of cabinet heads in order to get more information and independent advice (for a more detailed discussion of the collegial approach see Chapter 12).

As for Jimmy Carter, his management style is perhaps aptly characterized as embracing elements of both the collegial and bureaucratic models. As one observer has reported, Carter's national security policymaking system "is an amalgamation selectively drawn from the experiences of his predecessors."[14] As in Kennedy's case, Carter has strongly rejected thus far – even in the face of increasing criticism – a "chief of staff" system for organizing his work and contacts with others. Instead, Carter clearly prefers a communications structure in which he is at the center of the wheel with opportunity for direct contact with a number of officials and advisers. Further, again like Kennedy, Carter prefers to be actively involved in the policymaking process and at earlier stages before the system has produced options or a single recommended policy for his consideration.

At the same time, Carter differs from Kennedy in preferring a formally structured NSC system and has retained elements of the "formal options" system developed by Kissinger for Nixon. Carter restored the prestige of the NSC staff following the brief eclipse that occurred during the Ford years when Kissinger was secretary of state, and he relies on its studies for help in making decisions.[15] Carter's preference for underpinning the collegial features of his management model with formalistic structure and procedures is not surprising given his training and experience as an engineer. Carter brought with him to the White House a cognitive style and sense of personal efficacy that gave him confidence in the possibility of mastering difficult problems and of finding comprehensive "solutions" for them.[16] In his somewhat technocratic approach to policymaking, experts and orderly study procedures play an essential role, and so the features of the collegial model that he values had necessarily to be blended somehow with features of a formalistic model.

In this mixed system, policymaking is not as highly centralized as in the Nixon administration. Carter not only allows relatively liberal access to the Oval Office, he also has a more decentralized advisory sytem than did Nixon. This reflects not only his personality and management style, but also the lessons that he and others drew from the experience of his predecessors in that office. Carter's main concern was to set up his foreign-policy machinery in a way that would avoid the extreme centralization of power that Kissinger, as special assistant for national security affairs, had acquired during Nixon's first term and that led him to replace for all practical purposes the secretary of state. In Carter's administration, the special assistant (Brzezinski) is not as powerful as Kissinger was. Carter wanted his secretary of state, Cyrus Vance, to be his

leading foreign-policy adviser and the State Department to provide the
major backup in policy preparation. In line with this concept, the
number of committees in the NSC staff was reduced over what they had
been in Nixon's administration and, moreover, Brzezinski does not chair
all of the NSC committees as Kissinger had. Instead of allowing the
special assistant to become the dominant actor in the sytem and a virtual
"chief of staff," Carter relies on collegiality among his principal national
security advisers—the secretary of state, the secretary of defense, the
special assistant, the vice-president—to achieve the necessary interaction
and coordination. Accordingly, the NSC organization under Carter is
more modest than Nixon's both in centrality, structure, and
operations.[17]

Although Carter has succeeded in avoiding a highly centralized,
"closed" system of foreign-policymaking, it must also be said that he has
been much less successful in avoiding the potential difficulties of the
mixed formalistic-collegial model that he preferred. A number of
weaknesses have become evident in the Carter system that have seriously
affected its performance. The collegial model requires close contact and
continuing interaction between the president, his secretary of state, and
the special assistant. This they have achieved, but their respective roles
remain highly fluid and have not been well defined. There is, for example, no clear arrrangement for policy specialization and division of labor
among these three principals. (In contrast, the secretary of defense's role
appears to be well enough understood by all concerned so that his participation on policymaking appears to be relatively free of serious ambiguities or conflicts with others.) In the absence of role definition and
specialization, all three—the president, his secretary of state, and the
special assistant—can and do interest themselves in any important policy
problem. A shared interest in all major policy problems is to be expected
in a collegial system, but some understandings must also be developed to
regulate initiative, consultation, the articulation of disagreements, and
the formulation of collective judgment. Carter evidently counted on the
fact that the three men knew and respected each other prior to his elec-
tion to the presidency to make his collegial approach work. And, to be
sure, on the surface it has genuinely seemed to be the case that the three
men get along well. More than cordiality, however, is needed for effective policymaking in a collegial system.

Collegiality entails certain risks, and its preservation may exact a price.
Some evidence indicates that the preservation of cordiality was accompanied, at least in the first part of Carter's administration, with a perhaps
partly unconscious tendency to subordinate disagreements over policy

among the three men that should have been articulated, confronted, and dealt with in a timely fashion. One of the problems was Carter himself. He had a habit of suddenly taking the initiative or intervening in an important foreign-policy matter, as in the case of his human rights initiative, leaving Vance and Brzezinski with the embarrassing and difficult task of making the best of it or of trying to modify the policy.

Another weakness of Carter's system quickly developed and proved difficult to cope with. Foreign policy became badly fragmented in the first year of Carter's administration. It was characterized by (1) overactivism—the floating of many specific policy initiatives within a relatively short period of time; (2) a tendency to initiate attractive, desirable policies without sufficient attention to their feasibility; (3) poor conceptualization of overall foreign policy, and, related to this, a failure to recognize that individual policies conflicted with each other; (4) a poor sense of strategy and tactics; (5) a badly designed and managed policymaking system.[18]

These flaws cannot be attributed merely or even primarily to Carter's inexperience in foreign policy. After all, his administration included various high-level officials who were experts on foreign policy. Part of the explanation has to do with important aspects of his personality, which are attractive in and of themselves. Carter is a man of high moral principles, as exemplified by his sincere commitment to human rights. He wanted to imbue American foreign policy with renewed moral purpose; he is an activist in this respect, and therefore took genuine pleasure that his administration could launch so many worthwhile policy initiatives so quickly. He could see no harm in pushing ahead simultaneously with so many good initiatives.

What was needed to safeguard against an overloading of the foreign-policy agenda and the fragmentation of foreign policy was a strong policy planning and coordinating mechanism, one that would alert Carter to this problem and assist him in dealing with difficult trade-offs among conflicting policy initiatives by establishing priorities, and generally to better integrate the various strands of overall foreign policy. Such a policy planning and coordinating mechanism, however, was lacking. The need to develop it somehow fell between the two stools of Carter's mixed collegial-formalistic model. Thus, neither the formalistic nor the collegial components of Carter's system provided the necessary planning-coordinating mechanism and procedures. When criticism of Carter's foreign policy mounted, persons apparently close to Vance and Brzezinski let it be known, however discretely, that it wasn't always easy to curb Carter's tendency to take over important matters or to have an adequate opportunity to advise Carter beforehand. Whether determined efforts to do so were made by his principal advisers is not clear from the available record.

Another problem was that Vance and Brzezinski did have important disagreements over policy, particularly on matters having to do with assessment of Soviet intentions and the best strategy and tactics for dealing with the Soviet Union. The effort to preserve collegiality in the first eighteen months of the administration may have led both men to paper over their disagreements and to avoid the difficult but necessary task of coming to grips with these fundamental policy questions. But these matters could not be avoided indefinitely, and after jockeying and competing with each other to influence Carter's position on these issues, first one way and then the other, the controversy between Vance and Brzezinski spilled out into the open — with Brzezinski aggressively speaking out to undermine the positions taken by the secretary of state. Among other things, Brzezinski wanted the administration to exploit the Sino-Soviet conflict, "play the China card," in order to exert pressure on the Soviets. Vance opposed this effectively for some time. But Brzezinski continued his efforts and was successful in obtaining the president's approval for his trip to China. The special assistant's outspoken disagreements with the secretary of state became so damaging that Vance finally went to the president in the summer of 1978 and prevailed upon him to restrain Brzezinski from airing his disagreements publicly.

The roots of the problem lie deeper. It has to do with the question whether an expert on foreign policy, someone who wants to influence foreign policy, should be put into the position of special assistant for national security affairs. The most important responsibility of the special assistant ever since the NSC was created in 1947 has been to serve as the custodian-manager of the top-level policymaking process—i.e., to organize in an orderly, systematic way the flow of studies, papers—in other words, an administrator of the procedures that are needed to ensure that the president and his top foreign-policy advisers get high-quality information and analysis for a broad enough range of policy options before decisions are made, and then to communicate these policy decisions down the line and monitor their implementation. Until Kennedy became president, the person who served as special assistant for national security affairs was not an adviser on policy; rather, he was supposed to confine himself exclusively to being a neutral, efficient, sophisticated manager of the process and the flow of work. Since then, the special assistant, while retaining the role of custodian-manager of the process, has gradually acquired important new roles—that of a major policy adviser himself, that of public spokesman for and defender of the administration's foreign policy, and that of an operator actively engaged in the conduct of diplomacy.

This development came to a head with Kissinger, who as Nixon's special assistant, acquired and tried to perform *all* of these roles. The result was not only that he was overloaded, but also that he experienced serious conflict among these various roles. The most important role conflict was that Kissinger's roles as the major policy adviser and operator undermined his incentive to serve as the *neutral* custodian-manager of the process. Instead, being only human and quite self-confident regarding his own judgment in foreign policy, Kissinger succumbed to the temptation of using his control of the many NSC committees and over the policymaking process in order to enhance his influence with Nixon at the expense of others in the system who may have had different views. It was predictable that Brzezinski would experience similar temptations.[19]

There have been other weaknesses in the management of Carter's foreign-policy system. Under Brzezinski as special assistant, and given the character of his staff, the NSC has not functioned effectively to help coordinate the various strands of foreign policy and to help Carter with his difficult task of managing the various contradictions and trade-offs between different foreign-policy objectives. Neither Brzezinski himself nor his deputy, David Aaron, have earned a reputation in their positions for being good administrators or for defining their roles as high-level staff rather than as activists in making policy. In fact, both appear to be much more interested in influencing policy rather than in managing the policymaking process in a neutral, efficient manner. Moreover, many of the people Brzezinski brought into the NSC staff to work with him are also eager to influence policy as best they can from the vantage point of the White House.

As a result, the fragmentation of foreign policy at the conceptual level, to which many critics have called attention, was reinforced by the failure to develop an effective central coordinating mechanism for the organization and management of the policymaking process. More recently, in 1978 and 1979, Carter has turned increasingly to the creation of special task forces for each major policy issue in order to centralize authority in the White House and to improve coordination of agency and department officials on behalf of presidential policy. Following the successful use of ad hoc task forces to direct efforts to secure ratification of the Panama Canal Treaty and to deal with other major issues, in late 1978 Carter established an executive committee headed by Vice President Mondale to be responsible for dealing with the president's agenda and priorities. This committee endorsed a plan for forming task forces for all major presidential issues for 1979. Task forces have been established on a dozen issues of high priority, including domestic as well as foreign-policy issues.[20]

• • •

Each of these three management models tends to have certain advantages and to incur certain risks. These are discussed in some detail by Richard T. Johnson with respect to each of the six presidents he studied (see Table 1).[21]

In addition, Richard Johnson makes a number of useful suggestions for reducing the shortcomings and risks of each of these three management models:

> For example, a President who adopts the formalistic approach might choose [as Eisenhower did on occasion] to establish more fluid machinery or reach further down the information channels when facing a decision of particular importance to his Administration. [Similarly] a Chief Executive who adopts the competitive style might commission [as FDR did on occasion] formal study groups to ensure careful staff work on complex policy questions. . . . A President who chooses the collegial approach might utilize [as Kennedy did on occasion] a more formalistic structure for routine matters in order to concentrate his energies on the more sensitive policy areas.[22]

In concluding this discussion of the different management styles generally favored by different presidents, we should remind ourselves once again that our depiction of the communication structures associated with each of them necessarily oversimplifies the more complex reality and working of each system.[23] To some extent, elements of two or even all three models may be present in different mixes, with different emphases, in the policymaking system of each president.

Over the years, as the foreign-policy activities in which the U.S. government is engaged have multiplied, the organizational arrangements for dealing with them within the executive branch have proliferated. To some extent, the sheer magnitude and complexity of the foreign-policy enterprise forces every modern president to rely at least to some extent on formalistic procedures. It would be difficult in the modern era for even so gifted a politician and leader as Franklin Roosevelt to rely heavily on a competitive model. Of particular importance, therefore, are studies of variants of formalistic models that, in addition, attempt to make use of elements of the competitive and/or collegial models as well.

Finally, although each of these three management models has certain

Table 1. Three Management Models

Formalistic Approach

Benefits	*Costs*
Orderly decision process enforces more thorough analysis.	The hierarchy which screens information may also distort it. Tendency of the screening process to wash out or distort political pressures and public sentiments.
Conserves the decisionmaker's time and attention for the big decision.	
Emphasizes the optimal.	Tendency to respond slowly or inappropriately in crisis.

Competitive Approach

Places the decisionmaker in the mainstream of the information network.	Places large demands on decisionmaker's time and attention.
Tends to generate solutions that are politically feasible and bureaucratically doable.	Exposes decisionmaker to partial or biased information. Decision process may overly sacrifice optimality for doability.
Generates creative ideas, partially as a result of the "stimulus" of competition, but also because this unstructured kind of information network is more open to ideas from the outside.	Tendency to aggravate staff competition with the risk that aides may pursue their own interests at the expense of the decisionmaker.
	Wear and tear on aides fosters attrition and high turnover.

Collegial Approach

Seeks to achieve both optimality and doability.	Places substantial demands on the decisionmaker's time and attention.
Involves the decisionmaker in the information network but somewhat eases the demands upon him by stressing teamwork over competition.	Requires unusual interpersonal skill in dealing with subordinates, mediating differences, and maintaining teamwork among colleagues.
	Risk that "teamwork" will degenerate into a closed system of mutual support.

Source: Richard T. Johnson, *Managing the White House* (New York: Harper and Row, 1974). Reproduced with minor changes and additions in *The Stanford Business School Alumni Bulletin,* Fall 1973.

advantages and disadvantages, the effort to improve their performance by introducing modification of one kind or another encounters serious limits. The search for improvement in policymaking systems must go beyond general management models of this kind to more discriminating ways of improving information processing. Accordingly, in the next three chapters we discuss procedural tools—the "devil's advocate," the "formal options" system, and "multiple advocacy"—that are often recommended to widen the range of information, options, and judgment available to the president before he makes his decisions.

Notes

1. For a history and critical analysis of these efforts at reorganization, see I. M. Destler, *Presidents, Bureaucrats, and Foreign Policy* (Princeton, N.J.: Princeton University Press, 1972), chapter 2. Nonetheless, as Destler and other students of the problem recognize, organization design and structural parameters do affect foreign policy performance. For a sophisticated discussion, see Graham Allison and Peter Szanton, *Remaking Foreign Policy: The Organizational Connection* (New York: Basic Books, 1976); see particularly Chapter 1, "The Argument: Organization Matters." For a more general discussion applying not merely to foreign policy but the presidency as whole, see Stephen Hess, *Organizing the Presidency* (Washington, D.C.: The Brookings Institution, 1976).

2. The following paragraphs draw upon A. L. George, "Adaptation to Stress in Political Decision-making," in George V. Coelho, David A. Hamburg, and John E. Adams, eds., *Coping and Adaptation* (New York: Basic Books, 1974).

3. This general point is emphasized repeatedly also by Graham Allison in his study for the Commission on the Organization of the Government for the Conduct of Foreign Policy. For example: "The critical variable affecting which mechanisms [of centralized management] are used is the president: his personal preferences and style. . . . It follows, therefore, that efforts to legislate structure for high-level centralized management cannot succeed." Graham T. Allison, ed., *Adequacy of Current Organization: Defense and Arms Control*, vol. 4, Appendices, Commission on the Organization of the Government for the Conduct of Foreign Policy, June 1975 (Washington, D.C.: U.S. Government Printing Office, 1976), p. 35; see also pp. 10, 58.

4. These three management styles are described and evaluated in Richard T. Johnson, *Managing the White House* (New York: Harper & Row, 1974). See particularly chapters 1 and 8. A useful discussion of the evolution of the modern presidency and of the styles of different presidents is provided by Stephen Hess, *Organizing the Presidency* (Washington, D.C.: The Brookings Institution, 1976).

5. Richard Fenno, *The President's Cabinet* (New York: Vintage Books,

Knopf, 1959), pp. 44-46. See also Arthur Schlesinger, Jr., *The Age of Roosevelt,* vol. 2, *The Coming of the New Deal* (Boston: Houghton Mifflin, 1959), chapters 32-34; and Richard E. Neustadt, *Presidential Power* (New York: Wiley, 1960), chapter 7.

6. The following figures (with the exception of the one describing Nixon's variant of the formalistic model) are taken directly, with minor adaptations, from John Q. Johnson, "Communication Structures Among Presidential Advisors" (seminar paper, Stanford University, September 1975). The seminal work on communication networks is that of Alex Bavelas, "Communication Patterns in Task-oriented Groups," *Journal of Acoustic Society of America* 22 (1950):725-30. A summary of early work of this kind appears in Murray Glanzer and Robert Glaser, "Techniques for the Study of Group Structure and Behavior," *Psychological Bulletin* 58 (1961):2-27.

7. Recently available archival materials at the Eisenhower Library evidently require a substantial revision of the conventional image of Eisenhower as an apolitical military man, one who was generally uninformed about and not very attentive to his executive responsibilities, one who was prone to overdelegate his responsibilities, and one who was naive about the art of governing. What emerges, rather, is a different executive style that Fred Greenstein refers to as Eisenhower's "invisible hand" mode of leadership in which he sought actively to secure his goals by indirection (Fred I. Greenstein, "Presidential Activism Eisenhower Style: A Reassessment Based on Archival Evidence," [paper delivered to the 1979 Meeting of the Midwest Political Science Association, January 1979]).

8. Ibid., p. 9. See also Douglas Kinnard, *President Eisenhower and Strategy Management: A Study in Defense Politics* (Lexington: University of Kentucky Press, 1977); and Murray Kempton, "The Underestimation of Dwight D. Eisenhower," *Esquire* (September 1967).

9. Greenstein, "Presidential Activism," p. 10.

10. See, for example, James David Barber, *The Presidential Character* (Englewood Cliffs, N.J.: Prentice-Hall, 1972) and Johnson, *Managing the White House,* pp. 199-229.

11. Johnson, *Managing the White House,* pp. 210-11.

12. Ibid.

13. For a particularly detailed account of the structure, evolution, and performance of Nixon's NSC, *see* Chester Crocker, "The Nixon-Kissinger National Security Council System, 1969-1972: A Study in Foreign Policy Management," vol. 6, Appendices, Commission on the Organization of the Government for the Conduct of Foreign Policy, June 1975 (Washington, D.C.: Government Printing Office, 1976), pp. 79-99.

14. Don Bonafede, "Brzezinski—Stepping Out of His Backstage Role," *National Journal* (15 October 1977):1598. See also Elizabeth Drew, "A Reporter at Large: Brzezinski," *The New Yorker,* May 1978; and Marilyn Berger, "Vance and Brzezinski: Peaceful Coexistence or Guerrilla War?" *New York Times Magazine,* 13 February 1977.

15. Bonafede, "Brzezinski."

16. For a remarkably incisive set of observations regarding aspects of Carter's personality and outlook that have adversely affected the organization of his advisory system and his performance generally, see the series of articles published by his former speech writer, James Fallows, "The Passionless Presidency," *The Atlantic Monthly*, May and June 1979. Some of these difficulties were anticipated earlier by two political scientists, Jack Knott and Aaron Wildavsky, "Jimmy Carter's Theory of Governing," *The Wilson Quarterly* 1 (Winter 1977). An in-depth, thoroughly researched critical appraisal of Carter's personality and career is being prepared by Professor Betty Glad of the Political Science Department, The University of Illinois.

17. For a description of the NSC under Carter, see Bonafede, "Brzezinski"; and Lawrence J. Korb, "The Structure and Process of the National Security Council System in the First Year of the Carter Administration" (paper delivered at the annual meeting of the International Studies Association, Washington, D.C., 22-25 February 1978). On Brzezinski's role, see also chapter 11 in this volume.

18. *See*, for example, Stanley Hoffmann, "The Hell of Good Intentions," *Foreign Policy* 29 (winter 1977-78); and Thomas L. Hughes, "Carter and the Management of Contradictions," *Foreign Policy* 31 (summer 1978).

19. For a more detailed discussion of the evolution of the position of special assistant for national security affairs, *see* chapters 10 and 11.

20. Jack Nelson, "Task Forces Increase White House Efficiency," *Los Angeles Times*, 26 April 1979.

21. Johnson, *Managing the White House*, chapter 8; reproduced with minor changes and additions in *The Stanford Business School Alumni Bulletin*, fall 1973.

22. Ibid., pp. 237-39.

23. Important refinements in the description of each president's preferred executive work style are introduced by David K. Hall in his forthcoming Ph.D. dissertation at Stanford University.

9
The Devil's Advocate:
Uses and Limitations

In recent years much attention has been given to ways of ensuring that unpopular views are encouraged and given a proper hearing in small decisionmaking groups in which, as noted in Chapter 4, pressures for conformity often discourage expression of dissenting opinions. Among the organizational devices often recommended for this purpose is the time-honored institution of the "devil's advocate." Following the Bay of Pigs fiasco, in which President Kennedy's policy meetings had been marked by a seeming unanimity of opinion, his brother suggested that thereafter there always be a devil's advocate to give an opposite opinion if none was pressed.[1] Indeed, the president appears to have encouraged both his brother and Theodore Sorensen to take a more active "watchdog" role in foreign-policy matters. Later, President Johnson is said to have referred to Under Secretary of State George Ball as his "devil's advocate," thereby legitimizing as well as encouraging Ball's continued expresssion of his dissent over Vietnam policy.

While something like a devil's advocate role was perhaps played by these men and no doubt by other advisers on other occassions, remarkably little historical material describing activities of this kind is available to serve as a basis for evaluating the efficacy of this organizational device. Similarly, the experimental laboratory research on small groups that has been consulted in preparing this chapter has little to offer by way of an explicit assessment of the feasibility and utility of a devil's advocate, though it does provide support for the idea that a group's performance can be abetted under certain conditions by leadership practices that "protect" members who express minority views (see Chapter 4).

For the time being, therefore, the case for introducing a devil's advocate into policymaking groups rests largely on a priori grounds. While the case is a strong one in principle, the introduction and effective utilization of a devil's advocate is by no means a simple matter. Indeed, those who favor the idea of a devil's advocate often have different notions of what this would mean in practice. Some are content to suggest that the leader of a group should appoint one person on an ad hoc basis to serve as devil's advocate if no one in the group will challenge the dominant view in a given situation. Others have identified a much more complex set of requirements and procedures for institutionalizing the devil's advocate function, even going so far as to suggest that a subgroup rather than just one individual be assigned a continuing responsibility to make the opposition case even after a decision has been taken.[2]

Strictly speaking, the devil's advocate performs a *role*; it is understood that the person performing this role will argue an unpopular position that should be considered, but which no one else will speak up for and which the devil's advocate himself does not really favor. The fact that he is performing an accepted role and is not a genuine dissenter is designed, of course, to protect that person from incurring sanctions for challenging the groups's opinion or its leader's view. Thus defined, however, the limits as well as the potential utility of the role become manifest: for while the devil's advocate introduces some diversity into the group's deliberations or challenges some of the premises that enter into the leader's judgment, he cannot persist in his challenge nor, even more important, seek to develop a coalition within the group to oppose and, if possible, overcome the majority. Unlike a genuine policy dissident, the true devil's advocate is not a political actor with policy commitments and organizational resources of his own; he is not engaged in a competitive struggle to influence policy decisions but is merely playing a role that, at best, facilitates a dialetical, multisided examination of the problem that is being decided.

If the devil's advocate is not a dissident political actor, neither should the role of devil's advocate be confused with the much more comprehensive role of the "custodian-manager" of the policymaking process, which will be discussed in Chapter 11. The custodian-manager acts as a surrogate for the executive in attempting to assure the quality of the search and analysis phases of policymaking that precede final choice of action; in so doing, he attempts to insure that the executive will have a number of well-considered, well-presented options to choose from. To this end, to be sure, the custodian-manager (or the executive) may designate someone to play the role of devil's advocate when no genuine advocate for an unpopular option can be found. But the two roles are distinct and should not be confused.

Those who have observed with distress the repeated failure of policymakers to consider diverse views sometimes turn in desperation to the idea that installing a devil's advocate would help. But the mere provision of a devil's advocate in small decisionmaking groups is hardly a guarantee that the person will be able to perform the role well enough to contribute to improved policymaking. We know very little about what kinds of persons can perform effectively in this role, and how it can be introduced and maintained so that it is not regarded as an awkward or time-wasting gimmick by members of the group.

While there is much to be learned about how best to operate a devil's advocate, and while such knowledge might indeed be utilized to make this a useful innovation, one cannot be sanguine on the basis of recent experience. There is, first, some question whether the role can be performed with the integrity required to yield the desired impact. Second, there is sobering evidence that a devil's advocate can be put to uses other than those for which the role is intended. Let us examine both of these constraints on the utility of a devil's advocate.

Accounts of Vietnam policymaking suggest that the device of a devil's advocate can be misused in an effort to "domesticate" advisers who genuinely oppose policy decisions being taken. George Ball, for example, repeatedly disagreed with the development of U.S. policy in Vietnam. From an early stage President Johnson took to calling Ball his "devil's advocate" – a misnomer in this case since Ball was a genuine dissenter. Perhaps Johnson employed the euphemistic label of devil's advocate in order to soften the import of Ball's dissent and to indicate that he would regard it as legitimate and acceptable only if Ball provided his views as a service to the group and kept them within the confines of the group.

What this suggests is that in contrast to the often noted tendency in experimental laboratory groups for the majority to exert crude and extreme conformity pressures on dissident members (see Chapter 4), in real-world policy groups it is often unnecessary or undesirable to squelch or reject a dissident member. The possibility that dissidents are likely to increase malaise within the rest of the group is often accepted and legitimized in the expectation that they will strengthen on balance the ability of the group to cope with the problems of policymaking. But, in response, the dissident may moderate the style or manner in which he expresses his dissent, if not also the full extent of his disagreement, by falling into what James C. Thomson calls "the effectiveness trap" – i.e., the trap that keeps men from resigning in protest and airing their discontent outside the government. It is possible to be overly cynical and uncharitable about such behavior. The reality of the dilemma, however, cannot be ignored. As Thomson puts it, "To preserve your effectiveness, you must decide where and when to fight the mainstream of policy. . . . [by staying and not resigning] one may be able to prevent a few bad things from happening." As for George Ball, who presumably acquiesced in his "domestication," Thomson is quick to concede that matters might have gotten worse faster if Ball had kept silent or left before his departure in the fall of 1966.[3]

The inefficacy of devil's advocate has been strongly emphasized, but perhaps overstated, by George E. Reedy, a former press secretary to President Johnson: "It is well understood that he [the devil's advocate] is not going to press his points harshly or stridently. Therefore, his objections and cautions are discounted before they are delivered."[4]

There are a number of additional incentives, not mentioned by Thomson, that may encourage an executive to hold on to dissident policy advisers. Even a weakened form of multiple advocacy may be useful to the chief executive and his supporting advisers in several ways. First, hearing negative opinions expressed *and* rebutted may provide top-level officials with the psychologically comforting feeling that they have considered all sides of the issue and that the policy chosen has weathered challenges from within the decisionmaking circle. Paradoxically, then, having some dissenters within the group may help the others, in particular the leader, to cope with some of the stresses of decisionmaking.

Second, there is rehearsal value in listening to and debating dissenters within the policymaking group. Those who support the policy are then better equipped to reply when they encounter similar challenges in the public arena.

Third, the formal modalities of hearing diverse opinions can help hold the group together. The executive's task is not only to select as "wise" a policy as possible but to achieve some degree of consensus on its behalf among those actors in the system who are most concerned with the issue and those who will have to help implement it. If giving those advisers who disagree with policy a hearing does not always contribute as much as it might to achieving a wiser decision, it can be useful nonetheless as a vehicle for developing consensus. The feeling that consultation and debate took place before the executive made his decision may assuage some of the disappointment of those whose advice was not followed. It may be easier for them to close ranks, at least temporarily, behind the policy chosen.[5]

Fourth, if the "doubters" who have opposed policy in the private deliberations of the group can be cast into the role of defending it in public forums, they may well do a better job than firm, enthusiastic advocates of that policy.[6] Such a task forces the dissident policy adviser to confront his own doubts. To the extent that his original doubts are shared by outsiders, the defense of policy he manages to develop is likely to focus on considerations that will be especially salient for them.

Finally, there may be important public relations benefits for the executive who follows the practice of hearing dissident advocates and, more generally, who structures the policy-forming process to ensure orderly consideration of alternative options.[7] In an earlier era a leader could decide to do what he and his trusted advisers thought best on controversial policy matters without disclosing in detail how and why the decision was made. He could leave the question whether he had acted wisely to the "judgment of history" some generations hence. This possibility has been increasingly denied leaders of democratic governments in the modern era of rapid communications and of acute journalistic and public curiosity as to how the affairs of government are being decided. Important elements of the public are no longer satisfied to wait for the judgment that future historians will render. As a result, new expectations have been directed toward the presidency which its modern incumbents have incorporated into the performance of their role. Faced with the public's demand for "instant history," presidents and their advisers increasingly cooperate in enabling journalists to write inside accounts of how and why a recent decision was made.

One can see value in this. The demand of the informed, attentive public for orderly, "rational" consideration of alternative options in which all sides of an issue are considered and debated may indeed serve to strengthen such policymaking procedures within the government. This is not to ignore the possibility that the impact of these public expectations will be shallow; the administration may respond by routinizing the conduct of multiple advocacy, and "domesticating" devil's advocates in order to secure public relations advantages. As a result, top-level officials may learn to enact their policymaking in such a way as to meet the informed public's expectations as to how important decisions should be made and to project a favorable image into the "instant histories" that will be written shortly thereafter.

It is possible to be too cynical about this. Chief executives have been driven to find more effective ways of organizing and managing their policymaking machinery for a variety of reasons, not merely to satisfy public relations needs. And, in any case, one can hope that shadow and substance cannot exist wholly apart from each other and that the striving for a good image may serve to reinforce the hand of those in government who also strive for an effective system of policymaking.

With this in mind we turn in the next two chapters to examine two somewhat different policy making models—the formal options system and multiple advocacy—which have been proposed and utilized as vehicles for securing the equivalent of a rational system of policymaking. Both the formal options system and multiple advocacy are much more comprehensive in scope and objectives than is the device of a devil's advocate.

Notes

1. R. F. Kennedy, *Thirteen Days* (New York: Norton, 1969), p. 90. A more comprehensive case for a devil's advocate function is made by Joseph de Rivera, *The Psychological Dimension of Foreign Policy*, (Columbus: Charles E. Merrill, 1968), pp. 61-64, 209-11. See also Irving L. Janis, *Victims of Groupthink* (Boston: Houghton Mifflin Co., 1972), pp. 215-16.

2. De Rivera, *Psychological Dimension.*

3. James C. Thomson, Jr., "How Could Vietnam Happen? An Autopsy," *Atlantic Monthly*, April 1968. Albert Hirschman has expressed concern over the extreme reluctance of Americans in public office to resign in protest against policies with which they strongly disagree. Hirschman's general thesis is that "exit" has an essential role to play in restoring quality performance of government, as in any organization (*Exit, Voice and Loyalty* [Cambridge: Harvard University Press, 1970], pp. 114-19).

4. George E. Reedy, *The Twilight of the Presidency* (New York: World, 1970), p. 11. A sober evaluation of the devil's advocate idea is expressed forcefully also by Chester L. Cooper (personal communication): "A formal devil's advocate role would be an artificial and contrived one, empty of real meaning because the advocate is simply role-playing and is not arguing with serious conviction." Skepticism regarding the feasibility and efficacy of a devil's advocate is also expressed by Avi Shlaim in his analysis of the causes of "surprise" in the Arab-Israeli war of October 1973: "For devil's advocates to work effectively, therefore, it is not enough to appoint them and then to tolerate with ill-disguised impatience their questioning of agreed assumptions and their challenges to the conventional wisdom. Unless they are actively supported and encouraged by the people at the top, and are seen to be supported and valued, their views will carry little weight. . . . " ("Failures in National Intelligence Estimates: The Case of the Yom Kippur War," *World Politics* [April 1976]:374-75).

5. This is consistent with research findings in other settings which suggest that as long as the individual is satisfied that a proper degree of deference has been granted to his point of view by organizational superiors, his hostility reaction will, in all probability, be minimal if his superiors do not accept his judgement. See Murray Horwitz, "Managing Hostility in the Laboratory and the Refinery," in Robert L. Kahn and Elise Boulding, eds., *Power and Conflict in Organizations* (New York: Basic Books, 1964), pp. 79-82; cited by Louis G. Gawthrop, *Bureaucratic Behavior in the Executive Branch* (New York: Free Press, 1969), p. 42.

6. Philip Geyelin (*LBJ*, p. 210) notes that "It was a familiar Johnson stratagem to send known dissenters to argue on behalf of his policies."

7. As George Reedy puts it, the objections and cautions of the official devil's advocate "are actually welcomed because they prove for the record that decision was preceded by controversy." (Reedy, *Twilight of the Presidency*, p. 11).

10
The "Formal Options" System

In chapters 4, 5, and 6, we identified major impediments to information processing and serious malfunctions of the presidential advisory system that can arise from the dynamics of small policymaking groups and organizational behavior. It is clear that these impediments and malfunctions have deep roots in the internal complexity of the foreign-policymaking system. In view of this, relatively simple devices such as the devil's advocate, even if effectively implemented, cannot possibly meet all of the requirements for designing a more effective policymaking system. Clearly, more comprehensive prescriptive theories for models are needed. Two such theories will be considered in this chapter and in the next. Before proceeding to the first of these two design models, the formal options system, it will be useful to recall some of the tasks and problems that must be dealt with in efforts to design effective policymaking procedures.

The Need for Lateral Coordination
and Hierarchical Direction

The fact that responsibility for different aspects of foreign policy is distributed over a relatively large number of departments and agencies and that relevant information and competence is also widely dispersed within the executive branch, imposes on top-level officials the task of providing initiative, coherence, and control. An important part of this task is the requirement for internal coordination: those parts of the executive branch that have some responsibility for a particular policy problem must be encouraged to interact with each other in appropriate ways.[1] Lateral coordination through such mechanisms as interdepartmental committees, conferences, a system of clearances, etc., however, cannot be counted upon to produce the caliber of policy analysis, the level of consensus, and the procedures for implementation that may be required for an effective and coherent foreign policy. Also, lateral coordination by itself may be inadequate to cope with the dynamics of organizational behavior and the phenomena of "bureaucratic politics" that create impediments and malfunctions. Accordingly, all presidents have found it necessary to impose mechanisms for control and coordination from above; that is, to supplement lateral coordination with some degree of *hierarchical coordination and control.*

Hierarchical coordination and control attempts to provide for a number of presidential interests and purposes.

1. A president needs information and advice to make top-level foreign-policy decisions, and he must find ways of assuring that the quality of the information and advice he receives from departments and agencies is not distorted by their special interests and narrow perspectives.

2. The president must find ways of impressing his broader perspectives of the national interest on the functioning on lower-level foreign-policy officials.

3. A president must be alert to the harmful effect that actions by departments and agencies might have on "presidential interests" — that is, the personal political resources and the tactical and strategic flexibility that he needs in order to perform effectively on a continuing basis all facets of his complex role. The "national interest" and "presidential interests" are not necessarily one and the same thing, but to promote and safeguard one or both of them a president must "preserve his choices" over important foreign-policy decisions — that is, as Richard Neustadt emphasized so persuasively in *Presidential Power* (1960), he must make certain that the resolution of such foreign-policy issues is not preempted by lower-level officials but that they rise to the presidential level on a timely basis to enable him to make informed judgments and decisions of his own.

4. Hierarchical coordination and control are needed to ensure coherence and consistency in foreign policy and, of course, to assure implementation of presidential policy.

The nature and extent of hierarchical coordination and control have varied from president to president. Each incumbent of the office tends to define his own role and participation in foreign-policymaking somewhat differently. The structure and scope of hierarchical coordination and the nature of the advisory system around the president reflect his personal preferences and management style.

The Nixon-Kissinger NSC System

The most centralized and structured organizational model utilized thus far for securing hierarchical coordination and control has beeen the formal options system introduced in 1969 by President Nixon and his special assistant for national security affairs, Henry Kissinger.[2] We shall forego a detailed description of Nixon's reorganizaiton of the NSC. It will suffice for present purposes to recall its major features and to articulate some of its underlying premises in order to call attention to questions of theoretical and practical interest.

Under Nixon, it should be noted, the formal options system was linked with the choice of a White House–centered organizational model of foreign-policymaking. The president wished to enhance his personal role in dealing with major foreign-policy issues. The formal options system was designed not only to ensure that he would retain and exercise the power of final decision, but also, as he put it, "to make certain that clear policy choices" reached the top. Well aware that the play of bureaucratic politics could limit his choices, Nixon was determined not to be "confronted with a bureaucratic consensus that leaves me with no options but acceptance or rejection, and that gives me no way of knowing what alternatives exist."[3]

Kissinger created a structure of NSC-centered interdepartmental committeees that was designed to strengthen the intellectual and bureaucratic resources of the White House and to weaken the autonomy in foreign-policymaking of the departments and the agencies. Kissinger chaired all of the interdepartmental committees established at the next level below the NSC to identify and examine options before they were sent to the NSC and/or the president. Thus, he did not leave the important task of lateral coordination of policy *formation* to the discretion of and unregulated interaction between departments and agencies concerned with a particular issue; nor did he delegate this task to the State Department (as would be the case in a State-centered organizational model). Instead, lateral coordination of policy formation was integrated in substantial measure with hierarchical direction and control from the White House. In contrast, the comparable committees on policy *implementation* were chaired by the under secretary of state, and the policy studies generated by National Security Study Memoranda (NSSM) were assigned to a specific department or agency to ensure coordination and responsiveness to the deadline and framework imposed in the initial study request.[4]

As a result of Kissinger's chairmanship of the various NSC committees, the new NSC system greatly enhanced presidential control over the formulation of foreign policy and weakened the ability of departmental and agency officials to exercise independent judgment and influence. In effect, Nixon and Kissinger attempted to impose the model of a unitary, rational policymaker on the more loosely structured, pluralistic policymaking systems of previous administrations. The staff of the NSC, augmented in numbers and functions, reached deeper in to departments and agencies in order to identify and gain control over a wider range of issues at earlier stages in policymaking. It should be noted, too, that the NSC role went far beyond simple coordination of agency positions on security issues. Rather, the imposition of an interagency framework on many security issues (which in the past had been dealt with in semiautonomy by the Defense Department) forced many military questions to be examined in a broader context.

Kissinger's network of interdepartmental committees drew personnel from all agencies concerned with security and international affairs into the preliminary analytic work necessary for policymaking. As a result, it is probably the case that many foreign-policy specialists in the various departments and agencies were involved more systematically and more closely in the preparatory stages of policymaking, as individuals at least, than was the case in previous administrations. This was evidently the case, for example, with regard to personnel in the Arms Control and Disarmament Agency.

At the same time, however, the formal options model as employed by Nixon and Kissinger served to discourage the departments and agencies from maintaining or developing strong analytic capabilities of their own. For one thing, the fact that important policy issues were so often preempted by NSC directives commissioning an interagency study tended to discourage departments and agencies from undertaking independent studies of their own that might have to be redone or abandoned when the NSC launched a request for an interagency study on the same or a similar topic. It was often difficult for a department or agency to get its own thoughts on a question in order before being plunged into the interagency process, with all of its deadlines, often unwieldy meetings, and uneven expertise among participants. For another thing, departmental and agency analysts were either placed on interdepartmental committees or drawn into the task of preparing inputs to the work of such committees.

In other ways as well, the Nixon-Kissinger system discouraged and weakened competitive policy analysis at the departmental and agency levels that might differ from that produced by the NSC's formal options system. The studies produced by the NSC-oriented interdepartmental committees, available to all departments and agencies concerned with the policy issue in question, were considered to be authoritative and of superior quality. The few senior foreign-policy officials who participated in the final discussion before the president made his choice of policy were at times largely dependent upon these studies. Their own experts were often well versed in the policy issue that was up for decision and could brief the principals before they met with the president. But the process of examining options in the NSC or discussing them *tête-à-tête* with the president was allowed to atrophy. Indeed, many of the NSC policy studies would have provided a basis for wide-ranging discussions; but the airing of competitive viewpoints was frustrated by the inadequacy of presidential- and cabinet-level confrontation with the issues and with each other before the president made his choice.

Through the formal options system that has been described, Nixon and Kissinger attempted to obtain an "advocate-free" form of information processing, identification, and appraisal of options. (Hence, the appropriateness of the term "formal options," as against options developed and advanced by advocates in one or more agencies.) While departmental and agency specialists participated in the important early stages of policy analysis, agency viewpoints as such were not to influence the policy studies produced by the interdepartmental committees and, indeed, were not to be articulated and introduced into these preparatory studies.[5] Rather, the departmental and agency officials would presumably have an opportunity later, through the vehicle of another NSC committee—the Senior Review Group—and indeed in high-level policy discussions held in meetings of the NSC itself to introduce whatever special insight or wisdom their departmental perspective on the policy issue offered. But at that stage in the policymaking process their ability to perform as independent advisers, capable of challenging the authoritative options analyses produced by the prestigious NSC system, was obviously limited.

Not only was the role of leading departmental officials subtly redefined and delimited in Nixon's way of organizing and managing the foreign-policymaking system, the resources and opportunities available to them for influencing policy were curtailed. Cabinet officials and other senior officials were discouraged from performing as policy advocates and, as a result of the way in which the NSC system was structured, weakened in their ability to perform as forceful advisers who could back their judgment with independent analysis. As a result, when department heads finally had an opportunity—if indeed they did—at top-level meetings with the president to express their views on alternative options, as the system was supposed to provide, they were not always in a position to offer well-considered alternatives backed by solid independent analysis. Thus, even the most senior departmental officials were placed at a disadvantage in performing as advisers to the president in the final stages of decisionmaking.

Some Questions and Caveats

If we grant that the Nixon-Kissinger system curbed some of the dysfunctional features of "bureaucratic politics" and had other advantages as well, we are left with the question of the costs and possible risks of so centralized a system. Some reservations expresssed by critics of the Nixon-Kissinger system challenge theoretical assumptions underlying the formal options system; others are directed to the way in which this system worked in practice as against the way in which it was supposed to work in theory.

The Disadvantages of Separating Policy Analysis from Policymaking

It may be noted that the formal options system attempts to separate as much as possible the preliminary "search" and analysis phases of policymaking from the final process of "choice."[6] That is, the tasks of search and analysis are to be completed and the results, in the form of options analysis, then made available to the top-level decisionmaker for his choice. This is an orderly, sequential procedure which appears ideally suited for providing the executive with a well-considered, "finished" set of options from which to choose. The flow of policymaking in such a system is depicted in Figure 7.

It should be noted that the compartmentalized, formalistic way in which search and analysis are separated from choice in such a system can seriously interfere with the necessity for intellectual *interaction* between these phases of policymaking. Recognizing this, specialists in organiza-

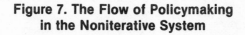

Figure 7. The Flow of Policymaking in the Noniterative System

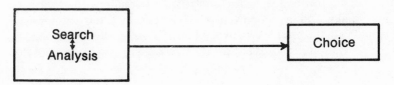

Search
Analysis

Choice

tional decisionmaking have regarded a strict separation of search and analysis from choice as highly questionable; they emphasize, to the contrary, that it is generally desirable to find ways of keeping specialists engaged in search and analysis in continuing contact with officials who will be making the final choice of policy.[7] Two-way communication between policymakers and specialists in search and analysis is valuable—some would say essential—in order to develop a more incisive and shared understanding of the policy problem that is to be decided.

Initial formulations of a foreign-policy problem for study and analysis are likely to be defective.[8] An *iterative* procedure is often required in which preliminary search and analysis on an inadequately formulated problem helps policymakers to reformulate the problem, which in turn generates a new round of search and analysis. Moreover, a policymaker's preliminary effort to come to grips with the problem of choice often generates new questions that were overlooked or inadequately dealt with in the policy analysis already completed by specialists in search and analysis, thereby posing a need for additional analysis or reconsideration of the previous analysis provided the policymaker. In other words, timely "rehearsals" of choice by policymakers have considerable value both for clarifying the problem, for indicating the need to search for additional information and somewhat novel options on the basis of new criteria of choice formulated by the policymaker during the course of his "rehearsal" of the decision.

There is considerable support for an iterative approach of this kind both in experimental laboratory research and in evaluations of real-world decisionmaking. Specialists who have studied the performance of problem-solving groups have called attention to the value of programming the group to ensure that it undertakes a "second solution" to the problem, since there is considerable evidence that an iterative approach of this kind improves performance.[9] A similar suggestion for a "second chance" meeting to review a decision just taken has been advanced by Irving Janis, whose studies of decisionmaking in small groups have emphasized the need to avoid certain types of group dynamics that can distort judgment and lead to poor decisions[10] (see also Chapter 4).

The flow of policymaking in a system which includes iteration, decision "rehearsals," and/or "second solutions" is depicted in Figure 8.

In this type of policymaking system, search and analysis are not compartmentalized and separated from choice in the same way as in the formal options system. Rather, this system is designed to encourage and permit additional search and analysis on the basis of the decisionmaker's rehearsal of choice. Thereby, the results of search and analysis are likely to be of higher quality and greater relevance to the policymaker's needs.

Figure 8. The Flow of Policymaking
in the Iterative System

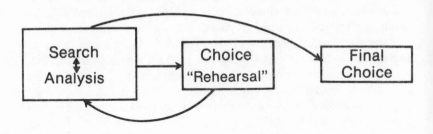

The Risks of Solo Decisionmaking
by the President

As noted elsewhere in this report, a president's style will dominate the process; any theoretical model of what constitutes an effective procedure of policymaking has to be adjusted to take this into account. Certainly the formal options system was nicely suited to Nixon's preference for solo decisions made in private. But this style of decisionmaking added to the risks of the formalistic separation of search and evaluation from choice. There is little in the record to indicate that Nixon made a habit of engaging in preliminary decision rehearsals; rather, having received the well-prepared formal options and heard some discussion of them, he preferred to withdraw in order to go through the final stages of deliberation privately prior to making his decision.

The combination of a formal options system and solo decisionmaking exaggerates the familiar risk that arises whenever, as often happens, an executive improvises at the last minute an option somewhat different from the carefully evaluated ones presented to him. As is well known, the utility of a complex option often suffers from last-minute alteration of some of its components. Unless the executive's improvised choice is resubmitted for careful evaluation, the value of meticulous preparation of options can be easily defeated. This danger is enhanced, moreover, in cases when time pressures are urgent.

Inadequacy of Formal Options
for Crisis Decisionmaking

More generally, when decisions must be arrived at quickly, the orderly but somewhat laborious collection and evaluation of formal options by the NSC apparatus may break down or work ineffectively. Evidently for this reason, Kissinger established still another committee in 1969, the Washington Special Actions Group (WSAG), to deal with international crises. Relatively little information is available for a rounded appraisal of WSAG's performance. But Kissinger himself has conceded that while he believes that the NSC system "works rather well" on the whole, it does "better in noncrisis situations than in crises."[11]

It would seem particularly important for crisis management, therefore, to backstop the NSC apparatus with a system of multiple advocacy in which the representatives of the departments and agencies who sit in WSAG can draw upon competent analytical staffs of their own.

Problems of Overloading

Another criticism leveled at the formal options system concerns the enormous bureaucratic effort that goes into the preparation of NSC study memoranda and policy papers by the various interdepartmental committees. Thus, the State Department has called attention to the "dangers that extensive use of studies [by the NSC] to deal with subsidiary issues may overburden the system . . ."[12]

It is also reported that recurrent delays have taken place in both the completion of staff work and White House action. This is not surprising since a highly centralized system of this type can easily overburden the top-level decisionmaker. It may be necessary, as has often been said, to centralize first before effective decentralization is possible. With the passage of time, however, signs multiplied that the Nixon-Kissinger system suffered from dangerous overload precisely because of its inability or unwillingness to build "centers of strength responsible to the president in other parts of the foreign affairs government."[13]

Selective Use of Formal Options by the President

The Nixon-Kissinger NSC system has been criticized also on the grounds that the president and his special assistant bypassed the formal options process on many important occasions. Professor Wilfred Kohl calls attention to a number of ways in which Kissinger and Nixon bypassed the NSC framework. In his detailed study of the patterns of policymaking employed by Nixon and Kissinger in dealing with eleven major issues in U.S.-European relations, Kohl finds that they utilized the formal options system, and then only in part, in five cases. What Kohl calls the "Royal Court" pattern of policymaking, in which high policy issues were handled outside the NSC system under Kissinger's personal direction, was employed in three cases. Three other instances of low-level policy issues were also handled outside of the formal NSC system, being left largely to the play of organizational procedures and bureaucratic politics among the most concerned departments and agencies.[14]

Restricted Range of Formal Options

As time passed, questions were also raised regarding the possibility that the search for options and their appraisal of the NSC system was not as "open" and broadranging as had been initially suggested. Certainly both Nixon and Kissinger had opportunities to use their control and influence over the NSC interdepartmental committees to shape the policy analysis and the formulation and assessment of options. One observer concludes a balanced appraisal of the workings of the NSC system with the following observation: "The kinds of analyses that are done, the way the choices are presented to the president and the NSC, and the shape of the resulting policies inevitably reflects the biases of the president and his leading officials, such as Kissinger."[15]

Another observer, in an otherwise sympathetic evaluation of the NSC, asked whether the often-repeated phrases such as "keeping the options open" do not have "more of a liturgical than intellectual significance"; he (and other critics) also noted the common complaint that the NSC-initiated studies imposed busywork on the departments while the special assistant and his own staff focused on the essential issues.[16]

The State Department, too, has questioned whether the formal options system does in fact succeed in identifying and prescribing to the president a full range of choices. "Experience has shown," the State Department observed to the Commission on the Organization of the Government for the Conduct of Foreign Policy, "that the presentation of options does not, of itself, ensure that all reasonable alternatives are placed before the President."[17]

The Multiple, Conflicting Roles
of the Special Assistant for National Security Affairs

Culminating a trend that can be traced to the Kennedy administration, the special assistant for national security affairs in Nixon's presidency emerged as an even stronger semiautonomous actor in foreign-policymaking. With the control of the NSC-centered formal options machinery in his hands and enjoying the increasing trust and confidence of the president, Kissinger gradually came to play a central role in influencing and shaping not only the procedures but also the substance of policy analysis throughout the executive branch.

To his job of "custodian-manager" of process and procedures, Kissinger gradually added a number of other important role tasks: that of "watchdog" over the president's personal power stakes in foreign-policy issues; that of implementer-enforcer of the president's decisions; that of administrative operator; and that of policy adviser-advocate. The assignment of so many additional roles to that of "custodian-manager" created the possibility of serious role conflicts that could easily interfere with the performance of his unique responsibility as neutral "custodian-manager" of the NSC–centered procedures for obtaining balanced views, objective review of policies, and multiple options for the president's benefit.

With the passage of time, it is reported that Kissinger would on occasion dominate meetings of the Verification Panel and the Senior Review Group either by force of personality or because of his strong advocacy of a particular position.[18] At one time reluctant to offer his own view when forwarding a set of options to the president, later on he began to add his own recommendation when doing so.

While the enormous enhancement of the special assistant's responsibilities and tasks no doubt reflected the president's wishes and expectations, it did introduce important new elements into the functioning of the formal options system. The latter was transformed into something quite different from what it had been at the outset of the Nixon administration, and the position of special assistant was converted into that of a second, or super secretary of state. (A more detailed discussion of the evolution of the special assistant's position and the performance of the role by various incumbents is provided in the next chapter.)

Indirect Effects on Role of Congress in Foreign Policy

It should be noted, finally, that by placing the president at the helm of a tightly controlled, depoliticized system of policymaking within the executive branch, the Nixon-Kissinger NSC system also strengthened his position in the foreign-policy arena vis-à-vis Congress. A less centralized system of policymaking within the executive branch contributes to a more "open" system; it generates more information and offers more opportunities for "outside" actors (Congress) to influence presidential policies. By weakening the struggle over foreign policy within the executive branch, the NSC system thereby also limited these opportunities.

Concluding Observations

Several general observations are appropriate and timely in concluding this review of the formal options system. The reality of a policymaking system is always more opaque and inconsistent than the clarity of the theoretical model which inspired the creation of that system and which justifies it as an effective way to make policy. The Nixon administration by no means made all of its important foreign-policy decisions in a manner consistent with its own NSC model. This is not offered as criticism, rather as a reminder that any president is likely to resort to a number of different ways of making foreign policy.

In effect, Nixon operated with a mixed system, employing a variety of procedures for making policy of which the formal options system was but one. Even multiple advocacy, an alternative to the formal options system which we shall discuss in the next chapter, could be noted from time to time in the Nixon administration's way of making foreign-policy decisions. Multiple advocacy occurred under two circumstances. Especially at the beginning of Nixon's administration, the formal options process was supposed to be supplemented at the last stages before the president made a final decision by discussion and debate, if there were advocates of different positions among senior advisers in the Senior Review Group or in the formal meetings of the NSC itself. But, in time, with his penchant for privacy and solo decisionmaking, Nixon utilized this procedure less and less, participating in few meetings of this kind and preferring to have policy disagreements among his advisers come to him in writing or as summarized by Kissinger. Multiple advocacy of sorts also took place when decisions were made outside the NSC system and were subject to the pull and tug among leading officials of different departments and agencies.

Moreover, as we have noted, the formal options system changed in important ways over a period of time. As one sympathetic observer noted in late 1971, "The NSC system today is not the tidy blueprint of January 1969. The older it has gotten, the more informal and overlapping its procedures have become."[19]

The experience of the Nixon presidency is quite relevant, of course, for evaluating the merits of a formal options system, but it must be used with care for the purpose. In addition to the preceding observations regarding the mixed and changing system of foreign-policymaking in his administration, we should note several other things that complicate the task of assessing the utility of formal options. In the Nixon presidency, the formal options procedure was combined with a highly centralized presidential control of foreign policy. But formal options can be combined with a State-centered organizational model rather than a White House–centered system. President Johnson's effort to move in this direction in the last few years of his administration proved largely abortive, as did Elliot Richardson's effort as under secretary of state to persuade Kissinger to move in this direction.[20]

Certain ways of strengthening Nixon's foreign-policymaking system, often advocated by sympathetic critics, were never undertaken or inadequately implemented.[21] Thus, for example, the formal options portion of Nixon's system might have worked better if multiple advocacy among senior advisers at the last stages had been encouraged and energized by the president instead of being discouraged and weakened. Despite paying lip service to the need for strengthening the role of the State Department and abortive efforts in that direction, essentially little was accomplished by way of enabling it to become a stronger participant in Nixon's foreign-policy system.[22]

Finally, of course, the performance of the centralized foreign-policy system of the Nixon administration depended on factors other than the inherent merits or defects of a formal options approach. Among these factors, relevant to the judgment whether as good or a better version of Nixon's NSC model can be institutionalized or utilized again in the future, is the fact that both Nixon and Kissinger were very special individuals. The successes and limitations of their NSC system may have depended as much, if not more, on them and on the accident of their collaboration as on the inherent utility of the organizational model they employed. Nonetheless, one can still hope that the review of the theory and practice of the formal options system in this chapter will be of help to those who have to decide how future presidents might organize their policymaking system.

Notes

1. A useful reminder that departments and agencies conduct a great deal of lateral coordination voluntarily and effectively on their own without hierarchical direction from the White House is contained in David Davis, *How the Bureaucracy Makes Foreign Policy* (Lexington, Mass.: Lexington Books, 1972).

2. See also the discussion in Chapter 8.

3. Richard M. Nixon, *U.S. Foreign Policy for the 1970s: A New Strategy for Peace* (A Report to the Congress, 18 February 1970, Washington, D.C.), p. 72.

4. A typical study might be assigned to the Department of State, which would convene a meeting of the interdepartmental group for (let us say) East Asia under the chairmanship of the assistant secretary of state for East Asian and Pacific affairs. Representatives of all other agencies concerned would attend, the work would be parceled out, and after several more meetings the finished policy study would be forwarded to the NSC staff for consideration by the Senior Review Group or another of the committees chaired by Kissinger. It would represent, at least in theory, a fully coordinated survey of options as developed by the entire government.

5. Nonetheless, it is stated that on occasion an agency would seek to ensure, as the price for its concurrence in a study, that its preferred option was contained in the paper and that the evaluation of options articulated the conflicting views of participating agencies.

6. In this chapter and elsewhere in this report, the terms "search," "analysis" (or "evaluation"), and "choice" are employed to refer to three essential functions in any policymaking system. The distinction between these three functions has been the focus of some of the most useful contemporary behavior theories of organizational decisionmaking. As usually employed by organizational theorists such as Herbert Simon, James March, Richard Cyert, and others, "search" refers to the processes of obtaining and sharing relevant information and identifying and inventing options; "analysis" (or "evaluation") refers to the processes of interpreting the significance of available information and evaluating the relative appropriateness of alternative options with reference to stated or alternative objectives and values; and "choice" refers to the procedures and decision rules followed in choosing from among the alternative options.

7. See, for example, Anthony Downs, *Inside Bureaucracy* (Boston: Little, Brown & Co., 1967), pp. 179-88.

8. Concern with this problem underlies one of the State Department's major reservations regarding the workings of the Nixon-Kissinger NSC system: "A critical element in the preparation of a satisfactory [NSC] study is a clear statement of the policy issue. Where this is lacking, options tend to become stereotyped and artificial rather than inviting a choice among genuine alternatives." Again, "it is important that the [NSC] study directive be as clear as possible in defining the problem, or set of problems, to be addressed. Otherwise, the interdepartmental working group may spend a great deal of time trying to formulate the scope and focus of the study" (Department of State Submission to the Commission on the Organization of the Government for the Conduct of Foreign Policy, February 1974, p. 45).

9. See, for example, N. R. F. Maier, *Problem-Solving Discussions and Conferences: Leadership Methods and Skills* (San Francisco: McGraw Hill, 1963).

10. Thus, among Irving Janis's suggestions for preventing Groupthink is the following recommendation: "After reaching a preliminary consensus about what seems to be the best policy alternative, the policy-making group should hold a 'second chance' meeting, at which every member is expected to express as vividly as he can all his residual doubts and to rethink the entire issue before making a definitive choice." (*Victims of Groupthink* [Boston: Houghton Mifflin Co., 1972], p. 219).

11. Quoted by Milton Viorst, "William Rogers Thinks Like Richard Nixon," *New York Times Magazine*, 27 February 1972.

12. Department of State submission, p. 45.

13. I. M. Destler believes that the failure to do so was one of the major deficiencies of the Nixon administration's organization of foreign-policymaking (*Presidents, Bureaucrats, and Foreign Policy* [Princeton, N.J.: Princeton University Press, 1972], p. 141). The creation of the planning and coordination staff in the State Department in 1969 was evidently not as successful in this respect as had been hoped. Moreover, the International Security Affairs Office in the Department of Defense, which played an important role in previous administrations, was allowed to become much weaker in the Nixon administration.

14. Wilfred L. Kohl, "The Nixon-Kissinger Foreign Policy System and

U.S.–European Relations: Patterns of Policy-Making," *World Politics* (October 1975).

15. Samuel C. Orr, "Defense Report/National Security Council Network Gives White House Tight Rein Over SALT Strategy," *National Journal* 3 (24 April 1971):881.

16. John P. Leacocos, "Kissinger's Apparat," *Foreign Policy* 5 (winter 1971-72):23.

17. Department of State submission, p. 45.

18. Kohl, "Nixon-Kissinger," drawing upon interviews with governmental officials, cites one of them as describing Kissinger's participation in these important committees as taking one or another of the following forms: (1) Kissinger knew what he wanted and argued for it from the outset, tending to dominate the group's deliberations unless taken on by another forceful personality who was sure of his arguments; (2) Kissinger remained "open" at the start whereas other agency representatives expressed strong views, in which case hybrid solutions generally emerged which Kissinger accepted as a consensus; (3) neither Kissinger nor others were sure of their ground at the beginning of the discussion of a new or unexplored policy issue and groped together for a position; and (4) everyone, including Kissinger, found it difficult to deal with the policy issue in question and, in effect, decided to put it aside.

19. Leacocos, "Kissinger's Apparat," p. 19.

20. According to the Kalbs, Richardson argued vigorously for an alternative NSC model that would have given the State Department the responsibility for coordinating foreign policy and for chairing the interdepartmental committees, reserving the NSC itself as an open forum in which senior officials would have an opportunity to influence the president's judgment and choice of policy (Marvin Kalb and Bernard Kalb, *Kissinger* [Boston: Little, Brown & Co., 1974], p. 88).

21. For example, Destler, *Presidents,* stressed the need to build "centers of strength responsive to the president in other parts of the foreign affairs government," that is, multiple centers of analysis and stronger staffs for departmental and agency officials who serve as advisers to the president and key figures in implementing his policies.

22. While the relative importance of the State Department in foreign-policymaking was, of course, enhanced when Kissinger moved from the NSC to the office of secretary of state, he does not appear to have made much effort to strengthen its institutional capability for playing a more important role. Kissinger did bring with him into the State Department many members of his NSC team and he was able, as secretary of state, to extend his direct use of State Department personnel.

11
Multiple Advocacy

We noted in the preceding chapter that many questions can be raised regarding the performance, as against the theory, of the formal options system. It is not easy to arrive at a well-informed, balanced, overall appraisal of the workings of the formal options system that was centered in the NSC during President Nixon's first term and continued, in part at least, after Kissinger became secretary of state. But even if the performance of the formal options warrants that it be continued in some form in future administrations, there would still be several reasons for considering alternative procedural models.

In the first place, it is doubtful that all future presidents and secretaries of state will want to rely as heavily on a formal options procedure as did Nixon and Kissinger. As noted in Chapter 8, the critical factor in a president's choice of a policymaking model is the personal style of decision-making he brings with him into the office. While Nixon (and Eisenhower before him) found a highly formalized NSC model preferable, other presidents have not. Indeed, variations in the personal styles and preferences of past presidents help to account for the zigzag in the degree of institutionalization and centralization of policymaking procedures under successive administrations, and in the degree of actual reliance upon them in making foreign-policy decisions. It is to be expected, therefore, that the personal preferences and styles of some future presidents and secretaries of state are likely to lead them to place far less reliance on a formal options system and to introduce different policymaking models. Some of them, we may expect, will prefer a more loosely coordinated, less formalistic way of conducting the search for effective policy. Or they may prefer to structure the advisory process to place greater emphasis on adversary proceedings, if not full-blown multiple advocacy, than did Nixon.

Besides, few presidents are likely to hew to but one way of making all of their foreign-policy decisions. Even Nixon and Kissinger departed from the formal options system on many occasions. And it may be re-called that the foreign-policymaking system they instituted called for a weak variant of multiple advocacy to be employed in the final stages of policymaking, when senior officials were to meet with President Nixon to discuss the formal options generated by the NSC system.

It behooves us, therefore, to consider other procedural models for achieving the necessary lateral and vertical coordination of efforts by the various departments and agencies concerned with foreign policy to col-lect and analyze information, to identify and appraise alternative op-tions, and to perform the advisory function for the chief executive. The formal options system is one way of attempting to cope with the serious impediments that the dynamics of organizational behavior and bu-reaucratic politics can introduce into the processing of information and the generation of options and their appraisal. Let us recall the principal features the formal options approach adopts for this purpose. It employs highly centralized management procedures to weaken and bypass some of the normal ways in which departments and agencies contribute to policymaking, and to rechannel their information, expertise, and judg-ment into well-defined and tightly controlled procedural "tracks" im-posed on the system from the presidential level. Thus, a formal options system attempts to order and "rationalize" the search for effective policy; it attempts to prevent latent or actual differences over policy from distor-ting or biasing "search" and "evaluation"; it attempts to "depoliticize" the expression of disagreements over policy within the executive branch, to reduce interpersonal and interagency clashes over policy, to discourage and repress efforts of individuals and agencies to employ bureaucratic resources, strategies, and maneuvers to influence the choice of policy.

Not surprisingly, the formal options system appeals to executives who are most committed to a "rational" and orderly approach to policy-making and who are most distrustful of a looser, competitive approach to policymaking. Other students of government, while also aware of the potentially dysfunctional effects of competitive internal processes, attach more weight to the potential advantages of a freer competition over policy within the executive branch. Moreover, they are concerned that much of the value of multiple viewpoints and disagreement over policy will be lost in a highly centralized, tightly controlled formal options system. In their view, disagreements over policy within the executive branch do not inevitably create abnormal strains that must be avoided in the interest of rational decisionmaking. Rather, they feel that the clash of opinion may help produce better policy *if* it can be managed and regulated properly.[1]

The present chapter outlines a policymaking system in which competition and disagreement among different participants is structured and managed in order to achieve the benefits of diverse points of view. The management model in question attempts to provide for a balanced, structured form of multiple advocacy. It should be made clear that achievement of the type of multiple advocacy outlined here is *not* left to the free play of internal organizational processes and bureaucratic politics; the top executive is *not* relegated to a passive role vis-à-vis the competitive struggle among his subordinates to define policy. Rather, the theory of multiple advocacy poses sharply defined requirements for executive management of the policymaking system. It requires considerable presidential-level involvement in that system. Strong, alert management must frequently be exercised in order to create and maintain the basis for structured, balanced debate among policy advocates drawn from different parts of the organization (or, as necessary, from outside the executive branch). As such, multiple advocacy encompasses but goes beyond what is usually meant by "adversary proceedings" or use of a "devil's advocate."[2]

Multiple advocacy is neither a highly decentralized policymaking system nor a highly centralized one. Rather it is a *mixed* system which requires executive initiative and centralized coordination of some of the activities of participants in policymaking. This management model accepts the fact that conflict over policy and advocacy in one form or another are inevitable in a complex organization. (Indeed, even the highly centralized system under President Nixon did not succeed in eliminating such disagreements, though it did not have a very effective way of utilizing such disgreements to supplement and improve the workings of the formal options system.) The solution it strives for is to ensure that there will be multiple advocates within the policymaking system who, among themselves, will cover a range of interesting viewpoints and policy options on any given issue. The premise of the model is that multiple advocacy will improve the quality of information search and appraisal and, thereby, illuminate better the problem the executive must decide and his options for doing so.

Requirements of the Model: Three Conditions

If a system of multiple advocacy is to function effectively, each participant must have minimal resources needed for advocacy, and certain rules of the game will be needed to ensure proper give-and-take.

A system of multiple advocacy works best and is likely to produce better decisions when three conditions are satisfied:

1. No major maldistribution among the various actors in the policymaking system of the following intellectual and bureaucratic resources:

   a. Intellectual resources
      1) Competence relevant to the policy issues;
      2) Information relevant to the policy issues;
      3) Analytical support (e.g., staff, technical skills);

   b. Bureaucratic resources
      1) Status, power, standing with the president;[3]
      2) Persuasion and bargaining skills.

2. Presidential-level participation in order to monitor and regulate the workings of multiple advocacy.

3. Time for adequate debate and give-and-take.[4]

The first of these conditions is a forceful reminder that *the mere existence within the policymaking system of actors holding different points of view will not guarantee adequate multisided examination of a policy issue.* Competence, information, and analytical resources bearing on the policy issue in question may be quite unequally distributed among the advocates. As a result, one policy option may be argued much more persuasively than another. There is no assurance that the policy option which is *objectively* the best will be presented effectively, for this requires that the advocate of that policy possess adequate intellectual resources.

Maldistribution of resources needed for advocacy can take many other forms. A marked disparity in the bureaucratic resources available to the advocates may well influence the outcome of the policy disagreement to a far greater extent than the intellectual merits of the competing positions. For example, an option put forward by an advocate with superior competence, adequate information, and good analytical resources will not necessarily prevail over an option advanced by an advocate who is less resourceful in these respects but operates with the advantage of superior bureaucratic resources or unusual persuasive skills.[5]

Implications for Presidential-Level Involvement

The potentially damaging effects on the policymaking process of maldistribution of the intellectual and bureaucratic resources relevant to effective advocacy pose some rather sharply defined requirements for managing the advisory system. There are three general tasks that the chief executive and designated staff aides will have to perform to ensure reasonably adequate forms of balanced multiple advocacy.

First, the executive may have to take steps if not to equalize resources among his chief advisors, then at least to avoid gross disparities in them.

Second, the chief executive and his immediate staff assistants in a given policy area must be alert to the danger that a sufficient range of policy alternatives may not be encompassed by those playing the role of advocates on a particular issue. In that event he may bring in outsiders or members of his own staff to serve as advocates for different interests or policy options.

Third, he may have to develop certain "rules of the game" to maintain due process for all advocates and fair competition among them, and to avoid "restraint of trade" among the advocates.

In brief, top-level authority in the organization — and at every lower level of decision making at which multiple advocacy is desired — has the task of maintaining and supervising the competitive nature of policymaking. Multiple advocacy does not just happen. The executive must want it and must take appropriate provision for securing it.

The NSC Special Assistant's Role as Custodian-Manager of the Policymaking Process

The president cannot be expected to personally carry out the three tasks identified previously as necessary for maintaining a system of multiple advocacy. Historically the responsibility for doing so has evolved to the executive secretary of the NSC, which was established in 1947. At the onset of President Eisenhower's administration, the position of executive secretary was strengthened and retitled as special assistant for national security affairs. While the range of duties and influence exercised by the incumbent of this position has varied under different presidents, the executive secretary/special assistant always has had major responsibility for ensuring that the foreign-policymaking apparatus effectively serves the president's special needs for information and advice.

Thus, from the inception of the NSC, the central role assigned to the executive assistant/special assistant has been what might be called "custodian-manager" of the procedures by means of which presidential-level national security policy is made. The role of "custodian-manager" has embraced a number of subtasks and functions, which may be described as follows:

1. balancing actor resources within the policymaking system;
2. strengthening weaker advocates;

3. bringing in new advisers to argue for unpopular options;
4. setting up new channels of information so that the president and other advisers are not dependent upon a single channel;
5. arranging for independent evaluation of decisional premises and options, when necessary;
6. monitoring the workings of the policymaking process to identify possibly dangerous malfunctions and instituting appropriate corrective action.

This "job description" of the special assistant's custodial functions is a composite of some of the most useful tasks performed on occasion by incumbents of the office. It seems useful to codify these tasks and institutionalize them as part of the duties of the special assistant, whoever he may be, in the future. In addition to his custodial functions, the special assistant's job has been broadened to include, from time to time, a number of additional major tasks.

The Special Assistant's Additional Roles and Potential Role Conflicts

Over time, since the inception of the NSC, occupants of the executive secretary/special assistant's position have assumed important roles in addition to that of custodian-manager. Such a trend has been particularly prominent since 1961. A list of the other activities assigned to or assumed by the special assistants from time to time includes the following functions or roles: (1) policy adviser-advocate; (2) policy spokesman; (3) political watchdog for the president's power stakes; (4) enforcer of policy decision; and (5) administrative operator.

To many observers it has seemed natural and inevitable that the special assistant for national security affairs should add one or more of these roles to his basic responsiblity as custodian-manager. Nor is this surprising, given the talents and personal qualities of some of those who have served as special assistant, their intimacy with the president, and the encouragement that he evidently has given them to participate more extensively in foreign-policymaking.

The acquisition of multiple roles, however, makes it likely that the special assistant will experience role conflict that will eventually undermine the effectiveness with which he performs his basic custodial functions. Once he becomes an adviser-advocate to the president as well as the custodian-manager, it will take a most exceptional person to continue to dispassionately oversee the flow of information and advice to the president; for to do so might well reduce his own influence as an adviser. Similar conflicts with his custodial responsibilities arise when the special assistant assumes the additional roles of policy spokesman and enforcer of policy. As a result, the special assistant may lack the incentive to encourage timely and objective reevaluation of ongoing policy, which is one of the custodian's responsibilities. As Thomas Cronin has observed, aides who might be able to fashion a fairly objective role in policy formation often become unrelenting lieutenants for fixed views in the implementation stage.[6]

Another role conflict is likely if the special assistant assumes the role of watchdog for the president's power stakes. As such, his concern for maintaining and enhancing the president's political influence is likely to interfere with the performance of his custodial responsibility for serving as an "honest broker" of information and advice.

The custodial role also can be undermined if the special assistant takes on important operational duties, such as diplomatic negotiations, "fact finding," and mediation. Not only are such activities likely to be time consuming, they may distract the special assistant from his duties as custodian-manager. Besides, once he is plunged into the role of administrative operator, the special assistant risks becoming personally identified with the "line" activities that he is pursuing, and this can interfere with his custodial responsibility for encouraging timely evaluation and review of ongoing policies.

In his detailed historical survey of the evolution and performance of the position of special assistant for national security affairs, David Hall finds considerable evidence that, beginning in the early 1960s, individuals serving in this capacity experienced appreciable role conflict. Hall also notes that the assumption of roles and functions in addition to those of the custodian-manager has overloaded the individual occupying this position. Both the phenomenon of role conflict and role overload became noticeable for the first time during the Kennedy administration with the assumption by McGeorge Bundy of additional roles and functions that his predecessors had not undertaken.

As noted already in Chapter 10, the role conflict and overload experienced by the special assistant were much accentuated in the Nixon administration. Not only did Kissinger's other roles—in addition to the basic one of custodian-manager—become more important than they had been in previous administrations; in addition, whereas McGeorge Bundy had moderated the potentialities for role overload by delegating and sharing his roles and functions with his senior NSC staff members, Kissinger was much more reluctant to do so.

The trend toward expansion of roles for the executive secretary/special assistant and the emergence of both role conflict and role overload are documented in David Hall's forthcoming study (see Table 2, prepared by Hall in summarizing his materials).

Table 2. Roles, Role Conflict, and Role Overload

	Custodian	Policy Adviser	Spokesman	Enforcer	Operator	Watchdog	Role Conflict	Role Overload
Souers (1947–1952)	YES ("neutral conduit")	YES (infrequently after 1950)	YES (infrequently, in private)	NO	NO	NO	NO (with minor exceptions)	NO
Lay (1950–1952)	YES ("neutral conduit")	NO	NO	NO	NO	NO	NO	NO
Cutler et al. (1953–1960)	YES ("active second guesser" on planning)	YES (infrequently)	YES (infrequently, in private)	YES (collective responsibility through OCB)	NO	NO (although Cutler campaign aide prior to terms as Sp. Asst.)	NO (with minor exceptions)	NO

Bundy (1961–1963)	YES ("active second guesser" on most issues)	YES	YES (particularly as background source)	YES	YES (from White House)	NO	YES	NO
Bundy (1964–1966)	YES	YES (with increasing frequency)	YES (increasingly visible)	YES	YES (from White House and overseas)	NO	YES (with increasing frequency)	NO
Rostow (1966–1968)	YES	YES	YES (highly visible)	YES (role diminished by SIG/IRGs)	YES (from White House)	NO	YES	NO
Kissinger (1969–	YES (unprecedented regulation with shaping inputs)	YES (chief adviser)	YES (chief spokesman)	YES	YES (from White House and overseas)	NO (though wiretaps & '72 campaign appearances raise doubts)	YES (often)	YES

Reproduced from Chapter 12 (of which David Hall is the author) in A. L. George et al., *Towards A More Soundly Based Foreign Policy: Making Better Use of Information*, p. 117.

This analysis is not carried beyond Kissinger's incumbency as special assistant. It will be recalled that when he became secretary of state, Kissinger retained for awhile his position as special assistant. Later, in response to increasing political criticism that Kissinger was allowed to wear two such important hats, President Ford appointed Kissinger's deputy, General Brent Skowcroft, as special assistant. In General Skowcroft's incumbency there was an appreciable shrinkage of roles and responsibilities and very little evidence of role conflict or overload; nor is this surprising since Kissinger was still secretary of state and was enjoying Ford's confidence and trust.

Upon becoming president, Jimmy Carter chose as his special assistant Zbigniew Brzezinski, a prominent academic specialist in international affairs and, what is more, one who was known to have pronounced views on foreign policy. It was made clear from the outset that Brzezinski would serve the president as a foreign-policy adviser as well as custodian-manager of NSC procedures, and that the president, Vance, and Brzezinski would work together as a team. Brzezinski announced that he would operate with restraint in his role as special assistant, thereby giving tacit assurance that he would not aggrandize the position as Kissinger had and would not in any way encroach on the prerogatives and responsibilities of the secretary of state, Cyrus Vance. With the passage of time, however, Brzezinski increasingly permitted himself to act as spokesman for Carter's foreign policy and as an occasional administrative operator. Whether this resulted in role conflict severe enough to distort Brzezinski's performance as custodian-manager it is not possible to say on the basis of available information. Neither is it clear whether Brzezinski also slipped into the roles of policy enforcer and "watchdog" for the president's personal political interests.

Particularly noticeable in the first half of 1978, as noted in Chapter 8, was that Brzezinski permitted himself to stretch his role as private adviser to the president to one of vigorous public advocacy on important foreign-policy issues having to do with the Soviet Union. On occasion he carried this to the point of tacit disagreement with the secretary of state. This ceased quite abruptly in mid-1978 when, it would seem, President Carter intervened, perhaps at Secretary of State Vance's request, to constrain Brzezinski from speaking out on foreign-policy issues in ways that differed from and undercut the secretary of state.[7]

The Executive's Role as "Magistrate"

In addition to balancing actor resources and maintaining the rules for effective multiple advocacy, the executive must consider how to define his own role. When making use of multiple advocacy, the executive should adopt the stance of a magistrate—one who listens to the arguments made, evaluates them, poses issues and asks questions, and finally judges which action to take either from among those articulated by advocates or as formulated independently by himself after hearing them. There are also some things the executive must *not* do since they would undermine the workings and utility of multiple advocacy. Thus, he should not convey policy preferences of his own or offer a particular definition of the problem or of the situation as he sees it that may constrain the options the group of advisers will consider or tilt them in the direction he seems to favor. If necessary to avoid this, the executive should absent himself from early meetings of his advisory group.

The magistrate role is of central importance to effective multiple advocacy. It is only because a magistrate presides at the apex of the policymaking system that a constructive, disciplined form of multiple advocacy can be assured. The presence of a magistrate, together with the rules and norms he imposes on the policy debate, means that the controversy among the advocates is not one which they must resolve somehow by themselves (as would be the case in a fully decentralized bargaining system that lacked an authoritative leader). Rather, the advocates in this system are competing for the executive's attention and are seeking to influence his judgment, at his insistence, via analytic arguments.

Emphasis on Disciplining Advocacy through High-Quality Analysis

Multiple advocacy does not attempt to eliminate partisanship, parochial viewpoints, and bargaining. Rather, it attempts to strengthen the analytical component of these familiar features of internal organizational politics. As systems analysts have suggested, analysis can usefully moderate bargaining processes and improve the quality of the debate.[8] To this end, multiple advocacy not only encourages competitive analysis, but, at the executive's insistence, it also forces the "partisan" analysis offered by the advocates to meet high standards. To ensure this, the executive needs to maintain a competent analytical staff of his own and use it in such a way as to evaluate and discipline the analyses offered by advocates in support of their positions.

As this implies, in his role as magistrate the executive and his staff aides do not passively accept the arguments of the advocates or simply decide in favor of the strongest coalition of advocates. Rather, the executive's central position, his own resources, and his ultimate responsibility give him the opportunity to force advocates to meet higher standards of analysis and debate. The executive's position also imposes on him the obligation to evaluate the relative merits of competing positions and, when necessary, to decide against the majority of his advisers. In order to discharge these responsibilities, the executive who employs multiple advocacy will require a strong, independent, analytically-oriented staff such as that of the NSC.

Selective Use of Multiple Advocacy

This is not to say that multiple advocacy must be used on every occasion; rather, it would have to be employed selectively and with some degree of flexibility. From time to time the executive will find it desirable to initiate policy advocacy himself, particularly when departmental officials do not become advocates for certain policy options that deserve serious consideration either because they do not attach high enough priority to them or perceive departmental disadvantages in those options. Presidential-level initiatives from time to time, then, are part of the "balancing" that is required to achieve more effective policymaking.

Even an executive who generally favors multiple advocacy will be well advised to bypass it as a vehicle for policymaking on occasion. Time constraints may not permit it; or some of the other costs and risks of multiple advocacy may make it inadvisable in certain situations. One can only hope that the executive will exercise good judgment in dispensing with multiple advocacy on occasion and will forego the temptation to do without it simply because he believes he already knows what the best policy is in a particular situation. We must deal in this connection with the observation that multiple advocacy would invariably be "bad advice" and "unwelcome" to an executive who already knows what he wants to do and regards his chief problem to be that of getting acceptance and understanding of his decision on the part of subordinates and those who would have to implement it. Certainly there will be many occasions on which an executive must, if necessary, eventually impose his policies on other actors in the executive branch.

Two observations, however, are relevant. First, the question remains whether the executive's preferred policy option is the most effective and desirable one. It may indeed be "unwelcome" but not therefore "bad advice" to an executive who already "knows what he wants to do" to expect of him that he subject his initially preferred options to serious scrutiny and debate. One can hope that a president will see that it is to his advantage to avoid reaching premature closure in his own mind as to the best course of action until the policymaking system — whether via multiple advocacy or other means — has generated sufficient information and appraisal of options to illuminate the issue and the choice that he must make. Certainly the final choice of policy has to remain with the president. Most everyone, however, agrees that he should have real alternatives from which to choose. It is not only other actors in the policymaking system who, when bureaucratic politics works badly, can narrow and delimit the president's choice; the president himself can deprive himself of genuine alternatives and an opportunity for a reasoned choice.

Second, even when the executive is confident from the beginning that he knows what the best course of action is and is concerned only with the task of imposing his policy and ensuring its implementation, it may still be useful as time permits to go through a process of multiple advocacy. This will enable those who favor another course of action to be heard and the executive and his supporters an opportunity to articulate the reasons for favoring their course of action and opposing alternatives. Policy discussion of the president's preferred course may result in marginal improvements of that option. And if properly managed, the policy debate can enhance understanding of the basis for the executive's preferred option. Finally, allowing everyone to be heard can facilitate acceptance of the decision.

Some Caveats

As do all other prescriptive theories for organizing policymaking, multiple advocacy, too, has practical limits and costs attached to it.

In the first place, the executive's receptivity to multiple advocacy is of course critical. This way of structuring the advisory process around himself is likely to suit the style and temperament of some presidents (and other officials who make lower-level policy at departmental and agency levels) more than others. Multiple advocacy is a poor prescription for a president who, as Nixon did, finds it quite uncongenial to his cognitive style and working habits. Some executives find it extremely distasteful, disorienting, and enervating to be exposed directly in face-to-face settings to the clash of opinion among their advisers. In addition, they may be reluctant to listen to the persuasive effort of any determined advocate, even in a private setting in which no other advocates are present, for fear of being swayed in favor of or against his position by nonrational considerations.

Such executives prefer a depersonalized presentation of the arguments for and against different options, either in writing or as presented orally by a neutral staff assistant. Insofar as multiple advocacy is acceptable to them, they can tolerate and benefit from it only if the element of interpersonal conflict is removed altogether from the development and presentation of options to them, or at least from the presentation. If sharp interpersonal disagreement among his advisers is altogether anathema to an executive, then he will have little confidence in or receptivity to multiple advocacy in any form. He is likely, then, to prefer some variant of a formal options system to any advocacy. If his personal antipathy to evidences of policy conflict among his advisers is less extreme, he may still be able to benefit indirectly from multiple advocacy that spares him face-to-face exposure to it. Thus, he may be willing to allow a trusted surrogate or alter ego to attend in his place meetings at which multiple advocacy takes place. Or he may be willing to read and benefit from written, well-prepared presentations submitted by advocate-advisers.

In the second place, multiple advocacy is not a panacea that can ensure high-quality policymaking. The content and quality of policy decisions is determined by many other variables — for example, the ideological values and cognitive beliefs of the policymakers and other factors discussed in Part 1. The way in which policymaking procedures are organized — whether via multiple advocacy or according to some other procedural model — often may make little difference so far as the substance and quality of decisions is concerned. It would be naive and misleading to suggest that any particular policymaking model can guarantee "good" decisions in every or even most instances. Rather, the case for multiple advocacy must rest on the more modest expectation that it will help prevent some very bad decisions and should generally improve the quality of information processing and appraisal. Thus, for example, when there are competing values and a variety of beliefs within the circle of policymakers around the executive, the procedure of multiple advocacy is more likely than a highly centralized policymaking system to secure critical examination and weighing of these values and beliefs before they are permitted to influence choices.

Third, an effective system of multiple advocacy is not easily achieved in practice. It is not easy to recruit able persons for all the senior positions in the policymaking system and to ensure that they will acquire and know how to use the intellectual and bureaucratic resources needed to become effective advocates. And, in any case, having the resources for advocacy does not ensure that the actors will actually engage in advocacy of all the options that need to be considered. They may avoid advocating options which run counter to the bureaucratic interests of their departments and agencies. They may decline to raise unpromising options, even if they believe in them, for fear of ending up on the "losing side" too often, thereby losing "influence" or tarnishing their "reputation" or expending limited bargaining resources in fruitless or costly endeavors.

Quite obviously, then, the policy system has to be designed and managed to give participants a stake in insuring multiple advocacy. Some things can be done to reduce to tolerable proportions the tendencies noted above. These would include selective recruitment of persons for senior positions, socialization of incumbents of these positions into their roles, management of incentives, and selective employment of multiple advocacy for problems and circumstances less likely to arouse these inhibitions. The executive (and surrogates charged with managing the policymaking system) must define the norms of the working of the advisory system in a manner consistent with the requirements of multiple advocacy. There is more latitude in defining policymaking norms than might be imagined: witness the widely different norms and role definitions for his advisers that Kennedy introduced into the policymaking group in the Cuban missile crisis as against the earlier Bay of Pigs. (See also Chapter 12.)

Even though the requirements for effective multiple advocacy are not easily or consistently achieved, knowledge of them on the part of the executive is useful. Such knowledge can sensitize him and his staff to defects in the way the policymaking process is operating when important decisions are being made. It can alert the executive and/or his chief staff assistants to the emergence of one or another of the procedural "malfunctions" in the advisory process that were noted in Chapter 6 and thereby encourage some appropriate balancing or remedial action. In any case, multiple advocacy need not work perfectly in order to be valuable. In some cases even a modest amount of multiple advocacy may suffice to highlight considerations that would otherwise be neglected or improperly appraised. In judging multiple advocacy one must compare it with some alternative system, not with an ideal standard. No policymaking system looks very good when compared with the ideal.

Fourth, it must be recognized that for an executive to submit to multiple advocacy may sometimes entail costs that he would rather avoid incurring. Thus, the time required for the give-and-take among advocates may on occasion impose undue delays on decisionmaking. Or competition and conflict within the advisory circle may occasionally get out of hand, strain the policymaking group's cohesion, and impose heavy human costs. Then, too, cast into the role of advocates, officials may be quicker to go outside the executive branch in search of allies for their internal policy disputes. This may encourage "leaks" and create political difficulties for the executive in his relations with Congress and the public; he may feel that the weakening of his control over final decisions outweighs on occasion the benefits he gets from multiple advocacy. There is no denying that multiple advocacy entails costs and risks which may be onerous and difficult to live with from time to time. But similar costs and risks are present in any but the most highly centralized policymaking system and were not altogether absent even in the centralized, formal options system of the Nixon administration. Besides, efforts to avoid and minimize some of these costs and risks, as the experience of the Nixon administration has demonstrated, lead to serious costs and risks of a different kind.

Fifth, since the executive is overburdened and cannot be expected to monitor and manage the system of multiple advocacy himself, he would have to delegate that task to one or more of his staff aides. The question arises whether a senior presidential assistant would have enough leverage to maintain and supervise the competitive nature of policymaking that is inherent in the system of multiple advocacy.[9] There is considerable historical experience that bears on this question, though it is certainly not easy to draw definitive conclusions. Insofar as all presidents beginning with Harry Truman have made use of multiple advocacy to some extent, or from time to time, they have generally relied upon the executive assistant or, as later retitled, the special assistant for national security affairs, to serve as "custodian" of the policymaking process. It seems clear that if the president turns to such an assistant to maintain and supervise multiple advocacy, he will have to provide the "custodian" with a strong presidential mandate and continuing support for his efforts to impose the procedures and norms of multiple advocacy upon departmental and bureau officials who participate in foreign-policymaking.

Notes

1. Support for this view also is available in some experimental laboratory studies of the performance of problem-solving groups. Under certain conditions, the presence of disagreement within the group has been found to have a positive impact on its problem-solving activity. Internal disagreement produces this effect by improving the quality of information processing and appraisal. Thus, the effect of internal disagreement within the group may improve the quality of "search" and "appraisal." See Joseph L. Bower, "The Role of Conflict in Economic Decision-making Groups: Some Empirical Results," *Quarterly Journal of Economics* 79 (May 1965):263-77. Empirical evidence in support of the view that *properly managed* conflict, such as in a system of multiple advocacy or in adversary proceedings, has a positive effect on information processing has been reported in a number of other studies as well. In a recent Ph.D. dissertation at Harvard University, Roger Porter presents evidence of the favorable workings of a form of structured, managed multiple advocacy in the Economic Policy Board during the Nixon administration. See also Henry Assael, "Constructive

Role of Interorganizational Conflict," *Adminstrative Science Quarterly* (December 1969); John Thibaut and Laurens Walker, *Procedural Justice* (Hillsdale, N.J.: Erlbaum Associates, 1975); Harold J. Leavitt and Louis R. Pondy, eds., *Readings in Managerial Psychology*, 2d ed. (Chicago: University of Chicago Press, 1973), p. 538; and Jay Hall, "Decisions," *Psychology Today*, November 1971. These and other studies are discussed in the forthcoming Ph.D dissertation by David K. Hall.

2. The concept of "adversary proceedings," which is often recommended for incorporation into policymaking procedures, is borrowed from the judicial system. What the exponents of adversary proceedings in policymaking generally have in mind is that explicit provision be made that any policy recommended by staff or subordinates to the top decisionmaker be subjected to critical scrutiny by someone other than those who advocate that policy. Thus, Task Force VII, "Stimulation of Creativity," of the State Department's *Diplomacy for the 70s*, notes that "the lack of a system for subjecting policy to the challenge of an adversary view" has been "a major weakness in the department's organization" (p. 294). However valuable this suggestion, it clearly falls short of a system of multiple advocacy.

3. This includes a number of different things that determine the degree of influence and bargaining advantages that an advocate can muster vis-à-vis other advocates and the president himself: (1) the formal and traditional responsibilities accruing to the incumbent by virtue of the office (e.g., secretary of state, secretary of defense, etc.); (2) access to and standing with the president and other senior officials and the ability to use their confidence and trust as a bargaining asset; (3) responsibility for implementation of policies decided upon, which amplifies one's voice in policymaking; and (4) the ability to go outside the executive branch to secure powerful allies in Congress, among foreign-policy specialists, and in the media.

4. The time pressures of international crises are likely to strain the workings of multiple advocacy even while making such advocacy more important than ever for obtaining a balanced, multisided examination of options. The range of effects that crisis-induced stress can have on information processing is discussed in Chapter 2.

5. This risk can be easily enhanced by personality factors. Individuals with hyperconfident, domineering personalities often rise to high levels in the advisory system. Once such individuals become convinced of the merits of a policy option, they can be exceedingly persuasive and forceful in selling it. The impact on the group's deliberations and on multisided analysis of options can be harmful if not countered by skillful balancing.

6. Quoted in A. L. George, "The Case for Multiple Advocacy in Making Foreign Policy," *American Political Science Review* (Sept. 1972):782-83.

7. The best single source on Brzezinski's performance as special assistant for national security affairs during the first sixteen months of the Carter administration is the profile "A Reporter at Large: Brzezinski," by Elizabeth Drew, *The New Yorker*, May 1978, pp. 90-130. See also Don Bonafede, "Brzezinski—Stepping Out of His Backstage Role," *National Journal*, 15 October 1977.

8. See, for example, Henry S. Rowen, "Bargaining and Analysis in Government," and William Capron, "The Impact of Analysis on Bargaining in Government," both in Louis C. Gawthrop, ed., *The Administrative Process and Democratic Theory* (Boston: Houghton Mifflin Co., 1970), pp. 31-37; 354-71. See also Alain C. Enthoven and K. Wayne Smith, *How Much is Enough?* (New York: Harper & Row, 1971.

9. This question was raised and argued forcefully by I. M. Destler ("Comment: Multiple Advocacy: Some 'Limits and Costs'," *American Political Science Review* [September 1972]:786-90) and rebutted in the same issue by A. L. George. Further discussion has resulted in clarification and convergence of their views, as reflected in Destler's statement in his article, "National Security Advice to U.S. Presidents: Some Lessons from Thirty Years," *World Politics*, January 1977. Recognizing the possibility of serious role conflict if the special assistant is given too many responsibilities in addition to those of custodian, Destler believes that sufficient additional leverage could be provided the special assistant by limiting him to the additional tasks "of managing the President's daily foreign policy business and over-seeing policy implementation, especially on issues of particular Presidential concern." (p. 171). Thus, in the latest formulation of his views, Destler does *not* advocate allowing the special assistant to play the roles of expert-adviser on foreign policy, policy-spokesman, watchdog of the president's personal political interests, or administrative-operator.

The question whether the special assistant will have sufficient "leverage" to perform the duties of "custodian-manager" if not assigned additional responsibilities and roles is examined in detail on the basis of relevant historical experience by David K. Hall in his forthcoming study.

12
The Collegial Policymaking Group

In Part One we noted that impediments to information processing may spring from the narrowness of perspective and interest often displayed by departments and agencies. Moreover, they tend to deal with new situations unimaginatively and inappropriately by drawing upon their standard repertoires of acting, and they frequently resort to the self-serving stratagems and maneuvers of "bureaucratic politics." Accordingly, it is not surprising that presidents have attempted to structure and manage the policymaking system so as to minimize the adverse impact of such behaviors. Several of the organizational models they have employed for this purpose were described and evaluated in chapters 10 and 11. And, as noted, the special assistant for national security affairs, in his role as custodian-manager, may undertake to balance actor resources and maintain a competitive relation among various advocates.

But neither the formal options system, multiple advocacy, or a strong and resourceful special assistant can provide a reliable safeguard against all of the impediments generated by the division of responsibilities and the bureaucratic organization of functional expertise within the executive branch. A president must necessarily draw upon heads of departments and agencies for information and specialized judgment. So long as these advisers adopt the narrow, specialized perspective of their own departments and participate in policymaking as highly partisan advocates, the president's dependence on them entails important risks that neither a system of balanced multiple advocacy nor the formal options procedure may be able to compensate for. The formal options system, it is true, attempts to do away with or seriously weaken partisan advocacy; but it, too, will encounter difficulties if leading departmental officials approach problems of foreign policy from a narrow perspective reflecting the functional expertise of their own agencies. The formal options system will encounter this difficulty particularly in crisis situations when the elaborate procedures on which it depends tend to break down, necessitating reliance on ad hoc policymaking or special committees such as Nixon's Washington Special Actions Group (WSAG).

Fortunately, "formal options," "multiple advocacy," and the "devil's advocate" do not exhaust the devices available to the chief executive for ameliorating the narrowness of perspective of departmental and agency officials. Many if not all of these senior departmental officials are, after all, cabinet and subcabinet appointees. If he chooses wisely, a president can place at the head of these functional departments and agencies individuals with the kind of personality, intellect, and experience that will lead them to maintain sensitivity to the dictates of the broader national interest even while discharging their responsibility to exert leadership of their agencies and to provide an effective voice for agency viewpoints in higher policy councils.

Indeed, cabinet officials are expected to bridge and reconcile presidential and departmental perspectives; and certainly they are strategically placed to undertake the task of mediating the conflicting imperatives of the White House's overall view of foreign-policy matters and their own department's expertise. But it does not always work out in this way. Caught in the middle and subject to conflicting demands and pressures, cabinet-level and subcabinet officials may seek to avoid the ensuing dilemma by leaning heavily in one direction or the other, or by behaving erratically. There is no assurance, therefore, that his appointees will succeed in achieving what the chief executive often needs most from them—namely, their help in bridging presidential and departmental perspectives. However carefully a president attempts to select his appointees to these positions, some of them will resolve the role conflict their position places them in by becoming loyal "president's men," at the cost of weakening their ability to provide leadership and representation for their own departments; others will come to identify largely with the specialized perspective of their own agencies.

A chief executive must, of necessity, find other ways of encouraging senior officials to retain a broader perspective alongside their identification with the department and/or agency for which they are responsible. A variety of procedures is available for this purpose. The president may set into motion policy-planning procedures that encourage critical, broad-gauged consideration of all of the relevant—and often competing—factors: political, diplomatic, economic, and military. Ad hoc interagency task forces can be set up for this purpose, staffed by personnel from the various departments who are known to be capable of taking a broad problem-oriented approach and for dealing with policy issues analytically rather than via interagency bargaining.[1]

There is much that a president can do to establish a similar climate in his top-level policy discussions with senior departmental officials. He can structure and define the roles of his top-level departmental advisers in order to discourage them from perceiving themselves as partisan advocates or functional experts. In encouraging them to broaden the perspective with which they view policy problems, he can make it clear at the same time that he does not wish them to abandon the valuable identification with agency viewpoints or to weaken their ability to draw upon the expertise of their particular departments.

For various reasons, a more loosely structured and not overly formal milieu — the collegial model of policymaking that was described in Chapter 8 — makes it easier for most participants to free themselves, and to encourage others to do likewise, from the constraints of organizational doctrines and from the tendency to overprotect the special interests of their subunits and constituencies. Particularly because these inhibitions and constraints tend to be implicit and deeply ingrained, they can easily stifle creative imagination and novel ways of looking at new policy problems.

It is particularly important to dissolve these constraints when foreign-policymakers are faced with novel situations which should not be responded to by drawing upon standard responses from the organization's repertoire.[2] To cope adequately with such challenging situations it is often necessary for the chief executive to make a special effort to rearrange the milieu and norms for the policymaking group so that they are able to ask questions at variance with the ideology and policy doctrines of the organization as a whole or of those of its subunits which they represent. This is difficult to achieve when the quest for an effective policy response proceeds within the context of a bureaucratically structured process of policymaking.

The possibility for fruitful restructuring of advisory roles and the introduction of new norms to guide policy deliberations was strikingly demonstrated by President Kennedy in the Cuban missile crisis. The lessons he and his close associates had drawn from his inept management of the policymaking group in the Bay of Pigs case were quickly put to use in improvising a quite different approach to crisis decisionmaking when they were suddenly confronted in October 1962 by Khrushchev's deployment of missiles into Cuba. Many questions arose for U.S. policy that required integrated evaluations from political, diplomatic, and military standpoints. The president immediately created a special ad hoc group of advisers from different branches of the government to consider the implications of the missile deployment for U.S. security interests and to identify, develop, and evaluate alternative courses of action for his consideration. This group came to be called the Executive Committee (Ex-

Com) of the National Security Council.

As has been emphasized in all available accounts, Kennedy quickly established a modus operandi and ground rules for the deliberations of the ExCom that greatly facilitated performance of the critical "search" and "analysis" phases of policy analysis before the final "choice" was made. The emphasis on "final" here calls attention to the fact that search and analysis were not separated bureaucratically or sequentially from the task of choice. Those who engaged in search and analysis also participated in thrashing out the choice; and an iterative approach to problem solving was employed, so that rehearsal and debate over choice were allowed to have a feedback for renewed search and analysis. (For additional discussion of the utility of an iterative approach and "decision rehearsals," see Chapter 10.) Moreover, the inept leadership practices Kennedy had displayed in managing the policy discussions that led to his Bay of Pigs decision were replaced by a much more sophisticated set of techniques for conducting policy discussions on what to do about the missiles in Cuba.

In Chapter 4 we noted various aspects of the structure, internal processes, and management of small decisionmaking groups that can create impediments to information processing. Kennedy's way of structuring and managing the ExCom in the missile crisis eliminated these troublesome features of group decisionmaking. The ExCom was given the character of an informal problem-solving group that was to concern itself with all relevant aspects of the problem. Each member of the group was encouraged to concern himself with the policy problem as a whole rather than to confine himself to that element of it — be it intelligence, military strategy, international affairs, diplomacy — on which he was an expert or for which he or the office to which he belonged was officially responsible. This mode of policy deliberation enhances the role of the "generalist" and gives him more scope for interacting with specialists and challenging their expert opinions. Though the importance of the generalist has often been emphasized by experienced policymakers, the role does not appear to be well defined or to have received much formal attention in studies of group problem solving. We need not see the ideal generalist as one who is broad-gauged without being, or having been, an expert of some kind. Even the expert can take the role of generalist on matters not within his expertise. The essence of the generalist's role is to ask the questions his very ignorance, naivete, and different perspective allow him to ask of experts, questions that might never occur to the experts or whose relevance would not be evident to them until pointed out.

As the detailed accounts of the missile crisis indicate, the meetings of the ExCom were marked by considerable give-and-take. Protocol was suspended. Second-level officials were encouraged to give their views even when they were at variance with those of superiors who were present. The president was encouraged by some of his close associates to absent himself from meetings when it was found that the process of mutual exploration of views was freer and more productive without him. Most participants are reported to have changed their positions at least once during the course of the six days prior to the president's final decision on a course of action.

The fact that time was available before the president would have to act and that secrecy was preserved proved to be highly useful. Time permitted the ExCom to pursue an iterative approach to its problem-solving task, which facilitated mutual education and made it possible for the group to close in on the critical facts on which the final choice of action depended.

The ExCom obtained specialized inputs on political, military, and diplomatic questions from functional and technical experts at lower echelons of the executive branch. Thus, the ExCom acted as an informal steering group for bringing to bear the best knowledge and analytical capabilities available in the more specialized branches of the government. The iterative approach to policymaking permitted an increasingly sharper edge to be put upon requirements for specialized inputs. But perhaps the major contribution the collegial mode made to effective policymaking was to maintain a broad perspective in which all relevant considerations could be identified, and the relationships among them kept in mind in devising and assessing alternative courses of action.

A collegial policymaking group has important advantages in dealing with broad policy problems over models in which participants reflect more closely the characteristic organizational features of hierarchy, specialization, and centralization. In the ExCom case, though the collegial model probably operated at something approaching optimal performance, it did so for reasons that may not always be present. Nonetheless, it deserves study so that we might understand what these special factors were and judge whether and how they might be replicated on future occasions.

To sharpen appreciation of these features let us compare the collegial style with an extremely bad variant of the formal bureaucratic model.[3] Planning and decisionmaking in this deliberate caricature are highly structured, expertise is compartmentalized along narrow functional lines, and system operation is highly formalized. Information and judgment on each of the relevant elements of the policy problem up for decision are provided the chief executive solely by the recognized functional expert on that element. Role playing is narrow and inflexible, and there is no devil's advocate. Further, the chief executive makes no provision for having the functional experts engage in a genuine dialogue in order to explore the problem as a whole and to examine the interrelationships among its elements. A formal procedure is followed by obtaining each expert's judgment on his portion of the problem—a judgment, it is presumed, that others are not competent to question. Each actor may also be asked for his overall judgement, but he gives it without having understood or studied the problem as a whole and because he is aware that he has not understood, he tempers his conclusions and holds to a conservative, even sterile, view.

Because there is little or no use of an iterative approach to problem solving in this process, the experts have no opportunity to revise their judgments. Further, the highly structured, compartmentalized approach casts each adviser in the role of spokesman for his group. This forces the participants to resort to bargaining and superficial compromises rather than to utilize analytic procedures as a means of dealing with disagreements over policy. A heavy if indeed not impossible intellectual burden is ultimately placed upon the chief executive and his immediate personal staff in attempting a blend or synthesis of the many elements of the problem. This variant of the bureaucratic model, therefore, fails to meet the critical challenge in problem solving, namely, analysis of the relationship of the various parts of the problem to one another, and of the relationship of the parts to the whole.

In sum, the collegial approach to problem solving strengthens the analytic component and reduces the influence of the bargaining component. It does so by restructuring the roles of special advocates, enhancing the role of the generalist vis-à-vis the functional experts, providing for interactive policy analysis, and introducing new norms for the process of deliberation.

However, as noted in Chapter 8, not every president will find the collegial approach to policymaking congenial. Even when a president's cognitive style and personality, as in John F. Kennedy's case, is a good "fit" with the collegial approach, he must still meet exacting requirements in order to establish and maintain an effectively functioning policymaking group of this kind. The risks associated with Kennedy's attempt to do so and his uneven success with this approach are noted by Richard T. Johnson in his perceptive study of presidential management styles.[4] The collegial approach not only requires unusual skill in interpersonal relations, it also demands a great deal of energy and attention from the president. When this is not forthcoming, a collegial system "tends to coast." Worse, as in the Kennedy administration's decisionmaking on Vietnam in October 1963, which led to the coup against Diem, the collegial policymaking group can disintegrate and split irretrievably into factions, thereby forcing the president to improvise an alternative policymaking approach.[5]

The conclusion to be drawn, however, is not that efforts to utilize a collegial approach to organizing and managing a policymaking group should be abandoned. After all, every management model must meet difficult requirements of one kind or another and is subject to malfunctions. Familiarity with the special requirements and latent difficulties of each model should assist a president and his advisers to make more effective use of whichever model he chooses to employ, and it may lead him to make more flexible and judicious use of different models at different times.

Notes

1. Francis M. Bator, who served as a specialist on economic policy in the NSC under Kennedy, has argued the merits and advantages of properly constituted ad hoc interdepartmental groups over formal standing committees, such as those that operate within the NSC structure. Ad hoc groups should be staffed, he says, by a small number of people "who are senior enough to marshall the resources of their agencies; not so senior as to make it impossible for them to keep up with detail, or spend the time needed for comprehensive and sustained exploration of each other's minds. . . ." Bator also stresses the critical mediating role that members of these ad hoc groups must play: thus, they should be "close enough to their secretaries and to the president to serve as double-edged negotiators (each operating for his secretary in the task group bargaining, and in turn representing the group's analyses of the issues and choices to his secretary)." He speaks also of the need for "constant and collegial interaction" among the members of a task group (Congressional Hearings before Committee on Foreign Affairs, "U.S. Foreign Economic Policy: Implications for the Organization of the Executive Branch," 20, 22 June; 25 July; 2 August; and September 1972). Bator's views are endorsed and elaborated in Graham T. Allison, ed., *Adequacy of Current Organization: Defense and Arms Control*, vol. 4, Appendices, Commission on the Organization of the Government for the Conduct of Foreign Policy, June 1975 (Washington, D.C.: U.S. Government Printing Office, 1976), pp. 33-35.

2. Relevant here is the distinction between "structured" and "unstructured" policy problems developed by Victor Vroom and Philip Yetton, *Leadership and Decision-making* (Pittsburgh: University of Pittsburgh Press, 1973), pp. 20-31. They cite empirical evidence that indicates that "unstructured" problems are better dealt with by decisionmakers within the framework of a less centralized network that permits and encourages interaction and exchange of information among subordinates—i.e., a "circle" policymaking similar to the collegial model.

3. While the description presented here is a deliberate exaggeration of all the worst features of a narrow, formalistic policymaking group, quite a few of these

features can be seen in the way in which some important foreign-policy decisions have been made in the past—for example, in the way Truman structured and managed the Blair House meetings when the decision to intervene unilaterally on behalf of the South Koreans was made in late June 1950, and once again in the way in which Kennedy organized and conducted the series of policy meetings leading to his approval of the Bay of Pigs invasion.

4. Richard T. Johnson, *Managing the White House* (New York: Harper & Row, 1974), Chapter 5; pp. 236-38.

5. Ibid., pp. 148-49. A fuller case study of the disintegration of Kennedy's collegial group in policymaking leading to the coup against Diem in November 1963 is presented in John Rogers, "In Pursuit of Survival: Presidential Leadership, Advisory Groups, and Decision-making" (Senior Honors Thesis, Political Science Department, Stanford University, June 1976).

13
The Concept of National Interests: Uses and Limitations

Alexander L. George
Robert O. Keohane

Foreign-policy problems, as was emphasized in Chapter 2, typically engage a multiplicity of competing values and interests, so much so that policymakers often have great difficulty in attempting to reduce them to a single criterion of utility with which then to judge which course of action is "best."[1] In principle, the criterion of national interest, which occupies so central a place in discussions of foreign policy, should assist decisionmakers to cut through much of this value complexity and improve judgments regarding the proper ends and goals of foreign policy. In practice, however, national interest has become so elastic and ambiguous a concept that its role as a guide to foreign policy is problematical and controversial. This chapter examines some of the reasons for this development and points to ways in which the concept can be clarified in order to strengthen the guidance it can give to foreign-policymakers.

An inquiry of this kind is especially pertinent in the current post–Cold War era. There is now substantial consensus among American leaders and public alike that the United States allowed itself to become overcommitted and overextended as a result of the Cold War and that henceforth American foreign policy must be guided by a more differentiated, discriminating analysis of the extent to which its interests are engaged by developments elsewhere in the world. Expressing agreement with this view, President Nixon stated in 1970 that his administration felt it necessary to reexamine U.S. commitments around the world "to see that they are consistent with our interests." His report to Congress on foreign policy that year underscored this point: ". . . Our interests must shape our commitments, rather than the other way around." On this and other occasions, most notably when he promulgated what came to be known as the Nixon Doctrine, the president signaled the intention of his administration to apply a more differentiated assessment of U.S. national interests with respect to commitments to help defend allies and weak neutrals than had been done during the height of the Cold War.

Criterion or Justification?

The concept of national interest continues to be important to foreign-policymakers despite its limitations as a theoretical and scientific concept.[2] They have used the concept in two different ways: first, as a *criterion* to assess what is at stake in any given situation and to evaluate what course of action is "best"; second, as a *justification* for decisions taken. Particularly with respect to the latter use of national interest there is reason to be uneasy and dissatisfied.

Admittedly, the task of justifying decisions has become increasingly important with the rise of public opinion and the remarkable changes in communications technology in the last century. Foreign policy is now conducted in a much more open environment than used to be the case, and the public's demand for an "instant history" of what is taking place and why a particular decision was made has created unusual pressures on leaders to explain and justify all of their important decisions and actions. It is not surprising that, under these circumstances, the national interest tends to become a somewhat shopworn part of the political rhetoric of every administration and at times a psychological crutch for leaders who become locked into disastrous policies.

Many thoughtful observers of foreign policy would readily agree that the national interest concept does indeed lend itself much more readily to being used as political rhetoric for legitimizing decisions and actions than as an exact, well-defined criterion for enabling policy officials to determine what those policies should be. But it is possible to be too cynical about this. For it is by no means the case that national interest has been without value to conscientious policymakers who were determined to set reasonable objectives, to judge carefully what was at stake in particular situations, and to act prudently in any given situation.

The surpassing need for a superordinate criterion such as the national interest is evident. Foreign-policy issues typically engage a multiplicity of values and interests which are often difficult to harmonize. Not only is much at stake, but the various values imbedded in the policy problem often pull the decision in different directions. In addition, uncertainty clouds the decisionmaker's judgment as to the benefits to be expected and the likely costs/risks of each of the options he has under consideration.

Under these circumstances it is understandable that the decisionmaker should attempt to apply the criterion of national interest in an effort to cut through the problem of value-complexity and to cope with the uncertainties affecting choice among alternative policies. A conscientious effort to consider the overall national interest can help to alleviate the psychological malaise an executive experiences in making difficult decisions of this kind. He can justify the ensuing decision both to himself and to others as one based on careful consideration of the national interest. However, the intellectual guidance the national interest criterion actually gives the decisionmaker in dealing with complex issues is another matter. It is of some importance to understand why this is so.

In the first place, national interest has the characteristics of what decision theorists refer to as a "nonoperational goal"; it does not provide a measuring rod for comparing alternative policies.[3] National interest is similar in this respect to concepts such as the general welfare and the public interest. Such concepts cannot be employed as a utility function in rigorous policy analysis. They can be related to specific choices of action only through consideration of the subgoals to which they are presumably related. Thus, national interest encompasses a variety of subgoals that compete for influence in the conduct of foreign policy. But there is lacking an operational common denominator for dealing with these subgoals. Hence, the relative weight to be given to various subgoals is a matter left to the authoritative (but subjective) judgment of top-level officials.

The limitation of the national interest concept was obscured in an earlier era by simplistic but influential arguments to the effect that national power is the supreme goal of national action. But power is, clearly, only one subgoal of national interest, and an instrumental goal at that, rather than a fundamental value in and of itself.

Other limitations of the national interest concept as a criterion of policy will emerge more clearly if we recall the historical transformation through which the international system has passed. The concept of national interest goes back several centuries and is associated with the emergence of the nation-state in the sixteenth and seventeenth centuries. The idea of national interest, or "raison d'état" as it was called, appears to have played a significant role at times in the determination of policy in the classical system of diplomacy before the French Revolution. As E. H. Carr puts it, "The essential characteristic of the period was the identification of the nation with the person of the sovereign."[4] The national interest was therefore unitary and relatively simple to determine, since it was considered to be merely the interest of the ruler.

With the "democratization" of nationalism, however, the relative simplicity of the concept of "raison d'état" was eroded, and the state itself came to be seen as composed of different interests. In the era of liberal democracy, "L'état, c'est moi" was no longer an acceptable answer to the question of sovereign legitimacy. The national interest came to reflect a weighing of various diverse interests within the state, held together, somewhat tenuously at times, by the doctrine of nationalism. It therefore became a more amorphous concept, as different groups within the polity competed to claim it as a legitimizing symbol for their interests and aspirations, which might by no means be shared by many of their compatriots.

With the transition from the laissez-faire to social service state after 1914, the character of the national interest changed further. More groups saw their interests affected by foreign policy, as foreign policy expanded much more deeply, and explicitly, into the realm of economics. Increasing numbers of individuals and groups asserted interests in, and claims upon, what foreign policy should be. It became less and less convincing to speak of the state as possessing superior interests of its own that were largely independent of, and transcending, those of its subjects and citizens. Thus, the scope of national interest was broadened appreciably, even in contrast to the situation prevailing during the nineteenth century.

Moreover, the traditional distinction between "foreign" and "domestic" policy has badly eroded during the past several decades. It has become commonplace now to observe that the most important problems of national policy, such as those having to do with energy, food, inflation, and trade, have both domestic and foreign implications. It is no longer possible for the federal government to deal with one dimension of one of these problems—either its foreign or domestic aspects—without careful attention also to the other dimension. As a result, the concept of national interest, if it continues to be utilized in determining foreign policy, must encompass the interface between the domestic and foreign sides of the policy issue in question.[5]

The calculation of national interests has therefore become far more complicated and more unpredictable than it was in the simpler system of classical diplomacy. As a result, some modern analysts have gone so far as to conclude that it is not useful to think in terms of an overarching national interest and that what we mean by the concept is simply whatever emerges from the policymaking process. However appealing this conclusion may be to academic authors concerned with precise definitions and clear delineation of empirical from value-laden terminology, it is hardly likely to satisfy policymakers, who need some reference point for comparing conflicting interests and coming to a judgment.

Is there, then, some way of salvaging the concept of national interest and strengthening the guidance it can give in the formulation of foreign policy?

Values and Interests as They Affect Foreign Policy

It is important to notice at the outset that the concept of national interest is heavily value laden. Interests can be seen as applications of values in context: values applied in the light of situations as they appear to people involved in them. As used by policymakers, the phrase "national interest" implies a choice among values standing behind those interests. Insofar as the concept of national interest is to be useful as a criterion for policy, it must specify some means by which leaders can determine which values, and therefore which interests, are to be included, and which excluded, from the set of national interests.

We shall attempt here to distinguish different types of national interests as a means of clarifying what the term may mean. Later in this chapter we will use these distinctions as a basis for arguing that different decision rules should be used to determine what to do when different types of national interests, broadly defined, are at stake.

Our first distinction turns on the question of whose interests are principally involved in a given situation. *Self-regarding interests,* for a state, refer to the attainment, preservation, or extension of benefits accruing to the state and its citizens. Preservation of the lives, liberty, and property of a given state's citizens are "self-regarding" from the viewpoint of that state. *Other-regarding interests,* by contrast, refer to benefits that accrue primarily to other states or their citizens, although action on their behalf may bring indirect and intangible benefits to a country's own people (as in the feeling of self-esteem one may feel on giving money to charity). *Collective interests* differ from both other types in that, as with collective goods, one cannot clearly separate benefits to oneself from those to others. All people in the world may benefit (although perhaps unequally) from preservation of a healthy atmosphere or a viable oceans environment; within a somewhat more restricted area, all may benefit from maintenance of an orderly world economic system and arrangements to assure adequate global food supplies.

Frequently the concept of national interest is used only to refer to self-regarding interests. Some advocates carry this view one step further when they contend that self-regarding interests must always be given priority over other-regarding ones, or even over collective interests. In time of extreme danger, when the autonomy of a government and the lives of its people are at stake, a strong argument can be made for doing this on the principle that the government has particular responsibility for the welfare of its own citizens. In a "war of all against all" it is every state for itself.

Most periods of history, however, are not properly characterized as "wars of all against all," with relative equals ranged against one another. Indeed, more characteristic of international politics is a situation of great inequality—inequality of power among states, and of welfare and living standards between populations of different countries. To argue a priori that self-regarding interests must always be given priority over other interests is not morally tenable. It would be difficult, for instance, to uphold, on moral grounds, the imposition of export quotas on American grain, for the sake of keeping beef prices lower in the United States, if the effect were to produce starvation in citizens of India or Chad. Trade-offs will necessarily have to be made between values, and in general, one can expect self-regarding interests to be given preference, in practice, over other-regarding ones; but it is not acceptable simply to assume that the values encompassed by national interests should have priority over all others.

The other important distinction for the concept of national interest rests on the seriousness of effects to the nation as a whole, to other nations, or to the international system of a given set of events. Frequently, for instance, claims are made on foreign policy by individuals and groups who assert that the intensity of adverse effects to their private interests necessarily implies that the national interest as a whole is involved. The weight these subnational claims have, as well as their legitimacy, needs to be carefully evaluated; it may be found that despite their seriousness to particular interests, from the viewpoint of the nation as a whole they are relatively minor.

Analysts using the concept of national interest for policy prescription have frequently found that much of its usefulness for them lay in allowing them to make and to dramatize precisely this distinction.[6] They have argued that while many different values are engaged by foreign-policy issues, it is not useful to regard even all self-regarding values, and the interests in which they are expressed, as essential to a concept of "vital" or irreducible national interest. Since power and will are both limited, the goals of foreign policy—and therefore the values such a policy seeks to promote and preserve—must also be limited.

These two distinctions cut across one another, so that six possible categories of state interests can be derived from them. Table 3 indicates the relationship of these various state interests to one another.

It should be clear that in order to pin down and delimit "irreducible national interests" we have differentiated this type from other kinds of interests that may lay legitimate claim to influencing a nation-states foreign policy. We do *not* thereby assert that only irreducible national interest should influence foreign policy but, rather, that it is desirable to sort out the other kinds of interests in addition to irreducible national interests having to be weighed in the formulation and conduct of foreign policy.

Table 3. Types of National Interests (for the United States)

Scope of Interests Principally Affected	Seriousness of Effects:	
	Major	Minor
United States	basic-self regarding ('irreducible national interests')	secondary self-regarding
International System Collectively	basic collective	secondary collective
Other States and/or their citizens	basic other-regarding	secondary other-regarding

It should also be clear from Table 3, in conjunction with the argument above, that the notion that "interests" should determine policy is incompletely specified until we know which types of interests are being referred to and what weights they are to be given. Furthermore, apart from "basic self-regarding national interests," no clear lexicographic ordering or these types of interests can be given. For reasons explicated above, it would not be justifiable to give self-regarding interests (however secondary) automatic priority over collective or other-regarding interests. In each case, the intensity of the interest needs to be considered along with the special degree of responsibility that a government has to defend the interests of its own citizens. No easy shortcuts are available.

If we cannot simply seize upon the national interest as a sound and reliable guide to policymaking, what use can be made of the notion? We attempt to answer this question in two steps. In the next section, we articulate our view of basic self-regarding national interests, attempting carefully to delimit these strictly. We refer to these as "irreducible national interests." In the following section, we discuss the different types of decisionmaking processes that should be followed, in our judgment, when irreducible national interests and other interests are at stake.

Irreducible National Interests

We consider in this section only self-regarding interests, and we take the standpoint of the United States, with its particular constitutional system, as one point of departure. Our first step is to distinguish "basic" from "secondary" self-regarding interests. Such distinctions among values are to some extent inherently arbitrary, but the familiar triad of "life, liberty, and property" (the last of these in the broad sense of economic well-being) provides a good place to start. We therefore identify three fundamental values, to which the term "irreducible national interests" seems appropriate. They are:

1) *Physical survival.* This refers to the survival of the country's citizens, not necessarily to the preservation of the territorial integrity and sovereign independence of the state. In an era of thermonuclear weapons, this value is, of course, always in jeopardy.

2) *Liberty.* Liberty here refers to the ability of inhabitants of a country to choose their own form of government and to exercise a set of individual rights defined by law and protected by the state. For the United States, liberty can be regarded as referring to preservation of the "democratic way of life." Liberty, unlike physical survival, is a matter of degree. Irreducible national interests are therefore best regarded not as including all claims to liberty, but more narrowly to the preservation of a significant degree of national autonomy and the maintenance of a nonarbitrary structure of laws.

3) *Economic subsistence.* Governments have always regarded it as vitally important to preserve the ability of their people to feed, house, and clothe themselves. This is once again a minimum definition as befits a notion of irreducible national interests. Maximizing economic welfare is generally a goal of governments, except insofar as other considerations interfered (as they often do); but it could hardly be considered part of an *irreducible* national interest to increase per capita income from, say, $4000 to $5000 per year. In times of great international stress, such as wars, it is economic subsistence at which governments aim. Economic welfare beyond subsistence is frequently sacrificed to other ends, such as maintaining liberty or ensuring physical survival against attack.

There was substantial agreement within the United States for many years after World War II that these three fundamental values—or irreducible national interests—should shape the basic purposes and objectives of American foreign policy.[7] At the same time, there was also sharp and persistent disagreement over the substance of foreign policy during this era. Quite obviously, the implications of even these irreducible national interests for foreign policy are not self-evident. There are several reasons for this, and it is instructive to inquire into them.

The first to be noted is that a value trade-off dilemma between precisely these irreducible interests can be experienced when important foreign-policy choices have to be made. A forced choice between physical safety and "liberty," for example, or between physical safety and economic well-being is difficult and often painful. Most American foreign-policymakers have felt, and continue to feel, that no one of these three irreducible interests should be subordinated to the others, or sacrificed or endangered in order to assure the other two. Shrewd management of foreign policy and good judgment are necessary to avoid drifting into (or inadvertently creating) situations in which a choice may have to be made between physical survival, liberty, and economic well-being. How to avoid this choice, on the other hand, has been the source of considerable controversy within the United States, which has periodically shaken the foreign-policy consensus.

Let us recall how this dilemma manifested itself during the Cold War and how it is generally dealt with by American policymakers. In each successive administration since World War II, whether Democratic or Republican, top-level officials agreed in perceiving *two primary threats* to these irreducible national interests. One of these perceived threats was, of course, the spread of international communism. The other was the danger of World War III. It was the objective of U.S. foreign policy to avoid *both* of these threats. On occasion American officials defended a particular policy (for example, economic and military aid) on the ground that it contributed both to preventing the spread of communism and the danger of World War III. But circumstances at times created a conflict between these two objectives, and when this occurred, or threatened to occur, policymakers were confronted by a difficult dilemma. For to take active steps to support the defection of a member of the Communist bloc could—as in Hungary in 1956—increase the risk of World War III. And, on other occasions, to adopt policies that would reduce the risk of a thermonuclear holocaust—as by accepting the overrunning of South Korea in 1950 without intervening militarily in its defense—could facilitate the spread of communism.

A major task for U.S. foreign policy during the Cold War, therefore, was to find a reasoned and reasonable basis for coping with the dilemma of deciding to which objective to give priority in situations in which the desire to curb the spread of communism clashed with the desire to avoid actions that significantly raised the risk of World War III. The general answer to this policy dilemma took the form of an effort to invoke the "balance of power" as the critical factor for determining which of the two competing objectives to adopt and which corresponding risk, therefore, to accept. In the minds of U.S. policymakers, the balance of power consideration meant that no adversary or *potential* combination of opponents should be permitted to gain *sufficient power* to impose their purposes upon the United States in a manner as to *jeopardize* its irreducible national interests. Quite obviously, this criterion could provide only a loose framework within which calculation of the national interest could be made. What constituted "sufficient power" in the hands of a "potential combination" of opponents that could "jeopardize" irreducible national interests could not be easily operationalized and measured. Nonetheless, the criterion served to structure and focus the judgments that had to be made. Thus, if a Communist success in a given area were thought by U.S. policymakers to be capable of seriously undermining the political and economic power of the non-communist world to contain the spread of international communism, then presumably the balance of power itself was at stake, and hence it could be argued that some risk of World War III had to be accepted in order to take action to thwart Communist success in that area. The converse of the argument also presumably applied.

The balance-of-power guideline lent itself reasonably well to attempts to resolve policy dilemmas having to do with Western Europe but encountered serious difficulties and generated much greater controversy when it was stretched to conflicts in other geographical arenas. It was much less plausible to argue that the overall balance of power and, therefore, our irreducible national interests, were really jeopardized by local communist or anti-Western successes in other parts of the world. Nonetheless, efforts to do so were made (even though it required analogies such as "row-of-dominoes" to make them more plausible) and were partly successful, at least so long as the costs of policies based on such premises were not excessive.

The difficulty of dealing with the trade-off between these three irreducible national interests is compounded by the fact, discussed earlier in this chapter, that national interest is a nonoperational goal which does not provide a measuring rod for comparing alternative policies. Hence, the weight to be given each of the three irreducible interests rests on the judgment of top-level foreign-policy officials and ultimately, of course, upon the president. The extent to which each of the irreducible interests needs to be furthered by means at the disposal of national-policymaking is not easily determined or agreed upon; nor, once determined and agreed upon, is the relative weight to be accorded them in the allocation of policy resources stable and fixed over time. Rather, it is subject to recalculation and adjustment to new circumstances. At the same time, the fundamental judgments of these matters, on which foreign policy is based, cannot be subject to constant reconsideration. Foreign policy must have a certain stability and continuity, and this, of course, invites the possibility that earlier judgments of threats to irreducible national interests and appropriate policy responses to meet them will be rendered obsolete by new developments. Yet, as was noted in Chapter 3, policy beliefs tend to persist in the face of discrepant information that challenges their validity and appropriateness.

Finally, the fact that national interest is a nonoperational goal encourages the tendency for particular subgoals of foreign policy with which departments and agencies identify to replace a broader, more balanced conception of what the national interest requires. Thus, parochial conceptions of the national interest are often advanced by different actors within the executive branch, each of whom tends to see the problem from the special perspective of his own department or agency. Often sharply competitive with each other, parochial conceptions of the requirements of foreign policy add to the internal struggle to define policy and become part of the dynamics of organizational politics that were discussed in Chapter 5.

The Irreducible National Interest and Other Interests

The strict notion of irreducible national interests that we have presented can be seen as an attempt to introduce discipline and restraint into the formulation of foreign policy. Specifying the components of the irreducible national interest makes it more difficult for other interests and values to be "smuggled" under the legitimizing umbrella of the term "national interests." Furthermore, including only *minimum* objectives of physical survival, liberty, and economic subsistence eliminates the objection, discussed above, to preferring self-regarding to other-regarding interests. If the irreducible national interests are fundamental as well as self-regarding, there is little reason not to give them priority.

Have we then solved the problem of national interest as a guide to policymaking? Hardly. What we have done is to delimit irreducible national interests strictly enough that a strong case can be made for giving them priority in foreign policy; but the very strictness of our definition means that many important foreign-policy situations will arise in which these irreducible national interests will not come into play. The concept of irreducible national interest becomes a useful tool of analysis only by explicitly acknowledging that as a guide to foreign policy it is incomplete.

We therefore need to consider the other types of state interests classified in Table 3 and the problem of deciding which objectives related to these interests to pursue. How should we go about doing this?

Recall that the chief *function* of the concept of national interest is to specify a means by which policymakers can make disciplined choices among interests and therefore among policy alternatives. Our concept of irreducible national interest has done this, for a limited set of situations, by specifying three criteria for judgment. This has only been possible, however, because the criteria were specified so strictly that problems of trade-offs with other, excluded, values did not arise. We could assume that the values included in the concept of irreducible national interest had priority. Where questions of trade-offs at the margin among scores, or hundreds, of different interests and values are involved, specifying unambiguous criteria for choice will be a hopeless task. Yet, if no standards, and no consistent procedures, are applied to determine what interests are to be pursued, and with what means, ideology in its worst forms can exercise undue influence. Vague and potentially dangerous notions of America's "world mission," or of the "battle against communism" may override careful and prudential judgment of values, interests, and policies.

It seems to us that one way out of this dilemma would be to specify a set of procedures, or "decision-rules," that policymakers would need to follow in order to assure the legitimacy of their actions. These decision-rules would not constitute formal or constitutional requirements, but if Congress, the press, and the public took them sufficiently seriously, the requirement that they be complied with would put real contraints on executive policymakers. The consultation procedures that our suggested decision-rules would require, furthermore, might lead to less hasty and better considered policy, thus saving the policymakers themselves from costly errors.

National-policymakers would retain full freedom of action, under the Constitution, for actions that were strictly necessary to safeguard irreducible national interests, as delimited above. In cases of serious threat to the basic values of physical survival, liberty, and economic subsistence (strictly defined), the use or threat of force could be sanctioned even if carried out unilaterally so long as the decisions were made in a careful and sober way, as discussed in the last two sections of this chapter. But the farther one went from irreducible national interest—in the direction of collective, other-regarding, or secondary national interests—the stronger the inhibitions on unilateral action would become. Congress, the public, and the press could be expected to become very sensitive to unilateral actions involving force on behalf of these interests.

Where the use or threat of force is contemplated, a carefully articulated fit between the interests threatened and the actions taken would be required. Employment of sanctions or coercive threats, at least beyond a certain threshold, might be excluded entirely for secondary national interests on the grounds that these could be sacrificed at less cost than they could be preserved through war. To protect basic collective interests, or basic other-regarding interests, however, a case could sometimes be made for using force, as in the widely discussed hypothetical "strangulation" by the OECD countries through a systematic oil boycott. In such a case, we would suggest as a *procedural requirement* for using sanctions agreement on action by an appropriate multilateral body, which fully represented the governments whose interests were supposedly threatened. This body could be either a pre-existing organization or an ad hoc multilateral forum; but it would have to be genuinely representative.

This does not mean that the United States would have to use force at the discretion of that body. On the contrary, the procedure that we suggest is meant as a *multilateral check* on the use of force rather than encouragement to it. Were our procedure to be accepted, Congress would exercise its supervisory role over foreign policy partly by asking the procedural question: have foreign-interested parties been consulted, and have they consented? Even if American executive officials wanted to employ sanctions to secure what they considered to be important collective or other-regarding interests, they would have to secure the consent of such a multilateral body, unless Congress, after serious deliberation, waived the principle. The *presumption* would be that unilateral actions, using force to secure alleged collective or other-regarding interests, would be illegitimate.

This procedure would strengthen self-discipline in foreign-policy decisionmaking where the use of force or other sanctions was involved and where self-regarding interests alone could not justify such drastic measures. Its rationale is clear: If it is not just American interests that are at stake, and if crucial American interests are not at stake, it is rather arrogant for the United States to use force (allegedly on behalf largely of others) unilaterally. From a policy point of view, although this procedure would be legally weak and not binding, it would at least legitimize the question to decisionmakers: "Why don't you secure the consent of other interested parties, particularly our allies, for your proposed action?"

To those who regard the suggestion as unduly restrictive or even utopian, we point out that a process similar to the one we suggest actually took place in 1954, with (temporarily) beneficial results. The Eisenhower administration at that time was considering military intervention in Indochina, but was informed by the Democratic congressional leadership that it could only support such action if the British consented. The British government was opposed to contemplated military measures, and largely as a consequence—in conjunction with opposition by General Ridgway and others within the American government—the project was abandoned. Here the multilateral check idea, while not hamstringing the U.S. government, forced it to consider the views of cooler, less committed governments before acting.

On the other side, it could be argued that the multilateral check is really no check at all. After all, the United States did secure support for its policies in Southeast Asia from a variety of Asian governments at Manila in 1966; and it could perhaps again secure the assent of assorted clients for misguided militaristic policies. Surely there is merit in this criticism: No formula or organizational device can protect the republic against bad judgment by all or almost all of its leaders. What our proposal would do is merely to *create a standard of legitimacy* that public figures opposed to military action could refer to in order to force wider and more dispassionate consideration of the problem. If Congress and the public were satisfied with the approval of a collection of dependent governments, there is little that any organizational device could do to prevent a multilateral check from becoming a sham.

The notion of a multilateral check may help to some extent to resolve a contemporary dilemma of American foreign policy: how much, and with what degree of self-confidence, to be involved in the world? The military and political events of the last decade, particularly in Southeast Asia, have taught us the need to be more modest about the quality of our own judgments and more restrained in pursuing grandiose military activities involving high moral, economic, and political costs. This had led some observers to suggest that the United States should withdraw to a great extent from the affairs of the world—which is what a strict definition of "irreducible national interests," *taken as the sole guide to foreign policy*, might imply.

This lesson, however, is in conflict with what the political-economic events of the last decade suggest: that economic interdependence is growing and that various international economic systems, such as the money-banking system and the petroleum-supply system, on which the United States depends, require active maintenance and periodic revision. There is strong evidence to suggest that to avoid system breakdown in a variety of areas, leadership from the United States will need to be forthcoming—and this means leadership that does not demand that every sacrifice on our part yield a direct and immediate benefit.[8] It is true that the United States might well be able to achieve its irreducible national interests in a world in which international economic cooperation had broken down.[9] But it would be a much poorer world, and the effects on millions of less fortunately placed people would be disastrous. To rely on the concept of irreducible national interest alone as a means to introduce discipline into our foreign policy would be to make the United States government powerless to affect developments that may determine the destiny of millions of the world's people during the next decade, and eventually its own fate as well.

The notion of a *multilateral check* on the use of force, as developed briefly in this paper, could meet the demands for self-discipline without destroying a number of essential collective and other-regarding values which, in our judgment, the United States ought to pursue. The policy could be consistent, however, not only with restraint but leadership. Positive action by the United States, in crucial political-economic areas, is not likely to be effective without considerable confidence not only in United States–supported policies but in American willingness to consult others as situations and policy requirements change. Self-restraint, through a multilateral check, in the use of force would help to engender such confidence and thereby contribute to the efficacies of policies in political-economic areas for which force was neither required nor desirable.

These ideas have been set forth with the intention of beginning a set of discussions about how one could develop more elaborately detailed procedures for dealing with situations where irreducible national interests were not involved. Even in the simpler situation where those interests are at stake, however, problems arise in applying the concept. Presumably, similar problems would arise, perhaps in more severe form, where collective, other-regarding, or secondary national interests were at stake. In the final sections of this chapter, therefore, we turn to problems of interpreting the national interest and of operationalizing it in crisis situations.

The Impact of Beliefs About the Opponent and the International System on Interpretations of the National Interest

Efforts to apply national interest as a criterion in policymaking have been complicated not only by the intrusion of ideological values, but also by the play of other considerations. Foremost among these are the policymaker's image of the opponent, his view of the nature of the conflict with the opponent, and his beliefs about the character of the international system. Such beliefs and images directly influence the policymaker's perception of threats to the national interest and his evaluation of what is at stake in different situations and what actions are necessary to safeguard the national interest.

Beliefs of this kind, as was noted in Chapter 3, are indispensable for enabling the individual to orient himself to a complex and often cloudy reality. But it is important to recognize that they often perform this function at the expense of simplifying and exaggerating important aspects of the situation. Moreover, once formed, such beliefs tend to be stable; they are not easily falsified or altered by new information that challenges their validity. Thus, beliefs about the opponent and the nature of the international setting often assume the role of axioms which guide and constrain policy-making. Their role in information processing and appraisal can be particularly important, but also questionable, when policymakers struggle with decisions characterized by great value-complexity and informational uncertainty. It is particularly tempting in these circumstances to fall back on stereotypic, simplified images of the opponent and axiomatic beliefs about the nature and imperatives of the continuing conflict.

Many thoughtful observers have come to the view that the Cold War was exacerbated and needlessly prolonged in part because of mutual misperceptions and exaggerated distrust and fears. During 1946-48, U.S. beliefs regarding the nature of the conflict with the Soviets hardened, primarily as the result of the way in which Soviet actions towards Iran, Greece, and Turkey were perceived. U.S. leaders came to feel that Soviet leaders were more hostile and were pursuing more ambitious objectives than had been thought to be the case. The first of these new beliefs was that the United States and Soviet Union were no longer limited adversaries but the relationship between them was one of acute conflict resembling a *"zero-sum"* contest.

The second new belief that emerged among U.S. leaders was that the international system was becoming, and necessarily had to become, increasingly *polarized*. Thus, according to this view, other countries who were not with us were not necessarily against us, but they were in danger of being coopted and absorbed into the enemy camp. Accordingly, in order for the United States to contain and frustrate Soviet ambitions, it had to organize and assume leadership of a Free World network of interlocking alliances.

The third new belief was that the international system was *highly unstable*. The different geographical parts of the world arena were seen as being tightly "coupled," so that a setback in one locale could have strong repercussions in other areas—a kind of "billiard-ball" effect, or what later came to be called the danger of a row-of-dominoes.

These new beliefs about the nature of the international system importantly reshaped American perceptions of threats to the national interest and the resulting requirements for foreign policy:

1. They led American policymakers to place a higher value on preventing distant areas, normally of peripheral interest, from coming under the control of anti-western elites, local communists, or the influence of major communist powers. American leaders were persuaded to commit the United States to the defense of West Berlin, to come to the defense of South Korea when it was attacked by the North Koreans, to undertake to maintain non-communist regimes in Indochina, and to risk war with

Communist China in order to help the Chinese nationalist regime to retain control of the Quemoy and Matsu islands, lying only a few miles off mainland China.

2. Those new beliefs about the international environment of the late 1940s encouraged a proliferation of U.S. commitments to defend weaker countries, a development which eventually led to criticisms that the United States had overcommitted itself and had assumed the role of "world policeman."

3. This set of beliefs encouraged a homogenized rather than a differentiated view of what U.S. interests were at stake in different parts of the world. This stood in sharp contrast with the normal practice of statesmen to make differentiated assessments of developments elsewhere in the world from the standpoint of vital, secondary, and tertiary national interests.

4. They also encouraged a belief in the "interdependence" of all U.S. commitments. As a result, American leaders came to feel that the failure of the United States to honor and implement effectively any one commitment would weaken the credibility of all other commitments and, hence, "invite" further communist challenges to other parts of the Free World.

5. Finally, these new beliefs about the international environment led U.S. leaders to rely almost exclusively on the policy of deterrence via military strength to influence the actions, policies, and attitudes of communist opponents. Left largely unused were the panoply of other means that statesmen normally employ for moderating the conflict potential in relations with other countries.

Problems of Operationalizing
the National Interest in Crisis Situations

When situations arise elsewhere in the world that pose a threat to American interests, policy makers face the task of estimating the character and magnitude of the expected damage to the national interest in order to fashion an appropriate response. This is what is meant by the task of operationalizing the national interest in a crisis situation. That is, policymakers attempt to determine just what is at stake in terms of the national interest in order to decide what level of cost and risk the United States should be prepared to accept in fashioning a response to prevent, undo, or limit the expected damage to its interests.

But it is often extremely difficult to assess the expected damage to U.S. national interests in a crisis situation, and there are various reasons for this. (1) The event may be wholly unexpected and shocking—a sudden military attack on a weak ally, the seizure of an American vessel, the overthrow of a friendly government, etc. (2) Information on what has happened may be incomplete, of uncertain reliability, or inaccurate. Is it a full-scale attack or a border clash? Was the friendly government overthrown by groups hostile to the United States? etc. (3) Limited time may be available to assess the information and to estimate its implications for national interests before having to decide on a response. (4) The crisis may generate strong emotions in policymakers themselves as well as among the public, generating psychological and political pressures for strong action to defend American interests.

Moreover, what has been called "value extension" (discussed in Chapter 2) often occurs in a crisis. Personal interests and political values other than those associated with safeguarding the national interest may intrude into the motivations and incentives of the decisionmaker and his advisers. Their perception of what is at stake may be colored by sensitivity to domestic political considerations, by the feeling that they are personally challenged in some way by the opponent's action, by the feeling that their ability to maintain effective power to govern or to get reelected will be affected by how they respond to the crisis. Depending on circumstances, additional considerations of this kind may lead policymakers either to exaggerate or downgrade what is at stake so far as national interest is concerned.

Optimal processing of available information in crisis situations can be impeded in other ways as well. Under the impact of emotional stress and the pressure of inadequate time and information, policymakers may fail to define the *magnitude* of the expected damage to the U.S. national interest. Instead, perceiving that American interests are jeopardized in some way, policymakers are impelled to act to prevent or minimize such damage. Consensus among policymakers on the objective of preventing damage to U.S. interest in crisis situations is often readily attained. But, for various reasons, it may be substantially more difficult for them to subject their agreement on taking some action to the test of a sober, realistic calculation of its costs and risks.

What level of cost and risk should be acceptable in responding to crises in which U.S. interests are being threatened or damaged? It is not possible to give a reasonable answer to this critical question if policymakers fail to estimate and to "bound" the magnitude of the expected damage to the U.S. national interest entailed by the events in question. Rational calculation and choice of policy requires not merely the selection of an objective; it also requires that a *value* be placed on that objective. How much is the objective worth? How valuable is it to prevent damage to U.S. interests in the situation at hand? To answer this question, however, requires policymakers to estimate the magnitude of the expected damage to U.S. interests. Only by doing so can they establish a ceiling on the level of costs and risks they are willing to accept, if necessary, in return for efforts to achieve that objective.

What we are calling attention to is the fact that, particularly in stressful crisis situations, a kind of generalized, unfocused consensus within the policymaking group on the "need for action to defend U.S. interests" can quickly emerge which can seriously impair rational decisionmaking. The fact that in a crisis atmosphere policymakers spontaneously agree upon the *desirability* of protecting endangered U.S. interests may in fact serve to discourage adequate discussion of the *feasibility* of doing so. The question of the level of costs and risks that would be commensurate with what is thought to be at stake is left unanswered. And, as a result, policymakers tend to drift into an open-ended commitment of incremental actions.

Impediments to optimal information processing of this kind characterized the policymaking discussions that accompanied Truman's decision to intervene militarily on behalf of South Korea in late June 1950. The decision may or may not have been the right one; in any case, one can hardly regard the way in which it was made as a model of policymaking. The president announced his determination to act at the outset, and this dominated the ensuing policy discussions. It served to discourage those advisers who were noticeably unenthusiastic about military intervention from articulating the reasons for their reluctance. Moreover, latent disagreements within Truman's policy group regarding the value of the objective of defending South Korea did not have an opportunity to emerge clearly enough to influence policy calculations. As a result, the expected costs and risks of a successful defense of South Korea were calculated in a most casual way and, not surprisingly under these circumstances, what it would take to turn back the North Koreans was grossly underestimated.

In the Korean case and in other crisis situations as well, policymakers have displayed a distressing tendency, not always successfully controlled, to slide into an open-ended commitment to absorb whatever costs and risks that may be entailed, and to engage in wishful thinking that clouds perception of the difficulty and costliness of the intervention that is set into motion. It is particularly when everyone seems to agree on the need for some action to prevent expected damage to the national interest that the most dangerous mistakes in policy calculation can occur. The typical error under these circumstances is a gross underestimation of the costs and risks of the action taken. Conversely, *disagreement* within the decisionmaking group on the proper objectives, the appropriate means, the kinds and level of risk present in the situation, is more likely to improve the quality of information processing and the advice that precedes final choice of policy by the president.

Thus, vigorous multiple advocacy within the Eisenhower administration in the Indochina crisis of 1954 helped to control the psychological impediments to rational calculation noted above and to arrest the initial momentum for U.S. military intervention during the Dienbienphu crisis. The expected damage to U.S. national interest was "bounded" in this case and, of particular importance, the price tag for a successful defense of Indochina was soberly calculated. A realistic cost-benefit judgment of the utility of American military intervention was then possible, and the president could make a reasoned decision against involving U.S. military forces. In the last analysis, the expected damage to U.S. interests that had earlier seemed a compelling reason for intervention was placed in calmer, more sober perspective. It was not, after all, of overwhelming importance to U.S. national interests to prevent a French defeat in Indochina; the "dominoes" would not quickly and inevitably fall; the administration could look to other ways of trying to minimize the damage to its interests of a French defeat. (See also Chapter 11.)

Notes

1. Since the writing of this chapter in 1975, several thoughtful analyses on this subject have appeared. See Fred A. Sondermann, "The Concept of the National Interest," *Orbis* (spring, 1977); Donald E. Neuchterlein, "National Interests and Foreign Policy: A Conceptual Framework for Analysis and Decision-making," *British Journal of International Studies* 2 (1976); J. Martin Rochester, "The 'National Interest' and Contemporary World Politics: A Case of New Wine in Old Bottles, or Old Wine in New Bottles?" (manuscript, Center for International Studies, University of Missouri–St. Louis [n.d.]).

2. For a critical analysis of the scientific and theoretical limitations of the concept, see James N. Rosenau, "National Interest," *International Encyclopedia of the Social Sciences* 11.

3. See, for example, James G. March and Herbert A. Simon, *Organizations* (New York: Wiley, 1958), pp. 156-57.

4. E. H. Carr, *Nationalism and After* (London: St. Martin, 1945), p. 2.

5. The erosion of the distinction between "foreign" and "domestic" policy has important implications also for the organization of the executive branch and for the way in which a president organizes his advisory and policymaking system. This development is discussed in several volumes of the report issued by the Commission on the Organization of the Government for the Conduct of Foreign Policy, June 1975.

6. See, for instance, the works of George F. Kennan, particularly *American*

Diplomacy 1900-1950 (Chicago: University of Chicago Press, 1951); and Walter Lippmann, *U.S. Foreign Policy: Shield of the Republic* (Boston: Little, Brown & Co., 1943).

7. This and the following paragraphs draw upon Seyom Brown, *The Faces of Power* (New York: Columbia University Press, 1968, part I); see also Morton A. Kaplan, *System and Process in International Politics* (New York: Wiley, 1957, chapter 8).

8. See especially Charles Kindleberger, *The World in Depression, 1929-39* (Berkeley: University of California Press, 1974).

9. See, for instance, Kenneth N. Waltz, "The Myth of National Interdependence," in Charles Kindleberger, ed., *The International Corporation* (Cambridge, Mass.: MIT Press, 1970).

14
Policy-Relevant Theory

In the last chapter we discussed ways in which the criterion of national interest, once it has been refined and clarified, can help policymakers to deal with the value-complexity imbedded in so many foreign-policy problems and to improve judgments regarding the proper ends and goals of foreign policy.[1] The present chapter is concerned with analytic components rather than the value dimensions of policymaking.

Foreign policy includes, in addition to questions about national interests, various analytic problems concerning the nature of one's adversaries, the characteristics of the international system and of the forces that are shaping it, the ways in which various instruments of policy can be appropriately and effectively employed in pursuit of foreign-policy goals, etc. In other words, foreign-policymaking has an important *cognitive* basis as well as a value dimension. Lack of adequate knowledge and theory about these various cognitive-analytic matters inevitably gives freer reign to the individual, group, and organizational sources of malfunctions of the policymaking process that were discussed in Part 1. At the same time, it is important to recognize that these various impediments to information processing may be avoided or minimized by improving the quality and relevance of knowledge available to policymakers about other actors in the international system and about the various strategies and activities—such as deterrence, crisis management, coercive diplomacy, alliance management, war termination, conciliation, etc.—that comprise the means of furthering foreign-policy goals.

Policymakers and their staffs develop theories of their own on these matters and rely on them in assessing available information about a current situation and in evaluating alternative courses of action. Since policymakers are actors and not theoreticians, they have no choice but to make decisions on the basis of what they think they know about the nature of opponents and the uses and limitations of various policy instruments. But even the best knowledge and understanding of these matters within the policymaking community is usually incomplete and often of uncertain or questionable validity.

Academic specialists on foreign policy and international relations have an opportunity, therefore, to contribute to the further development and refinement of the knowledge and theories needed in policymaking. To do so more effectively, however, academic scholars need to understand better the kinds of knowledge and theory that the policymaker needs and how he uses such information in making decisions. Accordingly, we shall present a brief discussion of two functions of theory in policymaking — the diagnostic and options-assessment functions.

The Diagnostic Function of Theory

Perhaps the greatest need of policymakers is an enhanced ability to comprehend the dynamic forces shaping international politics and to diagnose specific situations that arise to which they may have to react. The importance and difficulty of situational analysis in policymaking is perhaps not well enough understood by many academic scholars engaged in developing theories of international politics. The accumulation of knowledge in this realm, whether it concerns the nature of other actors on the world scene (e.g., their values, behavioral styles, internal politics, policymaking systems) or the proper use of certain instruments of foreign policy (e.g., deterrence, crisis management, conciliation, etc.) can be of considerable help to policymakers in making better definitions of the situation.

That theory can have this kind of important *diagnostic* function in policymaking is sometimes overlooked. Instead, scholars interested in contributing to improved policymaking often have bypassed the task of developing theories that aid in diagnosing situations and turned directly to developing rational choice theories for policymaking. Assistance in making better choices is, to be sure, an important function of policy-relevant theories. But rational choice theories often make only a limited contribution, since in making his choice the decisionmaker typically must be responsive to variables not considered in the available theories. In any case, correct diagnosis of emerging situations should precede — and indeed is usually a prerequisite for — efforts to make the best choice among policy options. The diagnostic function of a policy theory may be more important in many cases than its quite limited ability to prescribe the choice of the correct course of action in complex settings.

In the last analysis, the correct diagnosis of a new situation often depends on how available information about it is interpreted rather than on the accumulation of still more factual information. The policymaker must infer what other nations are up to in the situation at hand; he must assess their motives, goals, strategies, and tactics. The policymaker also must judge how the immediate situation relates to a wider context or pattern of events; i.e., its significance in terms of the dynamics and trends of the contemporary international situation.

Since the behavior of an opponent in a given situation is often capable of more than one plausible interpretation, policymakers have to rely upon their general knowledge of that particular adversary in order to assess the meaning and significance of his observable behavior. It is by now a truism that specific information for assessing an adversary's intentions in an emergent situation rarely speaks for itself. To interpret it correctly requires a theory or model of how *this particular adversary* perceives different kinds of situations and goes about calculating the utility of different options available to him. It is hazardous to assume that the adversary will perceive and respond to all situations the same way as one would one's self, or to operate on the assumption that a single general model of rationality can help predict the behavior of all actors. Rather, one must be able to understand this particular actor's peculiar approach to assessment of situations and calculation of utility; this will be a function of the opponent's ideological values, his belief system about the nature of political conflict and the best approach to strategy and tactics, the organizational and bureaucratic processes that affect his formulation and implementation of policy, his sensitivity to domestic political considerations, etc. The understanding that the policymaker has of these aspects of the opponent's approach to policymaking constitute what may be called his "image of the opponent," or his model of the opponent's "behavioral style." An incorrect or defective model of the opponent's behavioral style can distort even reasonably good factual information on what he may be up to.

Sound knowledge of the opponent's behavioral style is also necessary for deciding how best to respond to the situation, once it is diagnosed. To estimate correctly the expected consequences of alternative options requires the policymaker to assess the effects that these options will have on the adversary. An incorrect image of the opponent, therefore, can result not only in a defective diagnosis of the situation, but also in a faulty appraisal of the relative utility of different options.

While policymakers sometimes disagree on what constitutes a correct theory of the behavioral style of an adversary, there have been historical eras such as the Cold War in which a single general theory about the nature of the opponent dominated foreign policy. The effect of such a reigning, unchallenged image of the opponent may be to place blinders on policymaking, thereby reducing its flexibility and adaptability. Many historians and other foreign-policy specialists now believe, for example, that significant opportunities to moderate the Cold War were missed by American policymakers during the 1950s because the reigning image of both the Soviet Union and Communist China excluded the possibility that they could be genuinely interested in a mitigation of the conflict.

As noted in Part 1, there are many pressures—individual, group, and organizational—within a policymaking system that work toward the emergence and maintenance of a dominant, reigning image of other actors in the international arena. Disagreement within the policymaking system on such fundamental policy premises is discouraged by subtle pressures as well as by more overt means. Even when a potentially healthy disagreement about the nature of the opponent exists, it often leads to polarization within the policymaking community rather than to a concerted effort to state the points of disagreement more precisely and to set up analytical procedures for assessing relevant evidence in order to "bound," if not resolve, these disagreements so that the implications of these critical uncertainties about the nature of the opponent for policy can be better judged.

Much more can be done in this respect than, evidently, has been attempted or accomplished either within the government itself or by outside specialists. Disagreements on what is the correct basic view of the opponent tend to become linked somewhat prematurely and rigidly with competing policy preferences. The ensuing struggle over policy choices then tends to squeeze out the possibility of a more systematic and objective analysis of the fundamental disagreement over the nature of the opponent. One of the most challenging tasks for those interested in the further development of policy-relevant theory, therefore, is to find ways of reexamining dominant images and of adjudicating in a scholarly way disputes over the correct image of adversaries.[2]

The Option-Assessment Function of Theory

We have spoken of the policymaker's need for an enhanced ability to make accurate situational diagnoses. The policymaker also needs to improve his ability to judge the utility of alternative options under consideration. To do so requires him to assess the expected consequences of each of the options. Such assessments are in the nature of forecasts; in attempting to foresee the expected consequences of an option the policymaker, in effect, is making a contingent prediction.

Another way in which academic specialists can contribute to policymaking, therefore, is to develop theories about various aspects of international relations that will assist the policymaker to make better contingent predictions. As noted earlier, better knowledge of adversaries and the actors with whom the policymaker must deal will be helpful to him for making contingent predictions as to the impact on their attitudes and behavior that is likely to result from options under consideration. Other kinds of theories, to which we shall turn momentarily, also enhance the policymaker's ability to make better estimates of the expected consequences of alternative courses of action. But first we want to contrast theories that do help with the task of making contingent predictions with those that do not.

Many academic scholars define the task of developing theories of international politics in terms of formulating "comprehensive generalizations." That is, they seek to identify broad relationships that are valid in a large number of cases spanning a variety of times and places. Such comprehensive generalizations, however valid (and often they are held to be valid only on a probabilistic basis), are often of quite limited value in policymaking; for what the policymaker needs most in dealing with a specific situation are more refined generalizations that apply to the circumstances of that particular situation. Thus, the policymaker needs *differentiated* theories, i.e., theories that formulate a set of contingent generalizations about the phenomenon in question and tell him how it varies under different conditions. Each contingent generalization is valid only under certain conditions. A set of such contingent generalizations about the various manifestations of the activity constitutes a differentiated theory.

A differentiated theory of deterrence, for example, is more useful to the policymaker because it helps him to determine whether deterrence is a viable strategy to choose in a particular type of situation and, if so, what the requirements of a good deterrence strategy are in that situation (as opposed to some other type of situation). Thus, as we shall note later, such a theory of deterrence helps both in the diagnosis of situations and in the evaluation of alternative options.

Lack of systematic attention to contingent generalizations in developing theories about various aspects of international politics tends to obscure many questions of direct policy utility—for example, when and when not to expect one or another kind of deterrence strategy to be successful; the conditions that favor successful use of the strategy of coercive diplomacy and the types of problems encountered in attempting to "tailor" that strategy to the special context of a particular situation; and the requirements for successful crisis management and escalation control.

It is important to note that while the policymaker is generally aware of his need for what we are referring to as "differentiated theory," he is not adept at developing such theories himself. Instead, the harassed and action-oriented policymaker seeks substitutes for the contingent generalizations that a proper differentiated theory would provide, and he employs questionable shortcuts in attempting to develop such a theory. Thus, for well-developed contingent generalizations the policymaker substitutes a particular "lesson of history" drawn from a single historical case that strike him as providing the correct analogue for diagnosing and dealing with the new case at hand. And for a systematic procedure that would analyze a wide range of relevant historical cases, the policymaker overgeneralizes from a few cases to formulate a historical "law," overlooking the possibility that other cases might suggest a quite different historical law.

Since the use—and misuse—of history plays so important a role in assisting the policymaker to diagnose new situations and to decide how to deal with them, it is well to reflect further on this widespread practice.

From Lessons of History to Theory

The distinguished historian of the Renaissance, Jacob Burckhardt, once remarked that the true use of history is not to make men more clever for the next time but to make them wiser forever. Admittedly, it is not easy to learn from history, though almost every statesman and general has professed to have done so. In the first place, people often disagree as to the correct lesson to be drawn from a particular historical experience. For example, quite different lessons regarding military strategy for fighting limited wars were drawn from the frustrating experience of the Korean War and once again, quite ominously, from the failure of American military power in the Vietnam War.[3] Second, even if people agree on the correct lessons to be drawn from a particular historical case, they often misapply those lessons to a new situation that differs from the past one in important respects.[4]

If it is hazardous to draw lessons of broader applicability from single historical cases, how then can historical experience be utilized to understand better and to deal effectively with contemporary situations that bear a certain resemblance to past historical cases? The answer lies in stating lessons in a *systematic and differentiated way* from a *broader range* of experience that deliberately draws upon a variety of historical cases. In other words, the task is to convert individual "lessons of history" into a more diversified *theory* that encompasses the complexity of the phenomenon or activity in question. Achievement of this goal will be furthered by intellectual cooperation between historians, who are well equipped to provide detailed and discriminating explanations of single historical outcomes, and political scientists who specialize in techniques for generalizing from and explaining the variance among historical outcomes.[5] Let us consider further the contribution that historians and political scientists can make to the development of policy-relevant theory that is grounded in systematic examination of historical experience.

As any historian or literate person knows, the "lessons" of history are often inconsistent, if not contradictory, and generalizations are hazardous if not carefully qualified. The lesson drawn from a particular case may be contradicted by the lesson that springs from another case. Since historians know this better than others, they are perforce the custodians of relevant historical memory. Historians can make an important contribution to policymaking by providing timely reminders that the lessons of history relevant to a current policy problem are not always clear and that to view the current situation as analagous to an earlier historical case (or cases) may be inappropriate or misleading and lead to policy error.

The formulation of theory by political scientists builds upon but also attempts to go beyond this minimal but important contribution that historians can make. Theory attempts to absorb the lessons of a *variety* of historical cases within a single comprehensive analytical framework; it is the task of theory to identify the many conditions and variables that affect historical outcomes and to sort out the causal patterns associated with different historical outcomes. By doing so, theory accounts for the variance in historical outcomes; it clarifies the apparent inconsistencies and contradictions among the lessons of different cases by identifying the critical conditions and variables that differed from one case to the other.

For many years development of this kind of historically grounded theory lagged for various reasons, but, more recently, a number of scholars have been drawing upon the perspectives and special methods of both history and political science to produce examples of this type of differentiated policy-relevant theory. Studies of various foreign-policy problems and strategies such as crisis management, deterrence, coercive diplomacy, escalation, détente, conciliation and accommodation, etc., have begun to appear in some quantity in the United States. A field of knowledge and expertise is slowly developing that did not exist as recently as the time of the Kennedy administration.[6]

As an illustration of the nature of differentiated policy theory, four such theories will be discussed.

Crisis Management

Until recently, scholars could contribute comparatively little in the way of a theory of crisis management to help guide policy makers who wanted to protect important interests in a crisis without triggering escalation of the conflict. President Kennedy derived some of the most important principles upon which he relied in managing the Cuban missile crisis from his personal reading not long before of Barbara Tuchman's analysis in *The Guns of August* of how the statesmen of Europe had mismanaged the crisis triggered by the assassination of Archduke Ferdinand in the summer of 1914 and found themselves in a general European war.

More recently, by studying the problems and the requirements of crisis management in a number of historical cases, scholars have been able to formulate a more systematic theory of crisis management. Thus, working largely independently of each other, three scholars have formulated similar statements of the general tasks and requirements of crisis management.[7] One study lists seven criteria or principles of effective crisis management when force and/or threats of force are employed:

1. Presidential control of military options.
2. Pauses in military operations to give opponent time to assess the situation and to respond to proposals.
3. Military moves that constitute clear and appropriate demonstrations of one's resolve and limited crisis objectives.
4. Military moves closely coordinated with political-diplomatic actions and communications as part of an integrated strategy for persuading the opponent to alter his policy and behavior in the desired direction.
5. Confidence in the discriminating character as well as the effectiveness of military options.
6. Military moves that avoid motivating opponent to escalate.
7. Avoidance of impression of resort to large-scale warfare.[8]

The importance of these seven principles was recognized by Kennedy in the Cuban missile crisis and earlier, in the Laos crisis of 1961. These criteria were also relevant in other crises, though not always well understood and honored by policymakers. Many of these principles were violated, for example, by European statesmen in the sequence of events that led to the outbreak of World War I, and by President Truman in his inept handling of the threat of Chinese Communist intervention in the Korean War.

Coercive Diplomacy

Coercive diplomacy (or "compellance," as some prefer to call it) is a strategy that calls for employing military threats in an effort to persuade an opponent to halt or undo an encroachment in which he is already engaged.[9] Coercive diplomacy is a beguiling strategy insofar as leaders of militarily strong powers—as, for example, the Johnson administration in its effort to use air power in 1965 to coerce Hanoi—are tempted to believe that they can, with little risk to themselves, intimidate weaker opponents to give up their gains and their goals. Actually, however, this strategy can succeed only under special conditions; these happened to be present or were created by President Kennedy in 1962 as part of his effort to induce Khrushchev to remove the Soviet missiles from Cuba.

It is important to identify the conditions and processes necessary to the success of this strategy, since, in their absence, even a superpower can fail in its effort to coerce a weak opponent and find itself drawn into a costly military conflict. Systematic comparison of cases of successful and unsuccessful coercive diplomacy has led to the identification of a number of conditions. Three in particular appear to be of critical importance. It does not suffice that the action threatened against the opponent for failure to comply with what is demanded of him be credible. The success of coercive diplomacy depends on creating in the opponent's mind (1) a sense of urgency for compliance with demand; (2) a belief that there is an asymmetry of motivation that favors the coercing power—i.e., that it is more highly motivated to achieve its stated demand than the opponent is to oppose it; and (3) a fear of unacceptable escalation if the demand is not accepted.

The theory of coercive diplomacy emphasizes in this connection the importance of developing an asymmetry of motivation in one's favor by carefully limiting what one demands of the opponent. For, obviously, the strength of the opponent's motivation not to comply with the demand is highly dependent on what is demanded of it.

Coercive diplomacy also needs to be distinguished from pure coercion. It may not be possible to persuade an opponent to accept one's demand by relying solely on threats of punishment for noncompliance. It may be necessary, that is, to offer positive inducements for compliance as well. Coercive diplomacy—as distinguished from crude coercion—emphasizes the importance of negotiations, bargaining, and compromises as well as coercive threats. For the coercing power to succeed in creating an asymmetry of motivation in its favor may require it to offer a "carrot" to the opponent as part of a quid pro quo, as Kennedy did in the Cuban missile crisis.

Systematic study of actual historical instances of coercive diplomacy successes and failures also has drawn attention to the fact that the strategy is highly context-dependent. This means that the strategy must be tailored in a rather exacting manner to fit the unique configuration of each individual situation. But the special configuration of a crisis situation in which coercive diplomacy might be employed is seldom clearly visible to the policymaker, and, as a result, the strategy easily can fail. For this and other reasons, efforts to engage in coercive diplomacy rest heavily upon skill at improvisation. Six problems or tasks are involved in any effort to tailor the general strategy of coercive diplomacy to a particular situation:

1. Evaluating and controlling the risks of giving the opponent an explicit or tacit ultimatum—i.e., a deadline for compliance with the demand;
2. Dealing with the conflict between the necessity to create a sense of urgency for compliance in the opponent's mind—an important requirement for success in coercive diplomacy—and the requirement of effective crisis management to slow up on the momentum of events to give the opponent time to evaluate the situation;
3. Calculating the proper timing of the coercive threat to make certain that it will be regarded as credible;
4. Calculating the proper timing of negotiations with the opponent;
5. Formulating the contents of a "carrot and stick" that will be adequate to overcome the opponent's reluctance to comply with the demand;
6. Calculating the proper timing of the carrot and the stick.

It is important that before embarking on coerceive diplomacy policymakers be aware that these tasks of implementing the strategy are often difficult to perform satisfactorily.

Deterrence

Deterrence strategy attempts to dissuade an opponent from encroaching on one's own or an ally's interests.[10] Deterrence theory is most highly developed with respect to deterring military encroachment, though in principle it is applicable to other types of encroachments as well.

Though the practice of deterrence in interstate relations goes back to ancient times, theorizing about deterrence is a relatively recent phenomenon. The problem of deterrence took on new urgency in modern times with the advent of thermonuclear weapons and long-range delivery systems. Yet, it is surprising how slowly deterrence theory, and even clarity about the concept, developed after World War II. At first, deterrence was understood and conveyed in relatively simple terms. The doctrine of "massive retaliation" was invented by the Eisenhower administration in an effort to use the threat of strategic nuclear air power to deter not only a Soviet strategic attack but a variety of lesser encroachments on the Free World. Massive retaliation, however, was subjected to increasing criticism as Soviet capabilities grew and as its lack of relevance to low-level conflicts was demonstrated. Accordingly, the Kennedy administration and its successors moved to refine deterrence strategy and to differentiate its requirements for different types and levels of conflict. By the late 1960s, deterrence theory and practice were proceeding on several levels.

It is now necessary to reconceptualize the problem of deterrence somewhat differently for different levels of conflict. These are (1) the deterrent relationship of the two superpower's strategic forces to each other; (2) the deterrence of local and limited conflicts; and (3) the deterrence of "sublimited" conflict at the lower end of the spectrum of violence.

The first of these three levels has received the greatest attention in deterrence theory at the strategic level, dealing as it does with a relatively ticulating and refining the theory of strategic deterrence are the most advanced.[11] The quantity and quality of deterrence theory falls off sharply and steadily for the second and third levels. Deterrence theory at these levels remains relatively underdeveloped and is ridden with difficult problems both of conceptualization and methodology. Largely because deterrence theory at the strategic level, dealing as it does with a relatively simple structural situation, was so much better developed, theorists were tempted to employ the logic of strategic deterrence as the paradigm case for thinking about deterrence in general. This has proven to be quite unsatisfactory, however, for there are major differences in the problem of applying deterrence effectively at the second and third levels of conflict. Deterrence at those levels is much more context-dependent than at the strategic level, i.e., it is subject to the play of many more variables that change from one situation to another and, moreover, that are likely to be unstable over time for a particular situation.

As a result, not only are the requirements for deterrence often more complicated for the second and third levels of conflict, they are also more difficult to identify reliably and more difficult to meet. As historical experience amply demonstrates, conflicts at the second and third levels of violence are less easily deterred than the initiation of a strategic nuclear strike. And yet by far the largest volume of conflict-related developments in other parts of the world with which U.S. foreign policy has attempted to deal lie at the lower end of the spectrum. Many of these low-level conflicts are essentially nondeterrable, at least by threats of military intervention, for such threats either lack credibility or are irrelevant to these conflict situations.

What this brief review of the intellectual history of deterrence theory highlights, therefore, is that theorists have not had much success in extending the logic of deterrence from the simplest strategic case to the more complex cases at the second and third levels. The problems of deterrence at these levels cannot be squeezed into the analytical and policy framework of the logic of strategic deterrence.

The development of deterrence theory for the second and third levels has been complicated by the fact that U.S. interests are not equally engaged by all conflicts in third areas. It was one of the simplifying assumptions of general deterrence theory some years ago that deterrence commitments were of an "either-or" character—i.e., either the defending power (the United States) was commited fully to doing whatever was necessary to defend a weak ally, or it was not committed to doing anything at all. This fundamental assumption of deterrence theory seemed to be justified at first by the nature of the Cold War; not only did U.S. policymakers proliferate defense commitments to many countries during the 1950s particularly, but they spoke as if each commitment was equally important in engaging vital U.S. interests. Despite their frequent invocation of the "row of dominoes" analogy to enhance this impression, it was, of course, not the case. And with the passing of the acute Cold War era, it fell to President Nixon to discard this assumption. Early in his administration, he announced that henceforth the United States would differentiate among its commitments to other countries on the basis of a more discriminating assessment of its interests than in the past.

The assumption that U.S. commitments were unqualified and unlimited encouraged theorists to single out the credibility of a commitment and technical skill in signaling it to an opponent as the critical factor on which successful deterrence rested. As a result, early deterrence theory took on a narrow, apolitical, technocratic character; it focused on technical aspects of communicating a commitment and the tactics of strengthening the impression that it would make on an opponent. Thereby, early deterrence theory failed to comprehend that it was the real national interest that lay behind a commitment and not its rhetorical exaggeration that fundamentally determined its credibility in the eyes of the opponent.

Early deterrence theory also failed to capture the complexities of motivation and the resourcefulness of calculation that could lead a country dissatisfied with the status quo to find a way to test and challenge the deterrence commitments that the United States had undertaken on behalf of weaker countries. Deterrence theory failed to anticipate that the dissatisfied power usually has more than one option for challenging the status quo and that it will choose a strategy for doing so that takes advantage of any loopholes, weaknesses, or uncertainties in the deterrence strategy of the defending power.

Analysis of various failures of deterrence during the Cold War has shifted the attention of theorists away from the earlier preoccupation with signaling credibility to a broader analysis of the conditions under which a dissatisfied country (the "Initiator") will initiate action of some kind to alter the status quo (sometimes even in the face of some type of credible deterrence commitment!). To understand and predict the Initiator's behavior in this connection, deterrence theory now emphasizes that it is necessary to address two separate though interrelated questions: *whether* the dissatisfied country will initiate action, and if so *how* it will challenge deterrence (i.e., by what type of action).

Whether deterrence will be challenged depends in many instances on whether the dissatisfied country believes that it has an option for doing so whose risks are calculable and/or controllable—i.e., an option that constitutes an acceptable calculated risk that is commensurate with the hoped-for gains. *How* deterrence is challenged by the Initiator—i.e., which of several options at his disposal he will choose—depends on how he assesses the Defender's commitment. Three different patterns of deterrence failure have been identified. In the first place, if the Initiator believes (as in the case of the North Korean attack on South Korea in June 1950) that the Defender has *no* commitment to intervene militarily on behalf of a weak ally, then the Initiator is likely to regard as his best option a "*quick, decisive*" move against the weak ally to accomplish a fait accompli before the Defender can reconsider his policy and respond.

If, on the other hand, the Initiator believes (as in the Quemoy crisis of 1958) that the Defender's commitment is *uncertain*, then his best strategy for challenging deterrence is the "*limited probe*"—that is, an action that can be easily called off and reversed if the Defender responds more strongly and more threateningly than is acceptable to the Initiator. The purpose of a limited probe, in other words, is to clarify the uncertainty surrounding the Defender's commitment before proceeding to alter the status quo.

A third possibility arises when the Initiator believes that the Defender's commitment is *unequivocal but perhaps "soft"*—that is, subject to erosion or neutralization by the low-level challenge to deterrence that the Initiator can mount to manipulate and exploit various asymmetries latent in the situation. In this case, the best strategy for the Initiator is that of "*controlled pressure*," such as the Soviets exerted against West Berlin on several occasions.

These three types of initiation strategies differ in their implications for the Defender's effort to design and apply deterrence strategy. Moreover, the Defender's awareness that deterrence can fail in three different ways should enable him to make more accurate assessments of available intelligence on the opponent's intentions and what he is up to. Similarly, knowledge of the different initiation strategies should enable the Defender to respond more appropriately to available intelligence "warnings" that deterrence is about to fail or is in the process of failing, for the three patterns of possible deterrence failure may have quite different implications for the type of last-minute efforts that the Defender might make to shore up deterrence.

This aspect of deterrence theory exemplifies the point made earlier regarding the greater utility for policymaking of theories that offer a differentiated analysis of the phenomenon in question and greater assistance in diagnosis of emerging situations.

Still another weakness of early deterrence theory stemmed from the failure of theorists to draw a sharp dividing line between deterrence strategy and foreign policy. Reliance upon deterrence was so important and so integral a part of American Cold War policy that it did not seem necessary to distinguish more sharply between the two. A more refined analysis of the utility of deterrence strategy for foreign policy had to await the passing of the acute Cold War era. Only then did it emerge more clearly that deterrence is not an end in itself, but should be viewed as an instrument of foreign policy, and that, like other instruments, it has limitations as well as uses in promoting foreign-policy goals.

If viewed from the standpoint of *long-range* foreign policy, it is clear that deterrence is a *time-buying* strategy. Deterrence is a policy, which, if it succeeds, frustrates an opponent who aspires to changing some aspect of the international status quo in his favor. The consequences of continued frustration, however, are *not* easily predictable and are *not* always favorable to the deterring power. It is important in planning foreign-policy strategy to try to distinguish the conditions and circumstances under which successful deterrence is and is not likely to have favorable longer-term consequences. The argument advanced here, in other words, is that deterrence success in the *short* run is not always beneficial in the *longer* run.

The most reliable benefit that successful deterrence can bestow is more time—in which some of the conflict-generating or conflict-exacerbating elements in a historical situation can abate, so that deterrence will no longer be necessary or, at any rate, not be so critical for the maintenance of peace and stability. Successful deterrence gives the opposing parties time to work out an accommodation of their conflicting interests, thereby reducing existing tensions and the potential for overt military conflict. But in situations of this kind, time is precious. The failure or inability of the parties concerned to make good use of the time available—which successful deterrence provides—can easily transform deterrence strategy into a more permanent way of life.

It is certainly possible that successful deterrence may sometimes have benefits also in the longer run as well. Thus, if an expansionist, dissatisfied country is subjected to continued effective deterrence, its frustration may eventually lead it to abandon the expansionist objectives or at least modify the means it employs to pursue them. Thus, it may be recalled that at the onset of the Cold War, George Kennan (and others) hoped that if containment and deterrence were effectively applied to the Soviet Union over a period of years, this would gain time for internal developments to occur in Soviet society and in the character of Soviet leadership that would bring about a mellowing process, a lessening of the insecurities and strong ideological motives that gave Soviet foreign policy an expansionist thrust. In fact, something of the sort does appear to have occurred in the intervening years. Observers who believe that a mellowing has taken place disagree, however, on the dimensions, stability, and significance of this development. Other observers disagree; they do not believe that any real mellowing of Soviet policy has in fact occurred.

A similar mellowing some observers hope, may take place in the Chinese Communist leadership's attitude toward Taiwan. Not that Peking will abandon its objective of "liberating" Taiwan, but, it is hoped, Peking may be willing to renounce the use of force as a means of achieving this objective.

One should also be aware of the possible costs and risks of deterrence successes from the standpoint of foreign-policy objectives. Thus, sometimes deterrence that is successful in the short run can actually exacerbate conflict and increase the risks of war thereafter. There are situations in which one pays a high price for temporary deterrence successes. For example, a defending power that has successfully deterred an encroachment on a weak ally may find that its commitment to that weak ally has thereby hardened; and this can make it more difficult later on, after the crisis has subsided, for the defending power to recapture the political and diplomatic flexibility that is needed to find a diplomatic solution to the problem. Curiously, weak allies who have been successfully protected by a big power in a crisis often gain additional bargaining leverage with their protector. Relevant in this respect is the history of U.S. relations with Nationalist China (Taiwan) in the years after the Korean War. A gradual erosion of Washington's freedom of action vis-à-vis the future of the Nationalist regime occurred after Truman, in response to the North Korean attack on South Korea, extended what was presumably only temporary protection to Taiwan. In successive crises in the Taiwan Strait, the Eisenhower administration felt itself under considerable pressure—to which it yielded to a considerable degree—to harden and extend the U.S. commitment to the Nationalist regime. Moreover, deterrence success in the Taiwan Strait hardened U.S. policy on precisely those peripheral issues—the Offshore Islands—on which flexibility might have served overall American interests far better.

A similar danger may lurk in current U.S. policy toward Zaire. The question is not merely whether the United States can exert deterrence successfully on behalf of Zaire, which itself is problematical, but also whether it can afford deterrence successes if such successes strengthen the U.S. commitment to maintain the Mobuto regime in power.

Deterrence successes may be costly from the standpoint of overall and longer-range foreign policy in other ways as well. Thus, in some circumstances successful application of deterrence in a crisis may inflate the ideological and psychological dimensions of an existing conflict. In order to gain domestic support for their policies in the two Taiwan Strait crises of 1954-55 and 1958, Eisenhower and Dulles were forced to engage in rhetorical inflation of the extent to which U.S. national interests were at stake and to reinforce the "devil image" of the Chinese Communists. This contributed to a psychological escalation of the Cold War with Communist China and rigidification of U.S. policy.

Successful deterrence may also carry with it the penalty of hardening the opponent's conviction that the defending power is not responsive to his legitimate interests. As a result, the dissatisfied power that has been deterred in one crisis may resolve to prepare more effectively for the next round. The Berlin crises of 1958-59 and 1961 are possible examples of this type of delayed cost of a deterrence success. Eisenhower's and Kennedy's successes in thwarting Khrushchev's demands for a change in the status quo of Berlin undoubtedly contributed to Khrushchev's decision later on to place missiles in Cuba.

As these brief remarks suggest, the utility of deterrence strategy as an instrument of foreign policy cannot be assessed merely with reference to short-term successes of deterrence. Deterrence is only one instrument of foreign policy; it is not a substitute for a creative foreign policy that employs a variety of means—positive inducements as well as threats of negative sanctions—to reduce the conflict potential in relations with other states and to promote a more peaceful and viable international system.

In this connection, mention should be made of another characteristic of early deterrence theory that limited and at times distorted its utility for foreign policy. The work of early theorists was flawed by the assumption implicit in their thinking that a viable theory of deterrence could be developed independently of a broader theory of influence among nations. But, in fact, the nature of the Cold War notwithstanding, nations typically seek to influence one another not merely by making threats, but also by offering positive inducements. What is needed is not merely a better deterrence theory per se, but a more comprehensive formulation of the various means of influencing other states and an analysis of how they can be combined to achieve foreign-policy goals under different conditions. The need for a broader theory of this kind was obscured by the dynamics of the Cold War; the U.S. containment strategy seemed justifiably to rely exclusively on deterrence. The narrowness of this focus was not readily apparent to most policymakers and scholars at the time; emphasis on deterrence seemed to them a necessary correction to the earlier overreliance of the Western powers on conciliatory diplomatic approaches to adversaries—first toward Hitler in the 1930s, then toward Stalin during the latter part of World War II and immediately thereafter. As a result of these events, "appeasement" fell into such disrepute as to discredit more generally the traditional reliance of classical diplomacy upon negotiation and conciliation for adjusting conflicting interests and for reconciling change in the international system with the requirements for stability.[12]

Détente

With the passing of the acute Cold War, it became evident that policymakers would have to recapture and adapt the perspective of classical diplomacy, which, at its best, emphasized flexible, discriminating use of a variety of means for influencing adversaries and moderating the conflict potential in relations with other states. This was accompanied by a growing appreciation among specialists on international relations of the importance of supplementing deterrence with other kinds of influence resources and strategies.

Even earlier, during the height of the Cold War, a number of scholars had offered pragmatic theories of defusing the state of acute conflict between the two supernuclear powers. Strategies of this kind were advanced by an experimental psychologist, Charles E. Osgood, and a political sociologist, Amitai Etzioni. Osgood called for "graduated reciprocal reduction of conflict," i.e., a kind of step-by-step deescalation game in which the two antagonists would take turns making unilateral concessions that roughly matched each other and would continue to do so in successive rounds in order to reduce mutual mistrust and to build mutual confidence.[13]

Roger Fisher, on the other hand, urged that U.S. and Soviet leaders adopt the somewhat different tactic of "fractionating" the overall conflict between them into more manageable parts so as to loosen the rigidities of the Cold War and get the process of negotiation and limited accommodations started.[14] As a matter of fact, this tactic already had been employed since the end of the Cuban missile crisis. In pursuit of détente, both sides seemed to arrive at a tacit understanding that they would henceforth attempt to separate and "de-couple" as much as possible the issues on which they disagreed. Instead of attempting to resolve at one and the same time all the major outstanding conflicts between them, the two superpowers agreed in effect not to push, and thus risk exacerbating, their long-standing disagreements over Central and Eastern Europe, arms control inspection, Cuba, overseas U.S. bases, etc. Such issues, evidently deemed too difficult for early solution, were set aside for the time being by Kennedy and Khrushchev. Thus, the era of détente began with a mutual willingness to "fractionate" the overall Cold War conflict and to reach agreement on many single issues that could be separated from other, more important matters on which agreement for the time being would have been more difficult.

Still other theorists and observers spoke of the need for increasing communication flows between the East and the West and developing ties of one kind or another that would increase mutual interdependence to the point that the two sides would gradually modify the perception and reality of acute hostility and conflict in their relationship. Just as with the tactic of "fractionating conflict," elements of these ideas, too, were reflected in the efforts that Kennedy and his successors made to improve relations with the Soviet Union.

On the whole, however, the available academic theories of détente, conciliation, and accommodation were not very well developed and could offer relatively little guidance to American leaders in successive administrations. The most ambitious of the détente policies was that pursued by Nixon and Kissinger, and it is evident that its intellectual underpinnings — such as they were — were provided largely by these two leaders themselves. In Kissinger's case, the theoretical premises of his détente strategy were presumably influenced by his reading of history. However valuable Kissinger's knowledge of history, it contained important lacunae precisely with regard to the most ambitious of his détente objectives. The Nixon-Kissinger détente policy, it should be noted, aimed not merely at achieving and maintaining a relaxation of tensions in U.S.-Soviet relations and, going beyond this, not merely at a series of accommodations on specific outstanding issues. In addition, the détente policy aimed at persuading Soviet leaders to set aside ambitions to make advances elsewhere in the world at the expense of the West and, instead, to enter into a new constructive relationship with the United States. In other words, Nixon hoped to create a new regime in U.S.–Soviet relations that would serve as the bedrock for the development of a new international system to replace the Cold War. To this end, new "rules of the game" — and, indeed, a new "game" to replace the Cold War — were needed.

Nixon and Kissinger employed a complex strategy to achieve this goal: they emphasized conciliation, accommodation, and positive inducements but, as necessary, combined these with deterrence. Their détente policy, therefore, was more ambitious in objectives and more complicated in strategy than American Cold War policy had been. During the Cold War, the U.S. objective had been simply to contain the Soviet Union until someday, it was hoped, the force of Soviet ideology would spend itself; to achieve this long-range objective, the United States relied almost exclusively on deterrence strategy and various policies for reducing the vulnerability of Free World countries to communism.

Détente strategy, on the other hand, sought to bestow various benefits on the Soviet Union and to promise more for good behavior. The object was to motivate Soviet rulers to mend their ways and to stop meddling in Third Areas at the expense of the West. But Nixon and Kissinger did not rely solely on offering bribes and rewards; they stood ready, when necessary, to reinforce the positive incentives that they held out for good Soviet behavior with deterrence threats and sanctions. If and when the Soviets did not act with restraint in a Third Area, Kissinger believed and often insisted that the United States must react firmly. There were a number of occasions when the Nixon-Ford administration did so — in response to the Syrian tank invasion of Jordan in September 1970, in the Indian-Pakistani war in December 1971, in the Arab-Israeli war of 1973, and in Angola in 1974.

So Nixon and Kissinger did not rely solely on conciliation and appeasement but made use of the stick as well as the carrot. As a matter of fact, this strategy of rewards and punishments bears a striking resemblance to the psychological technique of behavior modification. Nixon and Kissinger were, at bottom, using a combination of rewards and punishments, promises and threats, in an effort to get Soviet leaders to modify certain behavior patterns, to resocialize Soviet leaders into new patterns of behavior — new "rules of the game" — that would be more consistent with the objectives and modalities of the new constructive relationship at which détente policy aimed.

While this aspect of détente policy was severely criticized in the United States on political grounds and because it did not produce enough of the hoped-for changes in Soviet behavior, surprisingly the theoretical premises behind the strategy and the way it was applied have not been subjected to a searching analysis. It is doubtful whether Kissinger's reading of history provided him with relevant historical analogs, let alone a theory, on which to draw in his efforts to resocialize Soviet leaders into new patterns of behavior. Efforts of the kind had been made in earlier historical epochs, but those that most easily came to mind—Chamberlain's effort to appease Hitler and to bring him into a strengthened Concert of Europe—were notorious failures. Nor had academic theorists other than Kissinger addressed this problem and attempted to formulate some working conception of how to apply a carrot and stick strategy to induce a "revolutionary" power to moderate its behavior and to accept a new set of restrictive rules of the game.

Several tentative observations may be offered that question the adequacy of the theoretical premises of Kissinger's use of carrot and stick strategy. His effort to resocialize the Soviet leaders violated two basic principles of behavior modification. Behavior modification works best when the therapist singles out *very specific items of behavior* that are to be changed; the approved items of behavior to be substituted in their place are also supposed to be specified. Kissinger, however, described the changes in Soviet behavior that he hoped for in very general terms. The "Basic Principles of Relations" agreed to by Nixon and Brezhnev in 1972 lacked specificity.[15] As a set of norms, or "rules of the game," they were somewhat ambiguous and certainly not easily put into operation. The two sides would not necessarily agree on how the Basic Principles would apply in a particular situation, whether and under what conditions the Principles would admit of exceptions, what behavior by one side would relieve the other side from the obligation to adhere strictly to the Principles, etc. Whatever the explanation, Soviet behavior in the events leading to the Yom Kippur war of October 1973 did not seem, in Kissinger's eyes, to be consistent with the Basic Principles. One may suppose that Soviet leaders entertained a similar complaint regarding the U.S. role in the Middle East.

Another important principle of behavior modification has to do with the timing of the reward to the subject. The reward is supposed to come *after* the subject behaves in the desired way; the function of the reward is to reinforce the new behavior pattern. But Kissinger, it would appear, often arranged benefits for the Soviets *beforehand*, i.e., as a bribe to induce the Soviet leaders to behave in the way he wanted them to.

It would be interesting to speculate whether a different version of the détente strategy, one more consistent with these two (and other) principles of behavior modification, might prove to be more successful. In any case, whether or not Kissinger applied behavior modification correctly, what he was trying to accomplish was very ambitious, and for this reason it may be only reasonable to assume that considerable time and repeated efforts would be necessary for the strategy to be successful. In the meantime, before Kissinger's therapy took full effect, one had to expect that the Soviets would occasionally "misbehave." But, if so, then how could one evaluate whether the strategy was succeeding? Kissinger's critics pointed to instances of Soviet meddling in Third Areas as evidence that his strategy had failed. Kissinger himself could only retort that Soviet behavior would have been even more aggressive had it not been for détente. Neither side could prove its case; but the possibility must be entertained that the critics pronounced the strategy of inducing self-restraints in Soviet foreign policy a failure prematurely.

Meanwhile, President Carter has abandoned this controversial component of the détente strategy. His administration does not pursue in a discernible or coherent fashion the objective of resocializing Soviet leaders into a new set of "rules of the game." And the intriguing but abortive Kissinger experiment lacks for an incisive analytical postmortem that might contribute to the formulation of a more useful theory governing these matters.

Concluding Observations

In contrast to Chapter 13, in which we dealt with value dimensions of foreign policy, the present chapter has focused upon its *analytic* components. We have called attention to the important cognitive requirements of policymaking regarding the character and dynamics of the international system, the intentions and behavioral styles of other actors, the prerequisites for effective use of various strategies and instruments of policy, etc. The policymaker needs adequate theories regarding these matters to help him make valid diagnoses of emerging situations and to choose viable courses of action.

Strong theories of this kind can play an important role, too, in disciplining and controlling the tendency of dynamics associated with individual, small group, and organizational behavior (noted in Part 1) to impair information processing within the policymaking system.

Finally, strong policy-relevant theories of the kind discussed in this chapter will be needed to make a success of *whatever* management model that a president chooses (see Chapter 8) and to get maximum benefits for policy from *either* the formal options system, multiple advocacy, or the collegial type of policymaking that were discussed in Chapters 10, 11, and 12. In the last analysis, effective foreign policy requires relevant substantive knowledge and policy-relevant theories. An important part of the task of structuring and managing policymaking systems is to find ways of bringing the relevant competence to bear in a timely and effective manner.

Notes

1. This chapter draws upon the earlier, briefer treatment of the topic in the chapter that Richard Smoke contributed to A. L. George et al., *Towards A More Soundly Based Foreign Policy: Making Better Use of Information*. For full reference, see note 37, Chapter 2.

2. The importance of improving assessments of other actors in the international system is emphasized and illustrated in a number of case studies also in Graham T. Allison, ed., *Adequacy of Current Organization: Defense and Arms Control*, vol. 4, Appendices, Commission on the Organization of the Government for the Conduct of Foreign Policy, June 1975 (Washington, D.C.: U.S. Government Printing Office, 1976), pp. 53-58.

3. See, for example, Ole R. Holsti and James N. Rosenau, "The Meaning of Vietnam: Belief Systems of American Leaders," *International Journal* 32 (summer 1977).

4. For an incisive discussion of the problem, see Ernest R. May, *"Lessons" of the Past: The Use and Misuse of History in American Foreign Policy* (New York: Oxford University Press, 1973); and Robert Jervis, *Perception and Misperception in International Politics* (Princeton, N.J.: Princeton University Press, 1976), chapter 6.

5. For an example of such collaboration between historians and political scientists, see the forthcoming volume edited by Paul Gordon Lauren, *Diplomatic History: New Approaches* (New York: The Free Press, 1979).

6. For a useful summary and discussion of some aspects of this development, see Lincoln P. Bloomfield, *The Foreign Policy Process: Making Theory Relevant*, International Studies Series, no. 3 (Beverley Hills, Cal.: Sage Publications, 1974).

7. Alexander L. George, David K. Hall, and William E. Simons, *The Limits of Coercive Diplomacy* (Boston: Little, Brown & Co., 1971), pp. 8-15; Ole R. Holsti, *Crisis, Escalation, War* (Montreal and London: McGill-Queen's University Press, 1972), chapter 8; Thomas W. Milburn, "The Management of Crises," in Charles F. Hermann, ed., *International Crises: Insights from Behavioral Research* (New York: The Free Press, 1972). An excellent discussion of crisis bargaining and decisionmaking is provided in Glenn H. Snyder and Paul Diesing, *Conflict Among Nations* (Princeton, N.J.: Princeton University Press, 1977). The problem of escalation, closely related to crisis management, is dealt with in exemplary fashion in Richard Smoke, *War: Controlling Escalation* (Cambridge,

Mass.: Harvard University Press, 1977). For an incisive critical appraisal – occasionally overstated – of the voluminous literature that has accumulated on the subject of crisis management, written mostly by political scientists and system analysts, see the essay by two well-qualified diplomatic historians, Arthur N. Gilbert and Paul Gordon Lauren, "Crisis Management: An Assessment and Critique" (1979; forthcoming).

8. George et al., *Limits of Coercive Diplomacy.*

9. This section is drawn from George et al. *Limits of Coercive Diplomacy,* chapters 1 and 5. See also Thomas C. Schelling, *Arms and Influence* (New Haven, Conn.: Yale University Press, 1966); Paul Gordon Lauren, "Ultimata and Coercive Diplomacy," *International Studies Quarterly* (June 1972), and the same author's "Coercive Diplomacy: Cases from Modern European History" (paper presented at the annual meeting of the American Historical Association, December 1975); and Phil Williams, *Crisis Management* (New York: Wiley, 1976).

10. This section draws upon A. L. George and R. Smoke, *Deterrence in American Foreign Policy: Theory and Practice* (New York: Columbia University Press, 1974). Of the many critical commentaries on deterrence theory and strategy (very few of which, incidentally, are based on systematic empirical research), the reader may find useful the summary and discussion in John Raser, "Theories of Deterrence," *Peace Research Reviews,* 3 (February 1969); and in Karl W. Deutsch, *The Analysis of International Relations,* 2d ed. (Englewood Cliffs, N.J.: Prentice-Hall, 1978), pp. 154-61.

11. For a recent critical analysis of strategic deterrence theory, see Patrick M. Morgan, *Deterrence: A Conceptual Analysis* (Beverley Hills, Cal.: Sage Library of Social Research, 1977).

12. See, for example, Evan Luard, "Conciliation and Deterrence," *World Politics* 19 (January 1967):167-89; and John Herz, "The Relevancy and Irrelevancy of Appeasement," *Social Research* 31 (autumn 1964):296-320.

Among those political scientists who have emphasized the neglected role of "positive sanctions" and incentives in the contemporary theory and practice of international relations, the writings of David Baldwin are of particular interest; see, for example, his latest essay, "Power Analysis and World Politics: New Trends *vs* Old Tendencies", *World Politics,* vol. 31, no. 2, (January 1979).

13. See Charles E. Osgood, "Suggestions for Winning the Real War with Communism," *Journal of Conflict Resolution* (December 1959); Amitai Etzioni, *The Hard Way to Peace* (New York: Crowell-Colber, 1962). For a balanced, critical appraisal of these theories, *see* chapter 3, "Deterrence, the Spiral Model, and Intentions of the Adversary," in Robert Jervis, *Perception and Misperception in International Politics* (Princeton, N.J.: Princeton University Press, 1976).

14. Roger Fisher, *International Conflict for Beginners* (New York: Harper & Row, 1969), pp. 91-109.

15. Among the agreements signed by Nixon and Brezhnev at their Moscow summit conference in May 1972 was one on "Basic Principles of Relations between the United States of America and the Union of Soviet Socialist Republics." While the Basic Principles were not in the form of a treaty and, in this sense, were

not legally binding, they constituted a set of agreed-upon norms and guidelines that not merely strengthened the crisis management regime that had already developed in U.S.-Soviet relations since the end of World War II, but added to it the beginning of a *crisis prevention* regime as well.

Thus, the Basic Principles document not only registered an agreement to conduct mutual relations on the basis of "peaceful coexistence"; it went on to define that relationship as prohibiting certain types of behavior that would threaten peaceful relations. In the second of the Basic Principles, the two sides also agreed to act constructively in their foreign policies to avoid the occurrence of crises. Thus, the document stated that both powers "attach major importance to preventing the development of situations capable of causing a dangerous exacerbation of their relations" and agree to "do their utmost to avoid military confrontations and to prevent the outbreak of nuclear war." To this end, the two sides further agreed that they "will always exercise restraint in their mutual relations and will be prepared to negotiate and settle differences by peaceful means." To this was added an injunction that always had been emphasized by Kissinger as of the essence of the détente process, namely, that "both sides recognize that efforts to obtain unilateral advantage at the expense of the other, directly or indirectly, are inconsistent with these objectives."

In the following year, at their summit meeting in Washington, D.C., Nixon and Brezhnev signed another agreement regarding the prevention of nuclear war. In it the two powers agreed to "immediately enter into urgent consultations with each other" to prevent the risk of nuclear war should developments in their own relations or those involving other countries create such a risk.

The texts of these two agreements and other documents bearing on détente are reproduced in Robert J. Pranger, ed., *Détente and Defense: A Reader* (Washington, D.C.: American Enterprises Institute for Public Policy Research, 1976). I have dealt with the difficult requirement of constructing a viable U.S.-S.U. crisis prevention regime in a discussion paper presented to the Pugwash Workshop on Crisis Management and Crisis Prevention held in Geneva, Switzerland, in December 1978.

Index

Acheson, Dean, 39, 69, 70, 75, 125, 126, 128, 151
Adams, Sherman, 153
Advisory systems, 81
  malfunctions of, 121-133
  norms, 98-101
  size of groups, 84-85, 86, 87
Allison, Graham, 116
Angola, 257
Arab-Israeli conflict, 59, 287. *See also* Yom Kippur war
Arms Control and Disarmament Agency, 178
Asch, Solomon, 90
Aswan Dam, 66
Attributional biases, 58-61
Availability heuristic, 60

Balance of power, 226
Baldwin, Stanley, 43
Bales, Robert, 84, 87
Ball, George, 124, 169, 171-172
Baruch Plan, 65
Basic Principles of Relations, 258
Bay of Pigs, 39, 94, 129, 130-131, 211
Beliefs and images, 19, 20, 45-47, 55-78
  and national interest, 231-233
  and simplified view of opponent, 71-72
Berger, J., 87
Berlin blockade, 70, 71, 75-76, 254
Bion, W. R., 109
Bissell, Richard, 130

Bolsheviks, 45-46
"Bolstering," 18-19, 37-39
Bowles, Chester, 131
Bradley, Omar, 128
Brezhnev, Leonid, 258
Brezhnev Doctrine, 76
Brzezinski, Zbigniew, 159, 160, 161, 162, 200
Bundy, McGeorge, 123, 127, 132, 197
Burckhardt, Jacob, 244
Bureaucratic politics, 115, 116. *See also* Formalistic management model
Butt, Archie, 7

Cabinet politics, 115
Carr, E. H., 219
Carter, Jimmy, 159-162, 259
Cartwright, D. C., 92
Castro, Fidel, 129, 130-131
Central Intelligence Agency (CIA), 129, 130-131
Chamberlain, Neville, 258
Chiang Kai-shek, 31, 36-37
China, 33, 36-37, 75, 77, 162, 232-233
Chinese communists, 69, 75, 125, 242, 246, 254
CIA. *See* Central Intelligence Agency
Clifford, Clark, 126
Coercive diplomacy, 246-248
Cognitive beliefs, 5, 19, 33
Cognitive psychology, 55-57, 77-78
Cognitive style, 147

Cohesion, 21-22, 87, 88-89
Cold War, 46, 65, 68, 70, 217, 225-226, 232, 242, 250, 251, 255
Collective interests, 221, 223 (figure), 228-229
Collegial management model, 148, 149, 157-159, 160, 164, 165 (table), 211-215
Commission on the Organization of the Government for the Conduct of Foreign Policy, 116
Committees, 84-85, 88. *See also* Small group subsystem
Compellance. *See* Coercive diplomacy
Competitive management model, 148-150, 164, 165 (table)
Conflict, 148
Conformity, 22, 87, 88, 89-96
Consensus, 1, 19, 42, 89, 90, 122-124
  illusory, 132-133
  and noncommunication, 127-129
Consistency seeker, 56, 58, 61-66, 77
Coolidge, Calvin, 35
Crisis
  management, 245-246
  situations, 47-49, 233-236. *See also* Values and interests, crises in
Cronin, Thomas, 197
Cuban missile crisis, 48, 69-70, 129, 211, 246, 247
Custodian-manager role, 196-197, 200
Czechoslovakia, 76-77

Decisionmaking
  consequences in, 3-4
  impediments to performance, 12, 17-24, 77-78, 103
  and national interest, 3-4, 26, 66-67, 141-143, 217-236
  and opponent's perspective, 66-78
  personality in, 4-9, 139
  procedural tasks in, 10
  psychological aspects of, 17-19, 25-49, 86
  quality, 1-4
  resources in, 2
  sequential, 41-42
  and size. *See* Advisory systems, size of groups
  solo. *See* Risk-taking

subsystems, 11-12
timely, 2, 37
tradeoffs in, 2 (figure), 27. *See also* Values and interests
See also Policymaking
Defense Programs Review Committee, 155
Defensive avoidance, 18-19, 25, 32-34, 37-39
de Gaulle, Charles, 43
Détente, 255-259
Deterrence strategy, 248-255
Devaluation, 33
Devil's advocate, 86-87, 124-126, 140, 169-173
Diagnostic function, 240-242
Differentiated theories, 243-244
Diplomacy, 114-116
Disagreement, 123, 235-236
Dispositional variables, 58-59
Dissonance-reduction biases, 61-66
Dominican crisis, 43-44, 64, 123, 130
Dulles, Allen, 130
Dulles, John Foster, 66, 153

Efficacy and competence, 148, 149
Eisenhower, Dwight D., 36-37, 102, 152-154
Etzioni, Amitai, 255
Executive Committee (ExCom). *See* National Security Council
Expectations, 20, 73-74
Expert's advocate. *See* Devil's advocate

Fiedler, Fred, 101
Finletter, Thomas, 125
Fisher, Roger, 256
Formalistic management model, 148, 150-157, 164, 165 (table), 192
  compared to collegial management model, 213-214
Formal options. *See* Options
Formosa, 33, 36
40 Committee, 155
Freud, Sigmund, 109
Fulbright, J. William, 130, 131

Geyelin, Philip, 123, 127
Graff, Henry, 95

Groupthink, 22, 89, 93-94, 96
Guns of August, The (Tuchman), 246

Haldeman, Robert, 102
Hall, David, 197
Halle, Louis, 55
Harriman, Averell, 71
Heradstveit, Daniel, 59
Heuristics, 60-61
Historical analogies, 19, 42-44, 244-245
Hitler, Adolph, 43, 68
Hoffmann, Stanley, 113
Holsti, Ole, 66
Hoopes, Townsend, 91
Hoover Commission, 150
Hull, Cordell, 44-45
Humphrey, Hubert H., 91
Hypervigilance, 37

Ideology, 19, 44-45
Incrementalism, 19, 40-42
India, 257
Individual subsystem, 11-12, 17, 26-49
Indochina, 236
Information
   adequate, 10, 25, 235
   and cognitive psychology, 56-57
   and cohesiveness, 95
   concrete, 61
   and consistency, 63
   and low-ranking committee members,
      88, 131-132
   need for, 81-82
   and organizational behavior, 111-114
   and scenarios, 61
   single channel of, 129-130, 210
   and uncertainty, 35-47
Initiation strategies, 251-252
Instant history, 218
Intuitive predictions, 60
Iterative systems, 181-182

Janis, Irving, 22, 82, 89, 93-94, 98, 130
Jervis, Robert, 64, 69
Johnson, Louis, 125
Johnson, Lyndon B., 39, 43, 95, 123, 126
Johnson, Richard T., 154, 164, 214
Johnson, Robert H., 124
Jordan, 257

Kahneman, D., 60
Kennan, George, 91, 125, 126, 253
Kennedy, John F., 39, 43, 70-71, 129,
   132, 157-159, 214, 246
Kennedy, Robert, 48, 91, 132, 169
Khrushchev, Nikita, 71, 129
Kissinger, Henry, 155, 157, 163, 177-179,
   186-187, 191-192, 200, 256-257, 258-
   259
Kohl, Wilfred, 183
Korean War, 31, 33, 39, 41, 69, 74-75,
   124, 125, 128, 235, 246, 251
Kowtowing, 90-91

Laissez-faire, 220
Lateral coordination, 145, 175-176
Leadership, 101-103
Lewin, Kurt, 88
Lippitt, Ronald, 92, 102, 103
Lovett, Robert, 70
Lowenthal, Abraham, 44, 64

MacArthur, Douglas, 39, 128-129, 151
McDougall, William, 109
Management models, 139, 145-166, 259-
   260
Marshall, George C., 128
May, Ernest, 43, 60
MLF. *See* North Atlantic Treaty Or-
   ganization
Mondale, Walter, 163
Moyers, Bill, 95
Multilateral check, 229-231
Multiple advocacy, 140, 155, 191-206, 236

Nasser, Gamal, 64
National interest. *See* Decisionmaking
National Security Council (NSC), 141,
   151, 152, 155, 159, 160, 163, 177-180,
   183-185, 186-187, 195-197
   Executive Committee (ExCom), 211-
      213
National Security Study Memorandums
   (NSSM), 177
NATO. *See* North Atlantic Treaty Or-
   ganization
Neustadt, Richard, 72, 116, 127, 128, 176
Nixon, Richard, 102, 154-157, 177, 186-
   187, 191-192, 256-257, 258
Nixon Doctrine, 217

Noniterative system, 180 (figure)
Nonoccurrences, 60
Nonoperational goal, 219
North Atlantic Treaty Organization (NATO)
  MLF (Multilateral Force), 126-127, 128
NSSM. *See* National Security Study Memorandums

OECD. *See* Organization for Economic Cooperation and Development
Operational code, 45
Optimizing decision rule, 40
Options, 10, 88, 124
  adequate evaluation of, 126-127, 242-244
  formal, 140, 175-187, 209
Organization for Economic Cooperation and Development (OECD), 229
Organization subsystem, 11-12, 17, 22, 109-118
Osgood, Charles E., 255
Other-regarding interests, 221, 223 (figure), 228-229
Overloading, 183

Pakistan, 257
Pearl Harbor, 72-73
Policymaking, 9, 25, 114, 115, 116-118, 228
  cognitive basis of, 239-260
  and consistency seeker, 61-66
  processes, 146-147
  provisions for, 122-133
  See also Decisionmaking
Presidential decisionmaking. *See* Decisionmaking
Presidential Power (Neustadt), 176
Problem solver, 56, 58
Procrastination
  calculated, 35
  defensive, 35-36
  rational, 36-37
Pruitt, Dean, 28

Quemoy crisis, 251

Rationality, 67-71
Receptivity to policies, 10
Reedy, George E., 172

Representativeness heuristic, 60
Ridgway, Matthew B., 229
Risk-taking, 97-98, 248
  of solo decisionmaking, 182-183
Role player, 31-32, 198-199 (table), 200-201, 213-214
Role systems, 84, 85, 87-88
Role variables, 5, 7
Roosevelt, Franklin D., 34, 43, 149-150
Roosevelt, Theodore, 6
Royal Court, 183
Rusk, Dean, 132

Satisficing decision rule, 19, 40
Schachter, Stanley, 90
Schilling, Warner, 114
Schlesinger, Arthur, Jr., 45, 94, 131, 132
Second solution. *See* Iterative system
Self-regarding interests, 221, 223-224, 228
Senior Review Group, 155, 157, 179, 185
Sherman, Forrest, 125
Situational variables, 5, 7, 58-59
Six Crises (Nixon), 154
Skowcroft, Brent, 200
Skybolt Crisis, 72, 116
Sloan, Alfred P., 122
Small group subsystem, 11-12, 17, 20-22, 81-103
Social service state, 220
Sorensen, Theodore, 48, 90, 132, 169
Soviet Union, 34, 60, 66, 70-71, 76-77, 129, 162, 232, 242, 252, 256, 258-259
Special assistant's role, 195-197, 200
Stalin, Joseph, 60, 68
Standard operating procedures (SOP's), 118
Strodbeck, F. L., 87
Structural reorganization, 146
Suez crisis, 64, 72, 116
Syria, 257

Taft, William Howard, 6-7
Taiwan, 253, 254
  Strait, 36-37
Task forces, ad hoc interagency, 210
Tavistock Clinic, 109
Thompson, Llewellyn E., 71
Thomson, James C., 171
Torrance, E. P., 88
Truman, Harry, 31, 32, 33, 39, 41, 43, 60,

69, 70, 75, 102, 125, 128-129, 150-152, 246
Tuchman, Barbara, 246
Tuesday Lunch Group, 95
Tversky, A., 60

Values and interests, 10, 17-18,67
  application of, 25
  avoidance of, 29, 32-34
  crises in, 47-49, 72-77
  and foreign policy, 221-223
  and resolution of conflict, 29, 30-31
  tradeoffs of, 29, 31-32, 34, 227-228
  value-complexity, 26-34
Vance, Cyrus, 159, 161, 162, 200
Verification Panel, 155, 185
Victims of Groupthink (Janis), 93, 130

Vietnam, 39, 69, 214-215
Vietnam Special Studies Group, 155

Washington Special Actions Group
  (WSAG), 155, 183, 210
White, Ralph, 102, 103
Wilensky, Harold, 110
Wilson, Harold, 126
Wilson, Woodrow, 43
WSAG. *See* Washington Special Actions
  Group

Yalta Conference, 34
Yom Kippur war, 258

Zaire, 254